FIVE PLAYS
BY THE TEAM

GIVE UP! START OVER!

A THOUSAND NATURAL SHOCKS

PARTICULARLY IN THE HEARTLAND

ARCHITECTING

MISSION DRIFT

OBERON BOOKS
LONDON

WWW.OBERONBOOKS.COM

First published in 2015 by Oberon Books Ltd
521 Caledonian Road, London N7 9RH
Tel: +44 (0) 20 7607 3637
Fax: +44 (0) 20 7607 3629
e-mail: info@oberonbooks.com
www.oberonbooks.com

A catalogue record for this book is available from the
British Library.

PB ISBN: 978-1-78319-190-1
E ISBN: 978-1-78319-689-0

Cover design by Wally Krantz

Printed, bound and converted
by CPI Group (UK) Ltd, Croydon, CR0 4YY.

Visit www.oberonbooks.com to read more about
all our books and to buy them. You will also find
features, author interviews and news of any author
events, and you can sign up for e-newsletters so that
you're always first to hear about our new releases.

CONTENTS

FOREWORD

I once told Rachel Chavkin that the reason I am in love with the TEAM's work is that the company are the frisky child of The Wooster Group and Robert Lepage. I had a glint in my eye but I was half-serious. Arriving in Glasgow in 1990 during the city's triumphant reign as European City of Culture, the work of the Wooster Group and Lepage stimulated a whole generation of theatre makers in Scotland, myself included. A good few years later and on the other side of the Atlantic, Rachel and many of the phenomenal group of artists that make up the TEAM were also experiencing a similar stimulation.

Jump to 2006 and the Edinburgh Festival. It was the inaugural year of the National Theatre of Scotland, where I was Associate Director, and I had just opened our Edinburgh Festival debut, *Black Watch.* Now it was time to see what else was happening. Several close friends had pushed people aside in noisy bars to tell me YOU HAVE TO GET TO THE TRAVERSE THEATRE. THERE'S SOMETHING ON THERE THAT YOU WILL LOSE YOUR SHIT FOR! And so I found myself at a daytime performance of *Particularly in the Heartland* being handed an egg to pelt at the actors on stage. I squealed with joy, inside and out, from start to finish. Our two companies quickly became cheerleaders for each other's shows, carousing through the city together, and to this day are great friends and colleagues.

As I write this I am reflecting on that year, 2006, and I now realise that it wasn't just the influence of those North American theatrical titans (or even hedonistic nights in Edinburgh) that were responsible for the deep bond that formed between the TEAM and I. *Black Watch* came out of a passionate desire both to investigate the Iraq War and acknowledge the unique traditions of Scottish Theatre. In the twentieth century these traditions found their clearest expression in the work of John McGrath and 7:84 Theatre Company, which was fuelled by vaudeville, music, visceral movement and a powerful political energy. When I write these words I could easily be describing the work of the TEAM.

After seeing *Particularly in the Heartland* and meeting the company I immediately asked them if they wanted to work with us at the National Theatre of Scotland and two years later we opened the groundbreaking *Architecting,* also at the Traverse, in a co-production between our two companies. *Architecting* may be the show I am most intimate with, having seen all of its incarnations, but it's also a good place to start discussing the TEAM's body of work as it is bursting with their trademark ideas, passions and extraordinary characters – real and imagined.

New Orleans is to *Architecting* what Kansas is to *Particularly in the Heartland* and Las Vegas is to *Mission Drift*. It's the anchor for the piece, the crucible and the cradle. Part of the TEAM's wonderful accessibility is that they explore the United States of America through exploring the United States of America. They care deeply about their country but their work also courses with fury and anger at what America has done, and become, over the last century.

Presidents, descendants of presidents and presidential candidates appear not just as characters but as titles of shows. Elvis, *The Wizard of Oz*'s Dorothy, Scarlett O'Hara and even her Mammy (played, brilliantly, by a white man) all have their place. American institutions from beauty pageants to the industry surrounding alien abductions are cogitated, masticated and often spat out. Even Shakespeare's *Hamlet* gets a look in, but only through the prism of Billy Joel's "We Didn't Start The Fire."

Time spent with the TEAM, in and out of their performances, is peppered with references to all these characters and institutions. There is also great political debate. *Architecting* was fuelled by their experiences observing America's attempts at reconstruction – both at home following the devastation caused by Hurricane Katrina and abroad following the military devastation of Iraq. *Mission Drift* is a raw critique of the American Dream, as two couples journey across the country, one arriving from Amsterdam in 1624 and the other during the recession of 2008.

Music Hall finds a welcome home in their work in ways which cross gender and smash taboos. I've already referred to their white male Mammy in *Architecting* but this is just the tip of the iceberg. A Scarlett O'Hara pageant, also in *Architecting*, finds its star in a young male gas station attendant. *RoosevElvis* has the double whammy of Teddy Roosevelt and Elvis Presley both played, in utterly transfixing performances, by women. These casting choices are not just intended to be entertaining – they have a profound sense of the political nourishing them – but gleefully entertaining they are.

However, it is the deep sense of empathy for their characters and the country they were born and raised in which marks the TEAM out as truly unique and makes me question whether they do actually have ancestors. This empathy is also what lingers after seeing the work. The TEAM's characters congregate to become an affecting tribe of lost souls searching for redemption and meaning in their vast land. Their work is certainly absurd, biting and satirical but also compassionate and optimistic. It's an optimism that feels fresh and innovative, a long way from that which yearns for fulfillment through the achievement of an American Dream. The TEAM's optimism calls for recalibration, regeneration and rebirth. It's suffused with hope and it has real power, as Carrie articulates so beautifully at the end of *Architecting*, in a passage that the TEAM adapted from Henry Miller's *Tropic of Cancer*, describing her utopian blueprint for national reconstruction:

'It's a memorial. Something – a…it's a vast building. It's a cathedral. It's a cathedral. In the building of which everybody will help who has lost his identity… Here… Here on this ground, in this place we need strong hands. We need spirits who are willing to give up the ghost, and put on flesh.'

John Tiffany
September 2014

A NOTE

In April 2011, on the advice of our friends and mentors the Rude Mechs (an Austin-based ensemble), we went on our first company retreat with two therapists who specialize in group communication. One of the things they taught us was to avoid using extreme language. Words that qualify as extreme include "always," "never," and hyperbolic language like "really." They are words that imply that things have always been, and will always be, as opposed to being a fleeting feeling in an isolated moment of time.

I am thinking about moments we've lived through as individuals and as a group, knowing how permanent (good or bad) they seemed at the time. Almost every word or image in these plays represents a battle won or lost, a contentious "casting" moment, a sleepless night, a well of resentment or satisfaction. Truly democratic collaboration is slow. The process of trying to inspire each other, the process of building consensus by trying to read people's eyes and silences and moods on ten-minute breaks.

We write through character-based improvisation (which we call "writing on our feet"), sitting around at computers, occasionally quoting other writers or films or YouTube videos. And now we increasingly edit as a group. We're getting more democratic as we age, and as our individual professional lives in more traditionally hierarchical rooms have taken shape.

These pieces represent many voices. That multiplicity is embedded in the bones of the work. It's often chaotic – bursting at the seams, overly long, hopefully ambitious. I'm far more interested in energy than polish. I'm interested in whether a production might career off at any point and become something embarrassing.

We are trying now to not take for granted that we know each other. It's probably one of the biggest acts of generosity we practice. These learned patterns are both shortcuts and traps. It's a bit ridiculous, because of course the great joy of company is that it's your family, and so you're starting from this incredibly thick base of shared values and inside jokes. And yet you sort of do, at a certain point, have to pretend you're back in the room with strangers…because your default with a collaborative stranger is to be forgiving. And encouraging. And maybe not so trusting, but maybe more supportive of the small victories. Because it is incredible when something flies in a room full of relative strangers; it's like magic. But when that's the baseline with a group of artists you've known at their best, so many days of rehearsal can feel pale by comparison.

And so I think, at ten, we're trying to unlearn each other. So that we can re-meet. Re-impress. It's why I think all of us have been so fulfilled by working on our own, and by working with each other in smaller groups. It's nice to feel like you exist in the larger world, but it's also good to learn that there is something unique about the way your company's room feels and operates, even if you don't want to do that all the time.

And the work remains. Or at least the messy scripts, which differed wildly from the archival videos, which differed wildly from our half-remembered memories of rewrites...we've assembled the scripts included here from all those sources. The editing process is no more objective than the initial writing process, but we've tried to represent the plays as we performed them the last time they were out of the box as accurately as possible, while still hopefully leaving room for future artists or ensembles who may someday want to tackle them themselves.

I hope this book is resonant for emerging ensembles. I want to say that even in an organization of our size – which at the time of this writing is somewhere between a quarter and a half million dollar operating budget – with 13 core members, one full-time and one-part time administrator (plus me, at all-time and no-time), one of our performers stated recently at a retreat that she didn't realize we, in the office, actually wanted our processes to be twice as long, that we wanted to pay our artists at least 75% more, or that we had hopes that were consistently compromised as we crunched numbers and put budgets together. And then I think about organizations many times the size of ours – the organizations for whom I work in my freelance life. The amount of communication and transparency necessary between two forces – artists and administrators – that can often feel oppositional. And then I think about different groups...not specifically artistic groups, just groups. And how varied their needs are. How firmly they each believe they are correct. How difficult it is to communicate through all that need and resentment... What is a deeply complicated conversation is often reduced, and each side becomes more extreme with more to lose, and a common ground becomes harder and harder to find.

We have to fight for complexity. We have to make space for it – when we collaborate, in the bones of the work or conversation itself. Efficiency is really useful (and cost effective), but it can be violent in the collaborative process. It can lead to over-simplification. And the TEAM has been the arena in which I get to help complicate the way we tell stories about ourselves, our past and present. Which has meant that the room has to be inefficient. We take pride in this.

Thank you to everyone who helped in so many different ways over the past ten years. Thank you families. Looking forward to seeing you all afterwards in the bar...

Rachel Chavkin, Artistic Director
Fall 2014

the TEAM

The TEAM is a Brooklyn-based ensemble dedicated to making new work about the experience of living in America today. Once described as "Gertrude Stein meets MTV," the TEAM's work crashes American history and mythology into modern stories to illuminate the current moment. We combine aggressive athleticism with emotional performances and intellectual rigor, keeping the brain, eyes, and heart of the audience constantly stimulated.

Founded in 2004, The TEAM has created and toured 9 works nationally and internationally. We are four-time winners of the *Scotsman* Fringe First Award, Winner 2011 Edinburgh International Festival Fringe Prize, 2011 *Herald* Angel, 2008 Edinburgh Total Theatre Award, Best Production Dublin Fringe 2007, and were nominated for the 2012 Drama League Award for Outstanding Musical. The TEAM was recently cited on "Best of 2013" lists on 3 continents, and is a recipient of the American Theatre Wing's 2014 National Theatre Company Grant.

The TEAM has performed all over New York (including the Public Theater, PS122, and the Ohio Theatre); nationally (including the Walker Art Center in Minneapolis, and the A.R.T. in Cambridge); and internationally (including London's National Theatre, Barbican Centre, Almeida Theatre, and Battersea Arts Centre; Edinburgh's Traverse Theatre; Lisbon's Culturgest; the Salzburg Festival; the Perth International Arts Festival; the Hong Kong Arts Festival; and multiple collaborations with the National Theatre of Scotland).

The TEAM is Jessica Almasy, Frank Boyd, Rachel Chavkin, Stephanie Douglass, Jill Frutkin, Brian Hastert, Jake Heinrichs, Matt Hubbs, Libby King, Jake Margolin, Dave Polato, Kristen Sieh, and Nick Vaughan.

Artistic Director: Rachel Chavkin
Producing Director: Manda Martin
General Manager: Lucy Jackson

138 South Oxford Street
Studio 1C
Brooklyn, NY 11217
theteamplays.org

vimeo.com/theteamplays
facebook.com/theteamplays
twitter.com/theteamplays
instagram.com/theteamplays

2004

December – Rachel, Jess, Jill, Kristen, Brian, and Stephanie meet at Atlas Cafe (East Village, NYC) to discuss the initial concept for *A Thousand Natural Shocks*, and the idea of taking two shows to the Edinburgh Fringe Festival. The TEAM is formed.

2005

Winter/Spring – Development of *A Thousand Natural Shocks* and *Give Up! Start Over!* First appearances of lighting designer Jake H. and sound designer Matty.

August – TEAM debut at the Edinburgh Fringe Festival: *A Thousand Natural Shocks* and *Give Up! Start Over!* Jess performing in both shows on a recently broken foot (broken by Brian in rehearsal). *GUSO* wins a Fringe First Award.

September – First appearance of writer/performers Jake M. and Libby as the TEAM begins work on *Particularly in the Heartland. Give Up! Start Over!* tours to London's Battersea Arts Centre (first TEAM tour).

November – *Give Up! Start Over!* tours to Glasgow's the Arches.

Fall – Rachel uses Columbia M.F.A. assignments to continue development of *Heartland.*

2006

January – *Give Up! Start Over!* performs in rep with the TEAM's adaptation of Allen Ginsberg's *Howl* at 59E59 (NYC).

March – *A Thousand Natural Shocks* tours to the Bath Shakespeare Festival (UK). *Heartland* residency at the Battersea Arts Centre, after which most of the script is scrapped, but the structure maintained.

July – *Heartland* preview production at Ice Factory Festival, Ohio Theatre (NYC). It is one million degrees. First appearance of scenic designer Nick.

August – Return to Edinburgh Fringe. *Heartland* premieres at Traverse Theatre with an entirely sold-out run; second Fringe First Award. The TEAM befriends the *Black Watch* company, who crush us in multiple games of American football and soccer/football. Director John Tiffany, representing the National Theatre of Scotland, offers first step towards a full commission for the TEAM's next work, and NTS resident playwright/director Davey Anderson begins periodic residency with the company.

September – *Heartland* run at the Battersea Arts Centre. First appearance of writer/performer Frank. Scratch presentation of a new work, *Three Simones Walk Into a Bar.*

Fall – Development on *Welcome Home, Carrie Campbell* (formerly *Three Simones*), including a workshop performance on the back of a flatbed truck for the Fourth Arts Block's FAB! Festival.

February/March – *Heartland* U.S. premiere at PS122 (NYC), and tour to Harbourfront Centre (Toronto). First appearance of stage manager Tater (Dave Polato), and producer Jeremy Blocker (eventually the first president of the TEAM's Board).

April/May – *Heartland* tours to the UK (Glasgow, Stirling, Kendal, Cambridge, Bristol Old Vic, Battersea Arts Centre), and development of *Architecting* (formerly *Welcome Home, Carrie Campbell*) while in Glasgow, during which 5 of the main characters are created. Associate Lucy Kendrick Smith takes over for Jess as Dorothy. First salaried tour.

Summer/Fall – *Heartland* performs at Galway Arts Festival and Dublin Fringe, where the TEAM wins Best Production and Libby wins

Best Actress. Scratch presentation of *Architecting* at Prelude Festival, NYC.

2008

January:
9 – 13 – *Heartland* reprise at PS122
15 – 19 – *Heartland* at Walker Art Center (Minneapolis)
23 – 27 – *Heartland* extended run at PS122
31 – February 1 – *Heartland* at Vanderbilt University (Nashville)

April/May – *Heartland* at the Quick Center for the Arts (Fairfield, CT). *Architecting* development at 3LD (NYC). First fully paid development period for TEAM artists. Kristen becomes obsessed with biography about young Theodore Roosevelt. Producer Jacqui Kaiser joins company for *Architecting* premiere, becoming first company administrator.

June – *Architecting* development at Orchard Project (NY). During a workshop with the OP Core Company, development begins on a new show, *Bowling for Dollars.* Jake M. and Nick get married.

July/August – *Architecting* (Part One) previews in Glasgow before Edinburgh Fringe premiere at the Traverse. Third Fringe First Award.

October – The TEAM becomes an official nonprofit organization.

2009

January – *Architecting* (Full production) premieres in NYC at the Public Theater, co-presented by the Under the Radar Festival and PS122's COIL Festival, and transfers to PS122 for extended run. Associate Heather Christian steps into the role as Scarlett for this run, and also begins collaborating with the TEAM as composer on *To the Boys and Girls of America, I'm Taking a Sick Day* (formerly *Bowling for Dollars*). Filmmaker Paulette Douglass begins filming the process for a new featurelength documentary about the TEAM. Producer Renee

Blinkwolt takes over administrative duties from Jacqui.

April – *The American Capitalism Project* (formerly *To the Boys and Girls of America*) residency at BRIClab (Brooklyn).

June/July – *The American Capitalism Project* development at Orchard Project and at the Almeida Theatre (London).

October/November – *Mission Drift* (formerly *The American Capitalism Project*) development, NYC. *Architecting* tours to The Arches, Barbican Centre (London), and Culturgest (Lisbon) in partnership with the National Theatre of Scotland.

Spring – Associate Ian Lassiter joins *Mission Drift* process. Producer Nate Koch takes over administrative duties from Renee.

2010

May – *Heartland* performances at A.R.T. as part of first Emerging America Festival (Cambridge, MA). Rachel makes brief return to the stage as Dorothy.

June – *Mission Drift* month-long residency at the University of Nevada Las Vegas. The TEAM lives in two foreclosed homes and interviews people daily from all over the spectrum of Vegas life. Libby and Rachel become obsessed with "Big Elvis," an impersonator on the Strip.

August – *Mission Drift* workshop performances at Ice Factory Festival, Ohio Theatre.

September – *Architecting* tours to Calgary. *Mission Drift* workshop presentation at Prelude Festival.

October/November – *Mission Drift* residency on Governor's Island with LMCC (NYC). Playwright Sarah Gancher joins the *Mission Drift* process.

2011	April – First TEAM company retreat at The O'Neill Theater Center (Connecticut).

May/June – Associates Amber Gray and Mikaal Sulaiman join the *Mission Drift* process. *Mission Drift* cast recording at the Motherbrain (Brooklyn), and preview presentation at the recently opened ArtsEmerson (Boston).

June – Development begins on *Town Hall*, a collaboration with Sojourn Theatre, at Orchard Project. Rachel and Jake H. get married.

July – *Mission Drift* preview performances at Culturgest and Universidade de Coimbra, Portugal.

August – *Mission Drift* makes its World Premiere in Edinburgh at the Traverse, winning the TEAM's fourth Fringe First Award, the *Herald* Angel, and Edinburgh International Festival Fringe Prize. Tours to Salzburg Festival Young Directors Program.

October/November – *Town Hall* development at Virginia Tech; *Mission Drift* performances at Williams College (Massachusetts).

December – Libby and Jaime Karate (now a TEAM Board Member) get married. |
| 2012 | January/February – *Mission Drift* U.S. Premiere in PS122's COIL Festival at the Connelly Theater.

May/June – Development begins on a new show, *RoosevElvis* ("Rose-of-Elvis") at The Bushwick Starr (Brooklyn) with Kristen and Libby playing Teddy Roosevelt and Elvis Presley, respectively.

June – *Waiting for You on the Corner of...* (formerly *Town Hall*) workshop at NACL (NY); Frank begins developing a character named Ray, a Kansas City jazz DJ. Development also begins on a new show, *Primer for a Failed Superpower*. |

July – *RoosevElvis* development and workshop at the Almeida Theatre.

August – *Primer for a Failed Superpower* development at National Theatre Studio, (London) and scratch presentation at Edinburgh International Festival as culmination of 2011 EIF Fringe Prize.

September – December – *Primer for a Failed Superpower* semester-long development and workshop production with students at NYU's Playwrights Horizons Theater School.

October – *Waiting for You on the Corner of...* residency at Georgetown University (Washington, DC).

January – The TEAM are named Creative Capital grantees for *Primer for a Failed Superpower*. Producing Director Manda Martin takes over administrative duties from Nate, becoming the TEAM's first full-time staff member.

January – March – *Waiting for You on the Corner of...* development and workshop production at Kansas City Repertory Theatre (Missouri). *Mission Drift* tours to Perth, Australia and Hong Kong.

May – Initial development of *Drive/Discipline*, a new collaboration with Taylor Mac, at Playmakers Repertory Theatre (North Carolina).

June – *Mission Drift* London premiere at The National Theatre's new Shed space (London). *The TEAM Makes a Play*, the documentary about the making of *Mission Drift*, streams for a single day on *The Stage* website, receiving over 1,000 hits. Development of *The Scottish Enlightenment Project*, a new collaboration with the National Theatre of Scotland, begins.

July – Libby, Kristen, Rachel, Video Designer Andrew Schneider and Assistant Director Kevin Hourigan spend 8 sweltering days in an RV on a road trip from the Badlands to Graceland (South

Dakota to Memphis) to film production footage for *RoosevElvis*.

September – Jess gives birth to Baby Ben, first TEAM baby.

October – *RoosevElvis* premieres at The Bushwick Starr.

December – *The Scottish Enlightenment Project* development at Cove Park, a retreat in bitterly cold northern Scotland (much wood chopping by collaborators Davey Anderson, Sandy Grierson, and Brian Ferguson). The TEAM is cited on "Best of 2013" lists on three continents.

2014

February – *The Scottish Enlightenment Project* development in London. Jess steps into the project, taking over initial character work from Brian and Libby.

April – General Manager Lucy Jackson joins the TEAM.

June – Development of *Tiny Emperors in the Land of Bicycles* (formerly *Drive/Discipline*) with Taylor Mac back at Playmakers Rep. Tater and TEAM Associate Heather Christian get married.

July/August – *The Scottish Enlightenment Project* development in Glasgow, scratch performances at Summerhall for Edinburgh Fringe.

September – The TEAM is a recipient of the American Theatre Wing's 2014 National Theatre Company Grant.

October – Matty and Rachel join (now Seattle-based) Frank to develop *The Holler Sessions* (grown out of *Waiting for You...*), in advance of January 2015 premiere at On the Boards (Seattle). Libby gives birth to Julien Heart King.

December – The TEAM celebrates its 10-year anniversary.

GIVE UP! START OVER!
(IN THE DARKEST OF TIMES I LOOK TO RICHARD NIXON FOR HOPE)

CREATED BY
JESSICA ALMASY and RACHEL CHAVKIN

WITH
JAKE HEINRICHS, DARRON L. WEST, and MATT HUBBS

The World Premiere of *Give Up! Start Over! (In The Darkest of Times I Look to Richard Nixon for Hope)* took place as part of the Edinburgh Fringe Festival at C Venue 34 on August 3, 2005 with the following cast:

EXPERIMENT (AKA ALICE)   Jessica Almasy

Rachel Chavkin   *Director*
Jake Heinrichs   *Lighting Design*
Darron L. West   *Sound Design*
Matt Hubbs   *Associate Sound Design*
Stephanie Douglass   *Stage Manager*

Give Up! Start Over! (In The Darkest of Times I Look to Richard Nixon for Hope) **was awarded** a 2005 *Scotsman* Fringe First Award.

CAST OF CHARACTERS

EXPERIMENT, a woman trapped inside her television.
Over the course of the play, she will become possessed by –
and struggle against – various television personalities.

A NOTE ABOUT *GIVE UP! START OVER!*

We began work over email during the summer of 2004. I was working at Barnes and Noble and reading George Trow's *Within the Context of No Context,* Daniel Boorstin's *The Image,* and Jean Baudrillard's *Simulacra and Simulation.* Jessica had become obsessed with Oliver Stone's *Nixon.* And at work, I came across *The Reality Television Handbook.*

We applied to Chashama for space to develop and present a one-person show from these building blocks. And we were thrilled when we were notified we'd received a space grant. And then we panicked when we realized that what we had actually applied for and received was in fact a *window* space: specifically a window display on the south side of West 37th Street in Manhattan. The idea was that Jess would perform in the window wearing a lavalier microphone, and her voice – plus any music – would be piped out on the street via speakers.

This unusual given circumstance, plus the texts we were starting with – which involved themes of surveillance and authenticity – radically shaped the metabolism of this show. It was built to be incredibly fast, and unfold in brief 2-3 minute increments that hopefully would be compelling to anyone walking by, but would also accumulate into a satisfying whole.

Other than the introduction, the show takes place in a box.

The fiction is that the Experiment has trapped herself inside to see whether she will still exist even if no one is watching her. There is a single safety net: a camera that projects a live feed – which others may or may not be watching – to the outside world. (This feed should be projected onto a television for the audience.)

The sound and lighting design for the original production were enormously intricate, and often harsh when it came to transitions.

– Rachel Chavkin, Director/Co-Creator

"You are in a reversed depth, which transforms you into a vanishing point."
Give Up! Start Over! at C Venues, Edinburgh Fringe, 2005
Photo: Rachel Chavkin

A prologue. The EXPERIMENTOR is onstage eating cereal as the audience enters. Onstage with her are a chair, a mini-refrigerator containing a video camera, and a large television displaying a blank, black screen. A square is delineated around these objects, signifying the box in which she will eventually seal herself. For the original production this was a simple tape line on the stage.

Quiet and intimate with the audience. House lights remain up through this section.

EXPERIMENTOR: Thank you for coming.

The Grid of National Life is very large now.

But the space in which one feels at home has shrunk.

There is the grid of almost 300 million.

And the grid of one.

The middle distance has fallen away, taking with it referentials, comfort, and reality. Itself.

> *An ominous moment.*
> *She marches onstage and launches into her introductory lecture.*

The Real!

The Real is produced from miniaturized cells. Matrices and memory banks. Models of control. And it can be reproduced an indefinite number of times from these. *(Stressing this.)* The Real can be reproduced an indefinite number of times.

(Off the record.) Reality television! For example. A reality television program may be filmed for fifteen weeks which is then edited into fifteen hours which is then edited into fifteen episodes which is then edited into five minutes of the most real confessional which will then cement your fifteen minutes and 0.2 megabytes of fame.

Fifteen weeks boiled down into five minutes you can watch an indefinite number of times. And from which you can learn everything that you need to know. About yourself.

This is the cost of your admission. These are the transactions of the Real.

And they are conducted in the "Language of Intimacy." So...

> *She sidles close to an audience member. Intimate conversation that serves as an example for the group.*

"You're a little bit famous?

I'm a little bit famous.

$0.2 + 0.2 = 0.5$ megabytes of celebrity.

You + me = us, which equals a little bit more famous."
(Back to the group.) The Language of Intimacy.

(On the record.) The Real. The Real no longer needs to be rational because it no longer measures itself against either an ideal or negative instance. The Real is no longer anything but operational. In fact, it is no longer really the Real because no <u>imaginary</u> envelops it anymore.
NEW YORK CITY.
For example.
The city is no longer anything but an immense scenario in which the stories of our lives can be played.
NEW. YORK. CITY.
It is a hyperreal – produced from a radiating synthesis of binary models in a hyperspace without atmosphere.

> *Eerie music begins creeping in. EXPERIMENTOR begins to go fuzzy. Something is changing.*

Sounds like a lot of science fiction if you ask me.
If you ask.

By entering into a space whose curvature is no longer that of the real, nor that of truth, the "Era of Simulation" is inaugurated.

> *Distorted presidential music.*

(Off the record.) Did you know Richard Nixon pigeon-proofed his inaugural parade? He commissioned an offensive chemical screen to deter the pigeons from their natural airspace. *(Doing a bad Nixon impression.)* "I assure you no pigeons were harmed in the making of this presidency."

(On the record.) The "Era of Simulation" is inaugurated by a liquidation of all referentials. And pigeons.

(Off the record.) There are no footnotes people. Authors cite themselves as references with impunity. Bono writes the forward to his own autobiography.

(On the record.) A liquidation of all referentials. There is this grid of almost 300 million. And a grid of one. Worse. Referentials get artificially resurrected in the systems of signs – a material more malleable than meaning in that it lends itself to all systems of equivalences, all binary oppositions, all combinatory algebra.

Sounds like a lot of science fiction... I already said that.

An eerie, lost moment.

What *is* the question?

Someone in the audience snaps a picture with a flash.

The EXPERIMENTOR is caught off guard, and becomes paranoid.

It is no longer a question of duplication nor imitation nor even parody.

Takes out a small piece of paper and begins writing a note. When she finishes, she crosses to the television, flipping through the channels to try to get it set to the correct station. But the screen remains eerily blank.

It is a question of substituting the signs of the real for the real.
It is a question of confusion.
Things are getting blurry.

Hands the note to an audience member. It reads "No more cameras."

You can pass this along for everyone, please.

Taking in the group one last time. She puts down her pen, showing the audience her open palms, her empty pockets, showing that she is about ready to begin the experiment. Mutters "Okay...Okay...I said that..." She makes sure <u>she</u> is ready. Finally:

Thank you and good night.

Turns upstage, begins to walk into the box.

Blackout. The blank glow of the television screen is the only light.

Wild sounds. A television being devoured. The dawn of cable television, of reality television, so many advertisements. It is deafening.

Time passing.

Sudden silence.

Stage lights slowly rise, tight on the EXPERIMENT now sealed inside the box.

She is crouching on the refrigerator.

She is thinking about the camera underneath her in the fridge. She has been thinking about it a long time. She continues to think about it for a long time in silence.

She is also staring at a spoon held outstretched in her right hand.

Her left hand reaches for the spoon.

The real is

> *She bends the spoon, badly hidden, behind her back.*
> *Pulls it back out, magically bent!*

Produced and

> *She straightens the spoon, badly hidden, behind her back.*
> *Pulls it back out, magically straightened!*

Reproduced and

> *She bends the spoon, badly hidden, behind her back.*
> *Pulls it back out, magically bent!*

Reproduced indefinitely.

> *Dropping the game.*

I watched this show on Spanish television where everyone but the cameramen were bending spoons. With their minds. The special guest was David Copperfield and he was leading them in an exercise and he wasn't speaking Spanish, but his voice was dubbed, and I could hear, faintly underneath the translation…"Bend the spoon. Bend the spoon. Focus. Focus. Pay ATTENTION." It made it clear. It made it so clear that an ILLUSION demands an AUDIENCE. *(Clapping.)* It's called a magic trick.

It's called a magic trick. Not a magic deal, or a magic pact, or a magic demonstration. No, it's called a magic trick.

And that, boys and girls, is why cameras are dangerous.

Point and shoot. Point and shoot. Do not fall prey to its whispers of truth. Yes, sure, you know at your core that these things are fabricated. You know Jennifer Aniston isn't really the real Rachel. And you know that Martha Stewart is a really bad woman. And you know that those people on *Fear Factor* won't be allowed to die. But on an even deeper level, you know, admit it, that the camera is something you can trust to focus reality into a form you can understand.

For the record, can you really look at the New York skyline and not think, "Oh. That's where that terrible mini-series about terrorism took place."

For the record. For the cameras.

NIXON: *(Exploding.)* Right! Get this on camera.

EXPERIMENT: *(As if goosed.)* Mr. Nixon!
Please! Stand up.

> *She addresses him, as if he's in the box with her.*

Nixon in your prime you ranked among the most hated men, two times
in fact beating Hitler for number one.
And for four years in a row you were voted the number one most
respected man in America.
You were so good at that game.

> *With a touch of admiration.*

NIXON: *(He slips back out.)* You're not so bad yourself kid.

> *She shakes him off violently and is now freaked out. Unsure if she is
> hallucinating or having a real vision.*

EXPERIMENT: I didn't say that…

> *She sits slowly. And slowly her body contorts into Nixon's hunch.*

Ha.

NIXON: Ha. Admit it. Just admit it.

EXPERIMENT: I can't.

NIXON: I will…
I confess…
I love Reality…

> *Throws arms up, extended. Victory. Now playing directly with audience.*

TELEVISION!

> *Canned audience applause.*

Maybe it's because I like to see the everyday drama of my life played
like a game by people just like (but a little bit better looking than) me!
Maybe it's because I like to see people just like (but a little bit funnier
than) me – win a million dollars, a beautiful bachelor / bachelorette's
hand, a post-show sponsorship deal, or a career.
In TELEVISION!

> *Moment of EXPERIMENT wrestling back from the possession, taking in
> what the fuck just happened.*

EXPERIMENT: It is a question of knowing things for sure. Or at least for a time.

It is a fantasy – the fantasy – of seizing <u>reality</u> live that continues. The hallucination is total and truly fascinating once the hologram is projected in front of the plaque so that nothing separates you from it. Instead of a field as a vanishing point for the eye, you are in a reversed depth, which transforms YOU into a vanishing point.

Several beats as she stretches back, fully taken over.

TELEVISION EVANGELIST: Yes-uh! Admit it-uh! And you too can – Come on Down!

IMMIGRANT CONTESTANT: *(Seated in chair.)* Me? Me? I won? Oh get out of town. I won?!?

Smiling, jumping up. Game show music.

AGGGGH!!

GAME SHOW HOST: *(Wink and pointing.)* Look at that girl smile folks! Look at that girl smile! *(Mugs for the cameras.)*

The more she smiles, the more certain it is that she represents something shocking.
Something trivial.
Something failed.

IMMIGRANT: AGGGH!!!

FAN: *(Kneeling, looking up.)* I am so in awe of you!

IMMIGRANT: *(Still smiling and jumping, kicking FAN aside.)* AGGGH!!!

GAME SHOW HOST: Somebody! Tell her what she's WON!

The IMMIGRANT runs in a jubilant circle around the stage. Waving and clapping to fans.

She comes to a stop and looks for prizes to arrive. Slowly the game show people around her begin to vanish. Studio lights turn out. She claps to will them back.

Looks into the audience. She regroups to speak just to them.

IMMIGRANT: I came from New Jersey. But now I am winner.
Reality shows want you.
How to find your show.

How to create you application.

Audition like an idol!

Ace a casting interview.

Most reality contestants are defined by – Where They Are From –
(Newark, Vietnam, Glasgow)

And – What They Do For Living
(Philosopher/Neurosurgeon/Model? Call me.)

These two elements make a neat, tidy frame for your Character.

And! They have the added advantage of fitting neatly in a text box
beneath your face every time you appear on camera.

Looks down at text box. Smiles up. Very positive to audience.

Smile! Be yourself!

If you are yourself then you never have to worry about falling out of
Character!

Who are you?

Take your pick.

Dress as the Character you want people to see.

Uh, a cunning vixen. *(Naughty meow at audience.)*

A country bumpkin! "Get on the farm."

An arrogant athlete! *(Pounds chest.)* "Give ME 25 million."

Be yourself!

Or!

Your most typecastable version of yourself.

Beat.

Tips! On Presenting the Real You.

EXPERIMENT: I hardly need any tips. I think I'm typecastable enough
already.

Surprised by what she has said. Nixon takes the opportunity to jump out.

NIXON: Tips on presenting the real you.

You want to make people <u>feel</u> like they are the only one in the room.
With you.

You want to make people <u>think</u> that only they can see you.

As if you've somehow… sneckled your true self.

(Posing.) This self.

(Posing.) This self.

The eyes.

You want to make people.

You want to make a PERSON feel as if no one before them has ever really looked into your eyes…

You want to speak intimately.

Hi.

Hello.

Good evening.

My fellow Americans.

I come before you tonight!

I come before you!

I am BEFORE YOU!!!

> *He takes on classic Nixon pose. He holds it for a long stretch, as if for photographs. Then breaking.*

How do you like my tie?

This tie?

When I'm talking to a woman about a tie, we're not just talking about the tie of course. *(Seeing the audiences' dirty thoughts.)* Now, I don't mean that. Ha. No. We're not even really talking. Really.

I'm not really "Dick Nixon" and she's certainly not "Alice."

Well.

I'm… "the President."

Or to be more precise,

I am "President."

I am an "American President."

And you are an "American citizen."

And WHAT A COUNTRY! When you and I can talk.

> *Hiking up pants, taking a seat.*

Just.

Like.

This.

On the Record.

For the Record.

This is for the Record.

When you've got a lot to say, don't say a lot. What are you gonna say? Our archives and airtime can't be wasted with the [unintelligible].

The nature of "the medium," the compulsion of "the medium," abhors silence and dead time.

Pause. Lights dim. Silence.

Restore.

That was a pause.

I cannot bear to suffer a pause.

ANCHORWOMAN: Fill it with programming!

ANCHORWOMAN rises, taking in (imaginary) auditorium of students waiting. University of Broadcasting Commencement Exercises.

Long silence.

What is programming?

Silence.

Programming is the daily product of men of good will.

Silence.

What is important programming?
Anybody?

Silence.

Important programming is programming that recognizes the problem.

Silence.

What is a problem?

Silence.

A problem is a disease in the demography.
Something sickening.
Something downright sinful.
Celebrities unsure about their weight and their future.
What's wondrous.
Yes.
What people want to watch.
Yes.
More.
More Programming!

Television Guide, for example.

A plan. "Uncertain Celebrities" at 7 followed by "What to be Afraid Of" at 9:30.

A plan. How else would we know that we had problems?

Problems we didn't know we had.

A plan. A system. A system of services designed to meet a social need.

> *She raises a hand like a sock puppet, and does the voice of "Problem."*

"I'm just a Hoosier."

> *She becomes herself, looking at the hand, coaching the "Problem" about how to become more compelling.*

No! No one cares.

> *She continues the role play.*

"I am youth."

It's better.

"I'm a battered child?"

Very good!

> *Dropping the game.*

The most important programming deals with people with a serious illness who make it to the Olympics!

> *Applause of the Olympic stadium. She mimes an earpiece. Thrilled to be reporting live from the games.*

Babies, given up for dead, who struggle towards national life and make it! For just a minute. It's a long distance to come.

People feel it very deeply and cheer the babies on.

> *Begins enactment, teaching students how to cheer; it's an educational simulation.*

Yea, babies. Yea, babies! *(To the students.)* Okay look up there, they're running. YEAH BABIES! Yea, babies! LOOK at those handicapped little babies. Isn't that wonderful. Go babies go.

> *In her imagination the babies have turned violent.*

Oh, oh my. *(Disgusted face, beat.)*

He's eating the leading baby's foot. That can't be fair. Where's the referee? Oh how horrible. How disgusting. I can't watch. *(Covers her eyes.)*
Damnit. *(Peeks out.)*
I'm watching.

> *Something else catches her half-hidden eye.*

Oh my, goodness!
Is that Susan Sarandon? Oh she looks fabulous! Susan!
Pssstpsstpsstpstpsst!
SUSAN!

> *SUSAN approaches.*

Oh would you LOOK at these babies.

> *SUSAN tells her about her charity work.*

Is that right. Isn't that wonderful. Who can I make the check out to?

> *Beat as ANCHORWOMAN steps downstage, switches gears back to students.*

Never be afraid to talk to celebrities. They are people too. It is so important to stay involved as a newsperson. A person of the news. It's important to show authentic concern. But then again authentic concern takes a lot of time to rehearse.

> *NIXON resurfaces. Struggle ensues as the two fight over the EXPERIMENT's body.*

NIXON: I get so impatient with the whole process that I refuse to take coaching. But as to shaking hands, I like to do that – it brightens people's lives to meet a celebrity; and as you may have noticed, I'm rather good at it.

ANCHORWOMAN: He is not. His eyes are here, there, and everywhere! The world as reported by television threatens him. It is a short and understandable step for him to conclude that television threatens him.

NIXON: I'm very good at one-to-one relationships! If there are just two of you, you can concentrate totally on each other. Not on image. Not on face.

> *A violent move. The EXPERIMENT is trying to regain control.*

EXPERIMENT: It is a question of knowing things for sure. Or at least for a time. It is a fantasy, the fantasy of seizing reality live that continues. The hallucination is total and truly fascinating once the hologram is projected in front of the plaque so that nothing separates you from it. Instead of a field as a vanishing point for the eye, you are in a reversed depth, which transforms you into a vanishing point.

> *A beat.*

> *The Rembrandt's "I'll Be There For You," (the music from the opening credits of* Friends*) blasts through the space.*

> *A vicious, aggressively cheerful dance as one after the other, the cast members of* Friends *possess and manipulate the EXPERIMENT's body like a ragdoll.*

> *The music winds to a close, as the EXPERIMENT pants, imagining herself joyfully splashing water in the Central Park fountain at the end of the show credits.*

> *Music Out. Long recovery.*

Isn't that a hell of a thing? *(Looking up.)*
47 seconds. And you wish you had an entirely different life.

> *NIXON begins to creep out again, taking advantage of her loneliness.*

NIXON/EXPERIMENT: ADMIT it. You WANT it.

EXPERIMENT: *(Giving up.)* I confess...
These are the hoaxes we play on ourselves.

> *She slowly opens the fridge, and for the first time the television downstage comes to life. Buried in the fridge is a video camera hooked to a live feed that projects on the television. It is an extreme close-up of her face peering into the fridge. She becomes Ashleigh, and tenderly relates to the camera like a confessor and best friend. We watch the following on screen.*

ASHLEIGH: I sent in another application today. "Ashleigh Abraham." Spelled A-S-H-L-E-I-G-H. To reflect my uniqueness and to get like a general yo no say quoi of nondenominational but nonetheless God-fearing all-American contestant.
Shoot.
Favorite foods are apple pie, paella, and cigarettes.

But willing to survive on cockroaches and sand for however long is necessary.

Is possible.

It's so important to show – in your application – your dedication to the utmost.

Your utmost fascinatingness.

You know you want to.

Admit it.

Your utmost ability to hold drama and create an audience.

Of millions.

Glued to their screens.

Plasma.

Dripping in it.

Like *The Fly*.

You gotta ask yourself, what do they wanna see?

Or even, "What do I want to see?"

I don't know about you but I like to see beautiful people. Glamorous people. It's so funny when you think about it. We all want to be famous. But we want our celebrities to be like, impossible.

I guess it's like Susan Sarandon said in that movie sometime.

You can't –

Have.

It.

All.

> *Jumping up on top of fridge, bending forward upside down so that her face is now upside down on television.*

I wanted to share this moment because it's an important one in my life.

This is my 150th application to different shows.

I applied to a show for the Home Shopping Network about new inventions.

And one on Fox about strippers with hearts of gold and one on NBC about good girls gone bad. I've done things I'm real good at and things I'm real bad at and things I don't feel so good about. Still. Sometimes. When I really think about it.

I've won approximately $124,300 on different shows in the form of prizes, cash, free trips, t-shirts, and booze. Drunken flings aside, I've had five relationships, two of which earned us our own specials. I keep a camera on me now just for practice.

Suddenly desperate. Back upright. Eyes boring into the camera.

How could you vote me off? It becomes difficult to see yourself without the eyes of others. Think of a boyfriend, a lover. I once heard that some movie star described the camera as the most faithful lover you could ever have. You see yourself for better or worse more clearly, more Technicolor, through their eyes. Take that away and it's like…
you've gone blind.

> *She closes her eyes to demonstrate.*

> *EXPERIMENT goes blind. The horrible "beep" of a lost signal.*

> *Groping toward camera. Feels camera like another face. Feels own face.*

> *Eyes open.*

> *EXPERIMENT looks at camera. Realizes she has lost her willpower and succumbed to this last thread connecting her to outside observers.*

> *She slams the fridge shut. The live feed stops. She barricades the fridge door with body.*

EXPERIMENT: *(Scolding herself.)* Sight must not be defined by how well you can be seen! Focus is your own clarity, clarity of purpose, clarity of mission… clarity… be clear!
(Losing it.) Am I in focus? Is this in focus? Are you getting this? Is anybody getting this?
Hello?
Hello? Am I in focus?
My background is receding rapidly…

> *She opens the fridge again, groping for the camera.*

(To herself.) Stop it. FOCUS!

> *She slams the fridge shut.*

(Back into lecture mode. Trying to sooth herself.) The grid of national life is very large now. But the space in which one feels at home has shrunk. Things very distant come powerfully close. But just for a minute.
They come powerfully close. Almost shoulder to shoulder. It's almost a conversation.
And they speak in the language of intimacy.
The language of YOU ARE NOT ALONE.
The grid is so large now.
The background is so distant.

The sense of protection is distant.

People are so frightened.

There is so much distance between them and their protection.

They reward anyone who can convince them that there is no distance.

> *Music. The hip intro to* Access Hollywood *or similar celebrity news show.*

> *She rises and becomes CELEBRITY.*
> *An interview "at home" in her kitchen. Seated.*

CELEBRITY: *(As music ends.)* Are we on? Oh goodness! Well...

For a long time I was afraid.

There was a period, very early in my career – Oh, long before "Alice." *(Referring to the television role that made her famous.)* Long before anyone knew my name at all, when I couldn't even go outside, really.

> *Nodding in recognition at the empathy of the interviewer.*

Yes, Yes, Agraphobia...

> *Continuing to nod smoothly, not acknowledging her mistake at all, but accepting the correction.*

AGORAPHOBIA. It was, well it was awful! I lived in this room, in this apartment, and I would try to step out, for an open call, or for soup! And I wouldn't even make it to the stairs. It was, it was, it wasn't like I was afraid of getting hurt or hit by a car or truck or something.

Nothing so literal as that.

No.

No, it was my vision. I could only see, like –

> *Holding up a hand a couple inches away from her eyes.*

THIS far in front of my face. It was a problem of focus! I could only see THIS.

My life.

My problems.

Serious problems, and I couldn't, I couldn't focus. But it wasn't my like eyesight. 20/15, pretty great, and now– *(To an offstage manager or agent.)* I'm fine. *(Back to camera and interviewer.)* There was me and there was this grid of, what, three hundred million other people, not to mention six billion!

Seven billion?!

And I couldn't focus, beyond my little speck. The grid was overwhelming...

And it was lonely. (I already said that.)

And I was so afraid.

But then I landed this job. My agent called and said, YOU CANNOT! – so I made it down, unable to breathe, and I remember as I was walking there were all of these signs that seemed to be talking directly TO me...

"Are you blue?"

"Under Pressure?"

"Do you want to go where everybody knows your name?"

And I did! And I landed this film! And it was hard still, focusing, breathing, sometimes. But finally, we wrapped, and I saw the rough cut of the film, and suddenly it was like the whole world <u>snapped</u> into focus. Two lenses just FINALLY overlapping! Near and far sightedness!

And it kept getting better, because at first I could see myself, and then somehow the two halves – myself here and myself up there – linked, and then I turned out.

And *you* were there.

You were there, and you were looking at me.

Not me here.

(Gesturing to an imagined "big screen.") Me there.

But the line between the two, it doesn't really...

It's a gift. It's a gift that you give me.

When you look.

At me.

Because I have my own eyes, and then I'm given the gift of hundreds, who knows MAYBE hundreds of thousands, of you looking at me, telling me I exist out there as well.

So you see me, and I see you seeing me, and I see myself being seen. By you.

And I don't think, I mean, it's a big responsibility, this gift you give me. To be a model.

A role model.

A reflection.

A refracted image.

And you know, the idol is the measure of the worshipper.

I'm a vessel, maybe.

We measure heroes as we do ships. By their displacement.

It's remarkable. I wish I could give this gift to everyone. What is it?
Living in three dimensions? Solidity at a geological level?
I feel complete.

NIXON suddenly bursts back out.

NIXON: *(Wants to get on the record.)* I want to tell you my side of the case!
I've got a theory too.

Henry Kissinger once told me (I've never said this out loud before,
this is an exclusive) a famous man looks up a word in the dictionary
because he wasn't sure it existed. Now what do you think is more
terrifying – that this man finds this word he thought was real never
actually existed? Or that he finds that he's the only one cited for its use?

CELEBRITY / EXPERIMENT: People who watch forget that we are not
the characters that we play. We make such a strong impression. They
think that maybe no one is behind these characters. But there is. There
most certainly is someone kicking in here, Dick. I am not just who I
am on Television. I mean, she is certainly not "Alice," although she's a
wonderful Character. And I thank my lucky stars and my producers I
get to play – Now, how to not get me wrong. No, seriously –

Her voice begins to drop and becomes strangled.

Don't – Get – Me – Wrong – Dick! But that's not me. I mean, this isn't
even me. Right now. Or now. This isn't even my real hair. Or my real
eyes. This isn't even my real voice.

Her voice and body are beginning to contort.

My real voice would probably be unintelligible. It probably wouldn't
even be able to form words.

ASHLEIGH: If you have trouble crying, and there's not a drugstore to run
to and pick up some saline, try rubbing sand in your eyes, or holding
your breath. Or yawning. I think about my mother dying. *(She does.)* It
doesn't work. *(Morphing into a sad face.)*

NIXON: *(Also making a sad face.)* Are you blue?

CELEBRITY: DON'T PANIC!!! I'm lost. But I can tell you exactly where I
am. I think.

How dull.

She stands.

The theme song for a nightly news broadcast blasts through the space.
She becomes a Walter Cronkite-esque ANCHORMAN.

ANCHORMAN: Good evening and thank you for welcoming me into your
home.

The grid of national life is very large now.

The middle distance has fallen away.

There is the grid of almost three hundred million.

And the grid of one.

People panic and start to want more in the way of company.

The background is distant.

The sense of protection is distant.

But

People Magazine.

Television.

Other Americans engaged in a process resembling the processes of
intimacy.

There is a context to which *People Magazine* grants access.

There is a context to which Television grants access.

Television is a context to which Television grants access.

It is a comfort.

What is comfort?

It is focus.

You bring this grid together with that grid.

You get the images to overlap and suddenly things have a bit of focus.

The Language of Intimacy.

The Language of "You are not alone."

EXPERIMENT: *(Trying to get out.)* I already said that.

ANCHORMAN: You are not alone.

EXPERIMENT: *(Trying to get out.)* I already said...

ANCHORMAN: YOU ARE NOT ALONE.

CBS *(Holds up left palm.)* and You. *(Holds up right palm.)*

It makes it clear.

It makes it so clear.

There is nothing else.

Nothing else exists.

Just CBS and You.

No city. No state. All those places where the series take place.

It's Miami.

It's Los Angeles.

It's New York City.

The city is no longer anything but an immense scenario in which the stories of our lives can be played like a game by people just like -

But a little better looking than –

A little bit funnier than –

You.

NIXON: *(Blasting through.)* You want comfort? I can give you comfort. I've got a real gem for you. Henry Kissinger told me once – I've never told this to anybody. This is an exclusive! – a biographer was doing research on a famous man. He read 15,000 letters that man had written. Including those on which the following words were marked up in big red letters: "Burn – This – Please." And they had obviously been ignored. Now isn't that reassuring?

How to Use this Medium Effectively.

How to Sell Yourself Like a Bar of Soap.

No long speeches, he said with a wink.

People don't have the stomach for a lot of attenuated ideas.

IMMIGRANT: Dick, I can't wait to spin!

NIXON: How to Sell Faces.

People will say a spot doesn't give an audience a chance to know a person.

Sometimes, that's a good thing.

Five minutes is smart.

One minute is smarter.

Saturate those airwaves!

Make sure!

Put your spots in the best time periods money can buy!

Now let me turn to the future.

You all remember the Checkers speech I suppose?

Well I want you to be the first to know.

> *EXPERIMENT rises to escape. Terrible screeching sound of television spasm.*

She is thrown back into the chair, and immediately NIXON takes over again.

I staged it.

Ha!

How to Not Get Me Wrong.

I meant every word of that speech.

I. Loved. That. Dog.

But let's be realistic. A dog is a natural.

(Suddenly tender.) My wife was a wonderful stenographer.

> *Romantic music croons through the space. A slow, surreal moment of NIXON picking up and dancing with a chair as if with his wife on their anniversary.*

Oh Patty, you look beautiful tonight.

> *Dancing with chair.*

> *Eventually and violently drops chair.*

But they were props!!!

But of course they were *more* than props.

People called Checkers a soap opera.

Any drama, to be successful, has to evoke sympathy.

I took, it took, two days to prepare that speech.

I'm a firm believer in off the cuff speeches that take a lot of time to prepare.

Sincerity is *essential* on TELEVISION.

I know those guys up front will say this is a phony.

Well I say:

> *Striking classic Nixon pose, as if for photographs.*

Complex and Devious!

Complex and Devious!

In the best sense of those words. Ha.

> *Long pause. He sobers up.*

Isn't that a hell of a thing. That the fate of a great nation can depend on camera angles.

> *A long, long beat. Exhausted. A quiet submission.*

The EXPERIMENT slowly picks up chair. Sets it down. Prepares to begin this final sequence, which is highly scored and choreographed. It starts quiet, but by the end should feel like running a mile at full sprint. It should also involve the EXPERIMENT breaking back into the fridge and using the camera as much as she wants to film herself and the audience.

EXPERIMENT: How to Find Your Show.

How to Create your Application.

Violent sound of television. Her body is thrust into classic Nixon pose.

NIXON: I am Captain Hook.

IMMIGRANT: How to Audition Like an Idol.

How to Ace a Casting Interview.

GAME SHOW HOST: How to Nail the Final Network.

How to Nail the Final Network Interview.

A pulse begins that continues to grow.

NIXON: How to Form an Alliance.

How to Maintain an Alliance.

How to Fly Under the Radar.

How to Manipulate Your Competitors.

How to Lie – and Get Away with It.

ASHLEIGH: How to Display Emotion on Cue.

CELEBRITY: How to Give an On-Camera Interview.

ANCHORWOMAN: How to Use Alcohol – to Your Advantage.

Playing herself, maybe snorting cocaine, at a party.

What a fabulous time! What a fabulous beer commercial it might have made!

NIXON: How to Manage Your Enemies.

How to Make the Most of Losing.

ASHLEIGH: How to Read a Bachelor or Bachelorette's Body Language.

How to Make the Most of Your Date.

How to Play for Time.

How to Discern Your Date is Actually Wealthy.

How to Escape the Microphones.

How to Hook Up On Camera.

How to Endear Yourself to the Parents.

How to Date Multiple Partners.

EXPERIMENT / ASHLEIGH: How to Make Fire.

How to Make a Water Pipeline.

How to Build Shelter.

How to Catch Food.

How to Cook in the Wild.

How to Deal with Wild Animals.

How to Treat Minor Medical Conditions.

How to Overcome Fear.

> *The pulsing music and lights drop suddenly out, and the EXPERIMENT is still and panting for a moment.*

EXPERIMENT: *(Quiet.)* How to Overcome Fear.

> *Beat, resume furious motion.*

ASHLEIGH: How to Eat Almost Anything.

How to Deal with Being Buried Alive.

How to Compete in Water.

How to Rappel Down a Mountain.

How to Maneuver a Team Through an Obstacle Course or Maze.

How to Get Help From the Crew.

How to Shine in a Talk Show Interview.

How to Extend Your Fifteen Minutes of FAME.

CELEBRITY: Move to New York or Los Angeles.

ANCHORMAN: Star in the next installment of the reality show in which you just participated.

NIXON: Write a book. Do a cameo in a situational comedy or television special.

ANCHORWOMAN: Allow a television network to film your wedding.

IMMIGRANT: Give the speeches on the college campuses.

CELEBRITY: Land a role on a soap opera.

ANCHORWOMAN: Dramatically alter your appearance by losing a significant amount of weight, getting breast implants, or having cosmetic surgery.

Crash celebrity parties and be photographed with them.

ANCHORMAN: Become a special correspondent on a tabloid television show.

Participate in a celebrity boxing match.

IMMIGRANT: Open a restaurant or bar.

Start your own line of clothing.

Start a band.

GAME SHOW HOST: Become a morning show radio DJ.

Climbing on the chair, like a starving beast.

NIXON: Co-host a cable game show.

Provide onscreen testimonials for infomercial products.

Get assassinated!

DIIIIEEEEEE!!!!

Stands on chair, arms outstretched in classic NIXON pose, waiting to be shot.

Sudden silence.

Nothing happens to her. Him.

Or rather: He's been voted off.

NIXON: *(Slow.)* Uhhhh... what can I say? *(Long quiet.)*

I totally didn't expect to be voted out tonight, so it's a big surprise for me. I thought me and Ike had something but I guess I was wrong – and anything can happen – and it happened to me tonight. Like I said, I'm a pretty honest person. And I played the game the best way I felt I think I knew how. I wasn't going to change my Character to play the game because I just felt that was fake.

So I played the game.

I competed as hard as I could. I did everything I think I could do without compromising my Character.

So, I mean...

Honestly...

I have no regrets.

NIXON slowly disappears.

The EXPERIMENT slowly comes back to reality, though still alone in box.

Quiet tender music creeps in.

EXPERIMENT: So I've been having these dreams.
I've been dreaming about Richard Nixon.
I've been having these dreams about Richard Nixon.
Actually. In my dreams I think, I think I'm Richard Nixon.

She quietly picks up the camera from wherever it has landed. She cradles it in her lap.

Or we're holding hands.
And we walk away together. We walk into the sunset...
The Technicolor, hyperreal, plasma screen sunset.

She looks into the camera. Her face is projected large and intimately for the audience on the television.

NIXON: You're gonna be so good at this game.

EXPERIMENT: You're not so bad yourself, Dick.

NIXON: Ha. Roll the credits.

She stares into camera waiting.

Waiting.

Waiting.

BLACKOUT.

A THOUSAND NATURAL SHOCKS

WRITTEN BY
JESSICA ALMASY, RACHEL CHAVKIN, JILL FRUTKIN,
BRIAN HASTERT and KRISTEN SIEH

WITH
STEPHANIE DOUGLASS, JAKE HEINRICHS and MATT HUBBS

The World Premiere of *A Thousand Natural Shocks* took place as part of the Edinburgh Fringe Festival at C Venue 34 on August 3, 2005 with the following cast:

HAMLET	Jessica Almasy
OPHELIA	Kristen Sieh
LAERTES	Brian Hastert
HORATIO	Jill Frutkin

Rachel Chavkin	*Director*
Jake Heinrichs	*Lighting Design*
Matt Hubbs	*Sound Design*
Stephanie Douglass	*Dramaturg/Stage Manager*

CAST OF CHARACTERS

HAMLET, Prince of Denmark, a student

OPHELIA, sister of Laertes, girlfriend of Hamlet

LAERTES, brother of Ophelia

HORATIO, friend of Hamlet, documentarian

A NOTE ABOUT *A THOUSAND NATURAL SHOCKS*

Shocks is in many ways the first work by the TEAM. Jessica and I had already begun work on *Give Up! Start Over!* and I had been the lead writer/conceiver on a work that involved her, Brian and Kristen (along with two other artists) called *Faster*, but we mark our founding as a company at the first *Shocks* meeting in December 2004. I came to the group with the idea of taking the four young characters from *Hamlet*, as well as that play's given circumstances, and transplanting them in a Denmark that resembled modern America.

We read and re-read *Hamlet*, and our version of Ophelia was largely informed by our shared frustration with how weakly she is often portrayed in productions. The character also took on a distinctly bizarre, comedic flavor when Kristen brought in an old traveller's guide to Denmark (snippets of which feature in the airport sequence), and I asked her to read it in her version of a Danish accent. The character of Hamlet was deeply informed by Evan Thomas' emotional biography of Robert F. Kennedy, which Jess and I both read; the image of this younger brother who had idolized John, and suddenly found himself in the spotlight following a violently created vacuum of leadership. Both Robert and John F. Kennedy's assassinations hung over this process, appearing as ghosts in the Zapruder footage we used, and ultimately embedded themselves in the text of *Particularly in the Heartland* (our next work, in which Robert is a character). In early drafts Horatio quoted a devastating Czesław Miłosz poem called "A Song on the End of the World." That poem's divide between apocalyptic visions and the eerie silence created in the wake of disaster was a guiding light. And Laertes grew out of the neocon project, and their authoritarian power grab following the September 11th attacks - at one point he even speaks an infamous Karl Rove quote.

The founding TEAM members were all at NYU on September 11th, 2001. One of the things that most remains with me from that day was a thought I had after watching the second tower fall: "Wait...buildings don't collapse." There was a dumbfoundedness - tied also to being 21 at the time - that came with seeing the sheen of permanence get rubbed away in a single Tuesday morning. That feeling of the ground radically shifting under one's feet threads through all our early work. And all the accompanying fury and grief and confusion linked to both that sensation, and the governance of our country at the time and in the years that followed, are at their apex in this play.

– Rachel Chavkin, Director/Co-Author

The given circumstances are familiar: Hamlet's father has suddenly died under shady circumstances. Hamlet has been away at school, where he meets Horatio (a scholarship student). Laertes has been away in France. Ophelia has been home...

The play takes place over 6 days, jumping back and forth between moments in time at a dizzying speed. As with periods of grief, the days may seem endless. There are times when the days overlap, and moments that exist out of time altogether. We used music as a placing device, so that recurring locations might be quickly recognized, and so that the edges of scenes could be distinct when necessary.

Day 1 - THE DAY OF THE SHOOTING.

Day 2 - THE RETURN HOME.

Day 3 - THE FUNERAL AND CONCERT.

Day 4 - THE DAY AFTER THE FUNERAL,
WHEN EVERYTHING FALLS APART.

Day 5 - THE DAY WHEN WE'RE SUPPOSED TO MAKE A
DECISION.

Day 6 - THE MORNING THE DECISION IS MADE.

OPHELIA is often noted as speaking in accent. This should be an overblown Danish accent, though performed with complete conviction.

HORATIO is portrayed as a documentary filmmaker, interested in capturing this moment in his country. The original production included a significant amount of rudimentary and live-feed video design.

Kristen Sieh as Ophelia and Jill Frutkin as Horatio in *A Thousand Natural Shocks* **at C Venues, Edinburgh Fringe, 2005**
Photo: Rachel Chavkin

Day 6.

A meeting room stands waiting. There is a pitcher of water with lemon and glasses on the table. HAMLET enters, terrified. He pours a glass of water and begins drinking.

HORATIO, who has been seated in his chair in the corner of the room, slowly turns. Though HAMLET has said nothing, he knows that HORATIO is there and waiting.

HORATIO: Hamlet?

> *HAMLET finishes drinking the water. Breathing.*

HAMLET: Do you know what time it is?

> *Blackout. Music.*
>
> *The past. Flashback to the beginning. In the playroom of the castle Elsinore. HORATIO has exited in the darkness – he is not a part of this reality yet.*
>
> *HAMLET, OPHELIA, LAERTES dancing, drunkenly singing. In original production, this was Sinatra's "One For My Baby," but could be replaced with another song that references time, as if in response to HAMLET's question in the preceding scene. The song will be sung again when coming back to this scene later in the play.*
>
> *This scene is about decadence. It's three people, who are going to be rulers someday, not being in charge of anything yet. Heavily scored by music that eventually overwhelms the scene.*

HAMLET, LAERTES, OPHELIA: *(Singing.)*
It's quarter to three, with no one in the place 'cept YOU and ME...

> *The teenagers begin to play their favorite game. They play with a real microphone, or one of those children's microphone and amp sets.*

HAMLET: How do you envision the end of the world Ophelia?

OPHELIA: *(Squealing laughter.)* I picture it all in the past tense! I am a VERY OLD WOMAN, hooked up to many many machines and I'm telling my great great great GREAT GRANDCHILDREN, "The day the world ended –" *(She is punched in the arm.)* OW!

HAMLET: Earthquakes! Mailbombs!

OPHELIA: Tsunamis?

HAMLET: Shit, wasn't that awful?

LAERTES: Did you make a donation?

HAMLET: Of course I made a donation.

LAERTES: I went to the concert.
Atomic bombs.

HAMLET: Oh, obvious.

LAERTES: I hate this game!

> *The MUSIC darkens. Under the music, the teenagers play at the microphone amidst making a mess. They imagine a mock speech to the people.*

OPHELIA: Let them eat cake. LET THEM EAT CAKE and DRINK CHAMPAGNE! Cake and champagne. Hostess cupcakes with cream and frosting and cake.

> *LAERTES and HAMLET do the* Titanic *pose.*

HAMLET: We're the king of the world!

OPHELIA: Keep the people downstairs well fed and we'll live forever!

> *LAERTES and HAMLET perform an Abbot and Costello routine at the mic.*

LAERTES: What do you wanna say to the people Hamlet?

HAMLET: Gee I don't know! What do *you* wanna say to the people Laertes?

LAERTES: I just want to thank everyone for coming out tonight. I love you all, people. I love this country! I love you DENMARK!!

> *Begins singing some awful song – or a song, awfully –perhaps U2.*
>
> *HAMLET begins talking over the song. This can barely be heard through the music, OPHELIA's giggling as she shoves cake in her mouth, LAERTES practicing boxing moves, as he sings... youthful cacophony.*
>
> *In the background, traces of the Zapruder film of President John F. Kennedy's assassination snake dimly through the din of home movies these three have made. Info overload.*

HAMLET: Who do you love, Denmark?!

OPHELIA: I LOVE YOU, DENMARK!

LAERTES: Yeah!

HAMLET: Start clapping for me, people.

> *HAMLET launches into a call and response into the mic quoting* Peter
> Pan.

I WON'T GROW UP.

OPHELIA AND LAERTES: I WON'T GROW UP.

HAMLET: I DON'T WANNA WEAR A TIE!

OPHELIA AND LAERTES: I DON'T WANNA WEAR A TIE!!

HAMLET: And I say to you people. My great people! My great Danes!

> *OPHELIA and LAERTES start barking/yipping like dogs.*

Shit.

Shhhit.

> *The scene devolves into full-blown chaos. LAERTES is blowing kisses
> to his imagined future crowds. OPHELIA is chugging a jug of water.
> HAMLET punching and reading.*
>
> *Somewhere in the future, HORATIO is knocking at a door.*
>
> *A gunshot rings through the air.*
>
> *Silence. Looking around.*
>
> *Day 1.*
>
> *A pause. A knock.*
>
> *HORATIO enters HAMLET's dorm room. He's there to deliver the news.*

HORATIO: Hamlet? You may wanna sit down.

> *Jump forward.*
>
> *Day 2.*
>
> *NOTE: Because of the time-jumping quick-cut nature of the play, the
> detritus from OPHELIA, HAMLET and LAERTES' party still covers the
> stage. OPHELIA's face is still covered with the cake she devoured in the
> previous scene.*

OPHELIA: *(Very quietly and slowly at first. And with accent.)* Clean up. Clean up!
We LOVE THINGS CLEAN in Wonderful Copenhagen.
King Claudius welcomes you home!

Music – 1950's idyllic. Airport. OPHELIA speaks in a demented Danish accent, and has put on a blonde wig.

On microphone, like at Disneyworld.

LOOK like a FRIEND on the REVITALIZED DENMARK!!! Copenhagen is laid-back the most out of everywhere! Our motto is *bare rolig*, "Take it easy." The language barrier is nowhere in Denmark! We speak everything! Danish, and English, and one or two other languages. Eating is everywhere! Restaurants serve salmon from the Baltic, ham from Danish porkers, opening-faces sandwiches, crispy vegetables from fertile Danish gardens, pastries with the lightness borrowed from the Vienneses, and sauces inspiration from the French. We're like the dining room at the United Nations! We like the eating so much that we never talk at ALL during dinner parties! Until maybe it's pass the dessert time. And speaking of dessert! A meal without one is, to a Dane, like a love affair with no kisses!

HAMLET and LAERTES meet at the airport urinals.

LAERTES: Hamlet!

HAMLET: Laertes.

LAERTES: Bonjour. How's school?

HAMLET: Great.

LAERTES: Glad to be home?

HAMLET: Not really.

LAERTES: Small bag.

HAMLET: I travel light.

LAERTES: *(Pressing.)* Hey Hamlet, how *are* you?

HAMLET: Been better. You?

LAERTES: Oh you know, comme ci comme ça. Can't complain. Work hard, play hard, living the dream!

Suddenly grabbing HAMLET and pulling him in.

Hey! I want you to know you can talk to me, man, about all this... tragic... tragedy. If you need to. I mean, you shouldn't keep all that stuff in. You know? I mean, grief man. Grief. Good God. FUCK! I mean, fucking grief, man.

Cell phone ring. Some shit music in the Coldplay vein.

Shit.

Answering.

Oui, ce Laertes...

Motioning just a second, but taking the call.

Meanwhile elsewhere in the airport, OPHELIA is continuing her routine.

OPHELIA: *(Latching on to HORATIO, who she thinks is an unsuspecting tourist.)* Children have delight to see wonders like Lego-land Park where there is a replica of Danish-made Mount Rushmore made in special beige Legos!

HORATIO: Thanks, but I'm here on business.

OPHELIA: Okey Dokey!

OPHELIA barrels on, growing a bit manic in her welcome.

Seals are everywhere! White sand is everywhere! Every day is Flag Day! We like to *le, tale,* and *spise!*

HORATIO suddenly recognizes her.

HORATIO: Ophelia!

HORATIO and OPHELIA: I saw your picture in Hamlet's room!

OPHELIA: *(She drops accent.)* Is he here?

HORATIO: He just landed. When did you start working here?

OPHELIA: My dad got me the job. It was either this or the mall. *(Back into accent/on mic.)* I'm the new minister of Danish Denmark.

Turning out, HORATIO makes a note on his pad? Blackberry? Or films this.

We LOVE GOOD TIMES HERE IN COPENHAGEN! Eat a pastry! Have a beer or Danish Aquavit! King Claudius welcomes you to the fairytale land of Hans Christian Anderson, and the existential playground of Kierkegaard!

Singing.

Fly me to Denmark, let me play...

Spotting LAERTES, still on the phone.

OH! That's my brother! He's the goodwill ambassador to France! Okay, he's very important! He has like a million frequent flyer miles.

Running over to LAERTES and grabbing the cell phone, which he's still mumbling, French into. She chatters with accent to whoever is on other end.

Okey dokey, we can't be talking to you now, but don't forget to give us a call when you're ready to go!

LAERTES: *(Annoyed.)* Ophelia!

She begins handing it back, but then yanks it back again.

OPHELIA: TEXT ME!!

She claps the phone shut giggling and hands it back to LAERTES.

LAERTES: OPHELIA!

OPHELIA: *(Giggling still.)* What?

(Seeing he's serious.) What?

LAERTES: This is not a time to be joking.

OPHELIA: *(Still in accent.)* Joking, no it is not.

LAERTES: We must be very quiet.

OPHELIA: *(Still in accent.)* Quiet! Yes very!

As the brother and sister catch up, HORATIO spots HAMLET in the airport, who immediately tries to hide.

HORATIO: Hamlet!

LAERTES: We must be very solemn.

OPHELIA: *(Still in accent.)* Slolem. Uh huh!

LAERTES: Nice accent.

OPHELIA: *(Still in accent, looking at audience.)* The tourists LOVE IT!

HORATIO: *(Breathless, catching up with him.)* Hamlet! Jesus Christ!

OPHELIA turns and catches sight of him as well. Temperature shift.

OPHELIA: Hamlet!

Flash forward.

Day 3.

The morning of the funeral. OPHELIA and HAMLET did not sleep together the night before. HORATIO is helping pick out what HAMLET will wear. LAERTES dresses himself in front of a mirror in another room. A camera is set up projecting this intimate scene on a television.

OPHELIA: *(Still in accent throughout the scene until noted.)* Did your mother hit you when you was a child?

HAMLET: Yes.

OPHELIA: Where? Like spanking?

HAMLET: Yes. And my face.

OPHELIA: Like a slap or a punch?

HAMLET: I don't really wanna talk about this.

OPHELIA: Slap or punch?

HAMLET: Is this interesting?

OPHELIA: *(Leaning over and speaking to HORATIO, who is filming this all.)* This is what you want to know, right? I was never hit as a child! Slap or punch?

HAMLET: Slap. She had a bad temper.

OPHELIA: But, you don't hit now do you?

HAMLET: No.

OPHELIA: And your temper is—

HAMLET: Not bad.

OPHELIA: Not bad!
So what is good for the goose is not so good for the gander.
Geese.
Group of geeses.
Gander—
I ALREADY SAID THAT!
(Offering.) You look good.

HAMLET: Thank you.

OPHELIA: In black. You look good in black.

HAMLET: I always wear black.

OPHELIA: You'll look just like the king when you are speaking today!
    (Falls on silence.) I'm really glad you're home.

HAMLET: Mmm.

OPHELIA: I'm having a good time!

HAMLET: Why are you talking with an accent?

OPHELIA: *(Beat. Dropping accent.)* I'm having a good time.

> *Day 2.*

> *Back at the airport, immediately where we left off.*

HORATIO: *(Breathless, finally catching up with him.)* Hamlet! Jesus Christ!

HAMLET: *(Automatically going to shake hands, not really looking at HORATIO.)*
    Yes, hi, thank you. Thanks for—

HORATIO: I'm so sorry again—you got my email, right?

HAMLET: Yes, tragic, yes I know—

HORATIO: Yes of course, I know how hard this has all been for you—

HAMLET: I know you.

HORATIO: *(Taken slightly aback.)* Yes. We were at school togeth—

HAMLET: I'm sorry, what was your name again?

HORATIO: *(A beat – after all, he delivered the news.)* Horatio.

HAMLET: Horatio... nope, not ringing a bell.

HORATIO: Yeah, I'm here to try and help you. Well actually I'm doing this
    piece—

> *The sound of the crowd at the airport begins to overwhelm the scene as
> a grieving Denmark welcomes back its prince. Unseen mob of reporters
> sprinting towards HAMLET and the gang.*

OPHELIA: Hamlet!

> *She runs to him, embracing.*

LAERTES: *(Taking over, on the mic which has appeared from a reporter in the "crowd.")* Visitors and Citizens, citizens and denizens, damerne og manden, a real treat for you, it's our very own Prince Hamlet!

> *Suddenly there is monstrous applause. HAMLET has officially returned. He and OPHELIA turn out to see the nation waiting, expectantly. LAERTES moves into the picture, waving.*
>
> *He hands the mic to HAMLET. All sound drops out.*
>
> *A heartbeat. HAMLET silent and struggling at the mic.*
>
> *This is the first time that he is supposed to speak to the people.*
>
> *He cannot get out a sound.*
>
> *NOTE: This will be the most important recurring image in the show, i.e. HAMLET unable to speak at a microphone.*

HORATIO: *(Swooping in, saving the day – the job he has in part come to do.)* We're all experiencing a lot of difficulty right now, none more so than Prince Hamlet. But I can tell you, he's just so happy to be back on Danish soil!

> *The applause is overwhelming.*
>
> *Over the applause, which is fading further away, as HORATIO ushers HAMLET away from the mic.*

HAMLET: *(Whispered.)* What was your name again?

HORATIO: *(Whispered.)* Horatio. I'm here to help.

> *Day 3.*
>
> *Evening. The funeral is ending, followed by a tribute concert at which Billy Joel is headlining. Huge roaring crowd sound.*
>
> *NOTE: This pre-concert moment repeats several times throughout the play and is linked with the sound cue of the crowd and music beginning.*

HAMLET: *(Shouting over the crowd.)* He always loved Billy Joel!

LAERTES: *(As the music gets underway, shouting.)* Do you wanna talk about it?

HAMLET: *(Over music.)* Don't really know what / there is to say...

LAERTES: *(As music gets going.)* Oh Billy! Yeah!

HAMLET and HORATIO: ... Awesome funeral!

Day 2.

Upon return home to castle from the airport. LAERTES, OPHELIA, and HORATIO finish press conference outside.

The three respond to questions rapidly back and forth, as if holding a dozen simultaneous press conferences.

LAERTES: Well, of course, I mean all our heads are spinning. King Hamlet was such a... really, really wonderful king, and a person. He taught me so much. It was an honor to serve him in any way I could.

Yeah, the grief. GRIEF. Good God. Good GRIEF. *(Tickled at his own word play.)*

HORATIO: Yes, well needless to say Hamlet is overwhelmed. Yes. Yes. This is so much to confront and such a sudden—

LAERTES: There are currently no details on that but I can assure you that I along with the new King Claudius—

OPHELIA: Well everybody uses some kind of recreational drug at some time or other!

HORATIO: No comment.
Me? No, no my position is not...
It's true I was at school with Hamlet.
Yes. *(Increasingly wary – accusations of taking advantage.)*
Yes.
No, currently I am just here to help Prince Hamlet, as well as, uh, whoever else—
No comment.
No comment.

LAERTES: *(Jumping in, swiping the mic from HORATIO.)* No, now, I mean, yes, Norway is the third largest oil-producing country in the world behind Saudi Arabia and Russia, but that is not where the conflict lies. The conflict with Norway, *my* conflict is a question of good and evil. Norway has insulted and degraded what we stand for. The freedoms that we stand for. And that is something I will not stand for. I hold my duty as I hold my soul, both to my God and to my gracious king. And to my new gracious king. And to my new gracious king's nephew/son. Thank you and good night.

Grand exit. HORATIO follows slowly behind, looking regretfully back. It didn't go great...

Day 3.

Morning. HAMLET is watching OPHELIA as she dresses for the funeral.
He is interrupted by HORATIO and LAERTES, who help dress him.
OPHELIA places a veil on her head. HORATIO is filming.

LAERTES: Is that what you're wearing to the funeral?

HAMLET: I hadn't really thought about it.

HORATIO: Never wear a red tie on camera

LAERTES: It's important, you know, it's your first public appearance, really.

HAMLET: Yeah, really.

LAERTES: Yeah. Wow. Wow. It's huge, I mean, fuckin' huge. People have expectations, you know?

> *This falls on dead silence other than the background music – "Blame it on the Tetons" by Modest Mouse or something equivalently quiet and melancholy.*

It's weird to be back, huh?

OPHELIA: *(Without accent.)* I'm always here.

> *Pulling veil over face, with accent and forced joy.*

Knock knock!

HAMLET: Who's there?

OPHELIA: Interrupting starfish!

HAMLET: Interrupting starfish wh–

> *She cuts him off smashing her splayed hand across his face, like a starfish suctioning on.*

LAERTES: So, Hamlet. What're you gonna say?

> *HAMLET looks at HORATIO.*

Day 3.

At the funeral earlier that evening. LAERTES looks good at the mic.
He has been talking for some time. Overly mournful music drenches the scene.

LAERTES: Generous and compassionate. King Hamlet was an inspiration to me, as I've told you, as I know he was to all of you. *(OPHELIA weeps loudly.)* But I promise now that we will continue his policy of compassion. Of caring. The state will not falter, so have no fear.

Continue to shop and ride the rollercoaster at the Mall of Copenhagen, and know that your purchases and you will be safe.

Continue to drive on our scenic highways, and drive assured that those of us in Elsinore are watching over you very very closely. Every single Danish day. In honor of King Hamlet. Yes, this tragic –

Tragedy. On an interpersonal and global scale.

I hear your fears. I know them.

Like I know my own face in the mirror. There are bad people beyond our walls. And you're asking, now, how do we carry on... in safety, and with hope?

I know these thoughts. You know, I never hoped to be here. I hoped, in fact, never to be here.

But Here We Are.

And now, HERE, to talk about his DAD, the man I know most of you have stood out here all night to see, back from school, my friend, mon frere, Damerne og Manden, please give it up for Denmark's NUMBER ONE SON!

> *Deafening applause. HAMLET stands, frozen and speechless and trying to grin. A long moment.*
>
> *Day 2.*
>
> *Very late at night. A pre-funeral/welcome home party. They have broken into the kitchen, which is stocked for the funeral tomorrow.*
>
> *HORATIO films all of this. It should be becoming clear that he is recording and molding the story of these three, especially HAMLET, using everything from a FlipCam to high-end digital technology. The three royals play to and with the camera.*

OPHELIA: *(In accent, which she drops in and out of throughout the scene.)* So much meat!

LAERTES: *(With derision.)* Cold cuts.

HAMLET: He always loved cold cuts. And they can use the leftovers at the wedding!

LAERTES: Is that a joke?

HAMLET: I don't know, is it?

OPHELIA: What was your name again?

HAMLET: Horatio!

LAERTES: So you're here to look after our young prince?

HAMLET: I'm seven months older than you.

HORATIO: I'm here to look after all of you.

OPHELIA: I'm older than both of them by almost a year.

LAERTES: Don't be silly Ophelia.

OPHELIA: *(Confiding to HORATIO.)* My brother didn't know how to read until he was almost 11.

> *HORATIO sets up the camera to capture the game. OPHELIA approaches it making faces.*

LAERTES: *(Not really listening.)* Do you know what you're gonna wear tomorrow?

HAMLET: Lederhosen. Whose turn is it?

HORATIO: *(Trying for a quiet moment with a strong close-up on HAMLET.)* I'm so sorry about your father.

HAMLET: Yes the house is full of people saying I'm sorry. Thank you.

HORATIO: You're welcome.

HAMLET: Ophelia, spin!

> *She spins a bottle as HAMLET provides a drum roll.*

HORATIO: I'm still not sure I get it. Is this a game?

HAMLET, OPHELIA and LAERTES: *(In unison.)* I don't know, is it?

> *The bottle lands. The result is indecipherable. LAERTES punches OPHELIA.*

HAMLET: Ophelia!

OPHELIA: Mothers!

> *They all switch places.*

LAERTES: *(While moving.)* Good one. Good one!

They land.

OPHELIA: *(Over enunciating.)* Liked to drink gin.

LAERTES: You're over enunciating. Shoulder pads.

HAMLET: Purple.

OPHELIA: Bread. Breasts!

HAMLET: Obvious.

OPHELIA: Oh! Milk. TISSUES!

HAMLET: Pet. Petting.

LAERTES: Champagne.

HORATIO: Free lunch ticket.

All look at him. Silence.

OPHELIA: Who wins?

HAMLET: Um, you win! HORATIO.

HAMLET turns the camera on him.

Tell us the story. Fill these sad times with clever antidotes.

OPHELIA/LAERTES: Anecdotes.

HORATIO: *(Uncomfortable in public gaze.)* My *mother* used to make beautiful sandwiches for me. Layered meats and cheeses. Lettuce. NICE BREAD. And I'd throw them in the garbage can when I'd get off the school bus. I'd eat the cookies. And we were poor. And she had no time or money to make those sandwiches. When she found out she put me in the free lunch program. I had to use the yellow ticket and everyone knew I was poor.

They sit stunned for a moment, except LAERTES who is texting.

OPHELIA: Wow.

HAMLET: You're a real Danish success story.

HORATIO: Actually I went to school on one of Ophelia's scholarships.

OPHELIA sighs. LAERTES begins giggling uncontrollably. They look and see he's texting. OPHELIA punches him. He looks up and figures it's his turn.

OPHELIA: Ok, hello?

LAERTES: Fathers.

> *Everyone switches places again, a little less enthusiastically. HORATIO watches HAMLET with concern at the topic. Perhaps he adjusts the camera to catch him closer.*

OPHELIA: Wool.

LAERTES: BEEF.

HORATIO: Sleeping bags.

OPHELIA: Birthdays.

LAERTES: Shopping bags.

OPHELIA and LAERTES: *(Together.)* Sock garters!

HAMLET: I don't want to play anymore.

OPHELIA: Woof!

HAMLET: Stop it.

OPHELIA: Woof!

LAERTES: Cold cuts. Law.

> *OPHELIA still barking.*

Law!

> *Deciding he's the winner.*

My father taught me to eat beef.

HAMLET: Game over.

> *Turning on music. Trying to drown the game and the others along with it.*

LAERTES: Don't be a baby.

HAMLET: Don't be a fuckface.

OPHELIA: Laertes!

LAERTES: Child.

HAMLET: Fuckface.

HORATIO: Hamlet—

OPHELIA: PASS THE DESSERT TIME!!

HAMLET: There's plenty of cake in the kitchen.

LAERTES: Whoever heard of cake at a funeral?

HAMLET: *(Right into the camera.)* He always loved cake.

> *Party breaking up, turning sour.*

OPHELIA: I'm really glad you're all home.

LAERTES: I think I'm headed back after the funeral.

HAMLET: Why bother leaving the airport at all?

OPHELIA: *(Perhaps inviting HAMLET.)* I think I'm going to bed.

HORATIO: Hamlet—

HAMLET: Yeah, me too. Goodnight.

HORATIO: Hamlet—

HAMLET: *(Beginning to wander away.)* My father—

HORATIO: If you want to talk about it—

LAERTES: He's not talking to anyone.

HAMLET: My father…

> *All fade away. HORATIO is the last to go and makes a decision to leave the camera running.*
>
> *Day 2.*
>
> *Even later at night. HAMLET in his room, very alone. He has been listening to music far too loud. Perhaps hours have passed since the game. Perhaps just now HAMLET is aware of having driven them all away.*

HAMLET: Cue the ghost!
    Don't blink.
    Don't blink!
    Blinking insults your audience.
    See I remember.
    It's not like I forgot everything.

Don't blink, don't breathe.
Hello?
Hello?!
I can hear you breathing.
I can feel you breathing in my ear.

He does and it feels gross and freaks him out.

HELLO?!

*Noticing the camera. Using it as a target more than anything else.
Perhaps speaking way too close.*

I am sitting in your lap, and you are whispering in my ear, and you
are telling me how a king never blinks. "Hamlet! Thou know'st 'tis
common. All that lives must die, passing through nature…"

He is beginning to cry, turning away from the camera.

Don't cry. Don't cry. No one likes a sore loser.

(Digging back.) "It is a fault to heaven. A fault against the dead. A fault
against nature whose common theme is DEATH OF FATHERS."

HAMLET opens his mouth to scream.

*Instead a noise <u>way</u> too loud pours forth and rocks the entire stage. It
drowns out HAMLET as he shrieks the "To be, or not to be" soliloquy
straight into the camera.*

Hands to head. Silence.

Day 2.

*Same time, late. Elsewhere in the castle. Nobody can sleep. OPHELIA
ambushes HORATIO, in the hallway.*

OPHELIA: Am I on camera?

HORATIO: No. Couldn't sleep?

OPHELIA: *(She speaks without accent.)* Not when everyone else is awake.
What are you doing here?

HORATIO: I told you I'm here to help.

OPHELIA: With what, what are you doing—

HORATIO: Him. I'm here to help him.

OPHELIA: Could you help me? With your camera?

HORATIO: What do you mean?

OPHELIA: Well you're telling our story right?

HORATIO: You know this is not just a home movie. This is national—

OPHELIA: I like your shoes! Can you help me? I could be Evita.

HORATIO: Well, yeah.

OPHELIA: *(Resuming accent.)* "I was dreaming again..." you should get this on camera!

HAMLET: *(Still with his camera.)* HELLO?!

> *Day 2.*
>
> *Same time. Elsewhere in the castle. LAERTES practices boxing in his room alone. He hears HAMLET shouting from many halls away.*

HAMLET: Hello?!!

LAERTES: *(Driven crazy.)* Whaaaaaattttttttt?!

> *LAERTES anxious. Examines his face. Takes his pulse. Takes out a rope. He begins jumping.*
>
> *Day 2.*
>
> *Same time. OPHELIA and HORATIO still in private hallway conference. HORATIO records this encounter.*

OPHELIA: *(With accent.)* I was dreaming again about tsunamis. The ground shook and the water in the harbor was cold and I was watching as the water kept rising until we were all underwater and it was freezing. And then when I woke up I had water in my ears. Wicked ends for wicked people.

HORATIO: Do you believe you're wicked?

OPHELIA: *(Looking at him, no accent.)* We all live on islands, if you really think about it. *(HORATIO doesn't respond. She resumes accent).* It might be because of all the cake I ate. It's not attractive for a woman to look so hungry. Particularly when she's surrounded by starving children with bloated bellies and covered in flies. She should be made saddened by how bad the world is. And how unfair. And then she should brush the flies away and show her beautiful white teeth.

She bares her teeth for HORATIO's camera.

So in my dream the poison got into the blood stream.

Into everybody's bloodstream.

The human body is 70% water, did you know that?

HORATIO: I think it's over 70%.

OPHELIA: Over 70%?

HORATIO: Right.

OPHELIA: Right. So, in my dream the poison got into the water system. And into the precious natural fluids. I told my father he should make a proposal! Guns at all the water towers, and at all the corners maybe and they could help you cross the street. Like grandmothers! I've been thinking about this a lot since –

HORATIO: You feel unsafe?

OPHELIA: *(Off the record.)* Laertes keeps talking about how easy it would be for someone to put poison in the water supply. *(Resuming accent. Melodramatic performance.)* Or in the milk supply. Think of all those school lunches!

HORATIO: I ate lunch all through school on your program. I went to university on your program.

OPHELIA: *(Dropping accent again. Flat.)* You said that.

HORATIO: I said that.

> *Beat.*

OPHELIA: *(For the camera.)* This is the first of my children I've ever met.

> *Long beat.*

What was your name again?

> *HAMLET still in the hallway. Horrific sound. All in the house stop. They just hear him screaming.*

HAMLET: *(Hands to head, silence.)* I apologize. Truly.

I am sorry.

I don't know, everyone else is so sorry. I can't tell what they're sorrier about. The fact that you're dead or the fact that I'm your son.

HELLO?!! HELLO?!!

See, someone comes! YOU come saying AVENGE ME Hamlet and I
do and things get better.

I make a good leader.

I look good in black.

I don't blink, but my eyes are dry.

Um I don't think I can do this.

Hello?

Hello?

CUE THE GHOST!

I am waiting for you.

I don't want to be here.

I'm waiting.

(Towards the camera.)

Turn it off.

> *HORATIO walks over and turns off the camera. Or moves it to position
> for final scene. Transition.*
>
> *Day 6.*
>
> *The present. The Boardroom. LAERTES enters and takes OPHELIA's glass
> and drinks it.*

HORATIO: Hamlet?

> *Long Silence.*
>
> *Day 4.*
>
> *The morning following the funeral. Breakfast.*

OPHELIA: Ok, ok, here's another one!

(French accent.) Monsieur Laertes, we zee people of France are
wondering what your King Claudius is intending to do about zee
negateeve international response to 'is continued war wiz Norway.
What does 'ee eentend to do wizout zee support of zis community?

LAERTES: Well, ma cherie, that's a question simple. Claudius ne donne
pas un damn about le comunite international. Il intend aller a la
guerre avec Norway, parce que Norway a fait un insult a notre pays,
et maintenant, nous pensons de nos citoyens, you know? We don't, en
autres mots, need the support of the international community on this
one, sucre.

> *Wink. He slaps her ass.*

HORATIO: *(Overlapping LAERTES and OPHELIA, as HAMLET enters.)* How are you feeling?

HAMLET: I've been better.

HORATIO: I heard you last night.

HAMLET: Hey Ophelia, Horatio heard us!

HORATIO: *(Embarrassed.)* Not that.

LAERTES: Hey!

OPHELIA: He's lying, I went to bed. Couldn't sleep though.

LAERTES: You shouldn't sleep on a full stomach.

OPHELIA and LAERTES: Weird dreams.
    Jinx!
    Double jinx!

HORATIO: Hamlet we should go over a few things.

OPHELIA: We should all go over a few things.

LAERTES: Don't be silly Ophelia.

HAMLET: Weren't you leaving today?

OPHELIA: You didn't hear!

HORATIO: Of course he didn't hear.

HAMLET: I didn't hear what?

HORATIO: They elevated the security level early this morning. They've cancelled all the flights out.

LAERTES: It's just a precaution, preventative method.

HORATIO: Preventative my ass, it's mass hysteria!

OPHELIA: Mass hysteria. Think of all those trembling Danish bodies.

HORATIO: The population's almost doubled since the funeral. We should go over a few things.

HAMLET: So, what did you wanna talk about?

Day 4.

Early afternoon. HORATIO and HAMLET. HORATIO adjusts the camera on HAMLET for a long time. Then they look at each other a long time.

HORATIO: Hamlet?

HAMLET: I thought the funeral was awful. I thought it was just awful. All those people crying crocodile tears.

HORATIO: I'm not sure where that comes from.

HAMLET: Crocodiles cry when they're hungry. How they capture their prey.

HORATIO: How did you know that?

HAMLET: I googled it...
I made Ophelia google it.

HORATIO: Do you have anything you wanna say about everything that has happened?

HAMLET: I wouldn't know where to begin. All these people, rubber faces and everyone looking and thinking, gosh Hamlet is so much shorter than his dad.

(Liking the alliteration.) His dead dad, dead dad, dead dad, dead dad, you know if you say the words enough they start to lose -

HORATIO: You might think about what you're going to do now.

HAMLET: Does the camera have to be on?

HORATIO: *(Sharply.)* This is not just the story of your life Hamlet.

HAMLET: Ooh, you're angry I messed up your speech aren't you? Aren't you?
Aren't you?
Aren't you?
Aren't you?
Aren't you? Just a little?

HORATIO: Don't be a child.

HAMLET: Oh, I am a child! *(Recalling the game.)* Fathers! Oh, I win! I never mouthed the pledge of allegiance and I never stole. I held hands and I watched him while he slept. I shut my mouth. I knew when to shut my mouth. Sometimes, he would sit me on his lap at meetings. Lap dog, lap dog. Dead dad's lap dog. He would lean in my ear whispering while everyone was talking: "Don't blink. Don't blink." That's what he said. Blinking insults your audience. Don't blink when you look in the camera especially. Because blinking means fear and fear means they never should've elected you in the first place.

HORATIO: We don't have elections.

HAMLET: I know.

HORATIO: Do you think the people will just sit through this?

HAMLET: They seem to be good at that.

HORATIO: It's not going to hold for very much longer. Everyone is tired–

HAMLET: I'm exhausted.

HORATIO: You're exhausting.

HAMLET: I could sleep for a week.

HORATIO: It's a lot. It's all a lot. But this is how things happen–

HAMLET: What things?

HORATIO: Change. Revolution. "We suffer youth like a serious sickness that is due to the time in which we have been thrown, a time of extensive decay and disintegration. Disintegration characterizes this time, and thus uncertainty." There are thousands of people sleeping in the streets right now for your father's funeral. They're all waiting. You know this is something those two – Ophelia and Laertes, they get it. "When you find yourself in the thick of a fiasco –"

HAMLET: Careful you're quoting yourself.

HORATIO: I'm quoting Nietzsche.

HAMLET: *(Laughing.)* Nietzsche was a nihilist.

HORATIO: Nietzsche was a rockstar.

HAMLET: You're angry I messed up your speech.

HORATIO: I could give a fuck about the speech.

HAMLET: That's not true.

HORATIO: You're right it's not.

HAMLET: Horatio, I think I am a nihilist.

HORATIO: I am not really sure what that means.

HAMLET: Well a nihilist is someone who—

HORATIO: I know what nihilism is.

HAMLET: Do you believe that we are about to change everything?

HORATIO: What do you think I'm doing here Hamlet?

> *Day 4.*

> *Earlier, the morning after the funeral. Breakfast.*

OPHELIA: You would have made a lovely king.

LAERTES: Don't be silly Ophelia.
But she's right. You would have. Especially in that suit. So dapper. You look gay. Like a viking.
I think the whole thing went quite well.
And actually a great buffet!

OPHELIA: *(Patting belly.)* So much meat!

LAERTES: It's not attractive for a woman to look so hungry.

OPHELIA: *(Beat. Reconsidering but trying not to let LAERTES see this.)* I think I'm giving up meat. For good this time.
And I should probably drink more water while I'm at it.

> *Beat. Turning to HORATIO, changing the subject.*

Show us a trick!!

> *She digs in her satchel or in her pockets to pay him.*

HORATIO: *(Looking to HAMLET for help, who has none to give.)* I don't know any tricks.

OPHELIA: Oh really? Not even for 50 dollars?

LAERTES: *(To OPHELIA.)* Is that play money? *(It is.)*

HORATIO: *(Showing the bill to the camera.)* It is.

HAMLET: Laertes, you dropped something...
Laertes, you dropped something!

LAERTES: I heard you the first time.

HAMLET: Then pick it up.

OPHELIA: Boys, boys.

HAMLET: Pick it up fuckface.

LAERTES: You pick it up, homo.

HAMLET: Pick it up or get out of my house.

LAERTES: I'm sorry, your house?

> *LAERTES grabs HAMLET and slams him on the table.*

OPHELIA: *(Attempting to diffuse.)* Pass the dessert time!

HAMLET: *(Against the table.)* SO! Laertes are you planning to follow in your father's shoes?

LAERTES: Footsteps.

OPHELIA: Laertes!

LAERTES: My father's footsteps. *(Steals HAMLET's glasses, tries them on.)* Boxing this afternoon? 3 o'clock. Don't blink.

> *Day 3.*

> *Early afternoon. HORATIO and HAMLET alone preparing for the funeral.*

HORATIO: You look great.

HAMLET: Yeah thanks that's what they tell me.

HORATIO: You know not to breathe too heavy into the mic.

HAMLET: You know I was raised, like they gave us classes. Like, don't blink, don't breathe too heavy into the mic.

HORATIO: Great, you're gonna be great. *(Pause.)* So what're you gonna say?

HAMLET: You sound like Laertes.

HORATIO: Laertes has a speech ready.

HAMLET: Fine.

HORATIO: Fine.
So here's what you're gonna say.

Day 4.

Late afternoon. After HAMLET's talk with HORATIO, OPHELIA ambushes him in the hallway.

OPHELIA: So how'd it go?

HAMLET: Oh. Jeez. Stupendous. Horatio is going to take care of the country while I write my memoirs.

OPHELIA: That's not funny.

HAMLET: You told me I wasn't funny.

OPHELIA: Well I was right wasn't I?

HAMLET: Why are you talking with an accent?

OPHELIA: Because I'm Danish!
Tell me what is going on.

HAMLET: I don't know. *(As if she and the world are totally deaf.)*
I DONNNN'TT KNNOOOOWW.

People keep looking, and thinking "OH the son, I mean that's part of the shame." And you and Laertes just keep on eating and eating –

OPHELIA: I know I eat too much–

HAMLET: Not the point. You're like those fucking dancing dolls.

OPHELIA: Well my father wasn't shot. Our father is still alive.

HAMLET: Do you want a fucking award?

OPHELIA: *(Dropping accent.)* This is not fair, Hamlet. I am here. I am trying for godsake, I'm working at the GODDAMNED AIRPORT!!

Suddenly catches sight of HORATIO eavesdropping. Resuming accent and poise.

I am trying to be a good person! All of these people are afraid and you're not helping.

HAMLET: I know. I'm sorry.

OPHELIA: You can be good. Adopt a school with me. Get into humanitarian work. There's so many people...

HAMLET: *(Suddenly.)* How's Dagmar?

Awkward beat. A sore spot has been struck.

OPHELIA: Fine.

HAMLET: Or Helga? Margarethe?

OPHELIA: Margaret.

HAMLET: Whatever.

OPHELIA: She's doing fine, thank you.

HAMLET: Did you ever write to Sofus?

OPHELIA: Yes.

HAMLET: Soren, Viktor, Kirsten? How about Laura? Marna? How many children do you sponsor now Ophelia? *(OPHELIA begins tallying under assault.)* How many sewer dwelling, malaria ridden, bloated bellied babies do you have running around in third world countries thinking, "Oh my saintly Danish mother, when will you send me more of those delicious butter cookies and some of that cough medicine?"

OPHELIA: 432!! I have 432 children in different countries. I maintain a brief but tender correspondence with all of them.

HAMLET: Oh yeah –

OPHELIA: With MOST of them. We pass for what we are and IAMAGOODPERSON!
(Resuming.) I tried to vote in last year's election.

HORATIO: *(Who has entered and is quietly watching.)* We don't have elections.

OPHELIA: *(No accent, bitter at the discovery she made.)* WE DON'T HAVE ELECTIONS!

> *Day 4.*
>
> *HORATIO and HAMLET.*

HAMLET: I am exhausted.

HORATIO: You said that already. Nihilism must be exhausting.

HAMLET: You wouldn't think so but it is.

> *The two suddenly share a ridiculous stint of laughter. OPHELIA and LAERTES join in, though it is a coincidence. They are in a totally different part of the castle.*

They are playing a game from childhood. It feels different.

LAERTES: Do you know what time it is?

OPHELIA: It's quarter to three.

LAERTES: That's right. And who is in the place?

OPHELIA: There's no one in the place. 'Cept –

LAERTES and OPHELIA: You and me.

> *Cutting back to HAMLET and HORATIO.*
>
> *Day 3.*
>
> *HAMLET and HORATIO continuing to prepare for the funeral.*

HAMLET: *(Reading the speech HORATIO has written.)* "When you find yourself in the thick of a fiasco" – that's a great word.

HORATIO: I know.

HAMLET: Man this is dark. "Where we still walk, soon no one will be able to walk." It's dark.

HORATIO: It's a funeral.

HAMLET: *(Long beat.)* It is a funeral.

> *Day 4.*
>
> *Late afternoon. Things are accelerating. The following takes place simultaneously, like a split screen – HORATIO and LAERTES in one room, and OPHELIA and HAMLET in another.*

LAERTES: *(Calling.)* Horatio!

> *HORATIO moves to him with the camera.*
>
> *Elsewhere in the castle, OPHELIA is on her own, gargling (perhaps with alcohol) and singing quietly to herself.*

OPHELIA: *(Begins gargling song from first scene.)* **We're drinking my friend**...

> *LAERTES and HORATIO get set up. LAERTES is preparing to film a statement.*

HORATIO: Are you ready?

LAERTES: You rolling?

OPHELIA: I should probably drink more water while I'm at it. *(Resumes song with more water. More gargling.)*

HORATIO: Yes, I'm set.

> *HAMLET is watching television. OPHELIA enters, still gargling. She stops and gulps it down.*

OPHELIA: Good my lord, how does your honor for this many a day?

LAERTES: *(Speaking into the camera.)* Good evening, damerne og manden. Thank you for welcoming me into your homes.

HAMLET: Ophelia.

LAERTES: This is a difficult time for us right now.
The king's death has struck hard. There are questions swirling about how quickly we have moved to stabilize the government... maybe even doubts.
These are hard times in which to keep your hearts open.
But I am here to tell you—

> *Breaking.*

Stop stop.
It's too wordy.

HORATIO: It's a little wordy, yeah.

OPHELIA: *(Trying to find her courage to start the scene she has to play. And he's not playing along. She will slip consistently in and out of accent during this.)* My lord, how DOES your honor? How DOES your HONOR?

HAMLET: I've been better.

OPHELIA: My lord I have remembrances—

> *She produces a cassette/cd mixtape HAMLET gave to her in the past, before the events of the play. She begins to play it on a boombox, underscoring their conversation like a movie (something like Avril Lavigne).*

HORATIO: I would think about "swirling,"

HAMLET: Don't be silly Ophelia.

HORATIO: It's flowery. You want to be—

LAERTES: I wanna be the guy they have beer with.

HAMLET: Can we just sit for a sec?

OPHELIA: I think it's time for a change.

HAMLET: I think I'm already nauseous.

OPHELIA: My lord I have these remembrances.

HAMLET: *(Picking up the game.)* No, not I. I never gave you aught.

HORATIO: Exactly.

OPHELIA: My lord you know right well you did.

HAMLET: Why are you talking with an accent?

OPHELIA: Why did you forget yours?

HAMLET: It sounded funny when I tried to speak. I sounded funny.

OPHELIA: You've always sounded funny.

HAMLET: You said that I wasn't.

OPHELIA: You're not. It's not the same thing, right?

LAERTES: Right.

HORATIO: Right. You want to go back?

LAERTES: *(Clearly hard on himself.)* Yeah, give me one second.

    Pause, HORATIO watching him.

HORATIO: Just, easy.

LAERTES: Yeah.

HORATIO: Take them closer.

LAERTES: Yeah.
    Yeah.
    Okay.
    Thanks for having me over damerne og manden.
    That's stupid.
    Keep rolling.

HAMLET: I don't really know where we are any more. I've got a lot of questions.

OPHELIA: Me too.

HAMLET: Me first.

LAERTES: Good evening, damerne og manden. Thank you for watching.

HORATIO: You don't want to seem desperate.

HAMLET: I think we should get married.

OPHELIA: That's not a question.

LAERTES: Right.
Keep rolling.
Good evening.
Good evening.

OPHELIA: I'm not really having a good time.

HAMLET: No shit. Not a question either.

OPHELIA: No shit. I think things are bad. I think things are really bad.

HAMLET: No shit.

OPHELIA: No shit. I'm starting a political party.

HAMLET: We don't have political parties here.

LAERTES: Hello damerne og manden and thank you for welcoming me into your home.

> *HORATIO nodding.*

We are in the midst of
Shit
Shit

> *The mixtape song is reaching its tween emotive climax. OPHELIA caught between who she is supposed to be in this classic story, and how she is actually feeling.*

HAMLET: I did love you once.

OPHELIA: Yeah you told me.

HAMLET: I did?
What did I say?

OPHELIA: You said you loved me. You said you wanted 432 children. You said you were happy.

HAMLET: Well then I must've been.

OPHELIA: I think so.

> *They move into a wrestling sequence, part fight, part making out. She yanks his pants down. They embrace and kiss. She chugs water and spits it in his face as he stands, arms open. They race to shut off the boombox.*

> *This combat overlaps with LAERTES becoming more and more rigid in the sights of the camera.*

LAERTES: We are—
These are hard times damerne og manden.

> *Staring.*

> *Staring.*

HORATIO: Laertes?

> *Silence.*

> *HAMLET and OPHELIA abruptly stop the blaring mixtape. They are panting.*

OPHELIA/HAMLET: *(In the sudden silence, shouting in each other's faces.)*
What should such fellows as I do crawling between earth and heaven?!

OPHELIA: *(No accent.)* Grow up.

HORATIO: Laertes?

HAMLET: What do you want me to do Ophelia? Tell me what to do.

> *She carefully and coldly resumes accent, and fixes herself from the previous struggle.*

OPHELIA: Write a memoir.
Buy a humvee.
Go on a roadtrip.
Find yourself.

HORATIO: Laertes?

LAERTES: *(Staring.)* Keep rolling.
(Staring.) Ladies and gentlemen, I know you are afraid...

> *Quiet. Or extended drone.*

Day 6.

The present. The three of them stand around the table. HORATIO looks at them.

HAMLET: Am I supposed to...

They all look at him, completely out of patience.

Horatio.

HORATIO: Hamlet I've been double tasking. I came into this blind with nothing but the best intentions. The material I have isn't necessarily going to help.

HAMLET: *(Taking in this information. After a few beats.)* Ophelia?

Ophelia screams with revolutionary fervor in Danish.

HAMLET puts his head in his hands. ALL a bit stunned.

After another few beats.

HAMLET: Laertes?

LAERTES: *(Sharp.)* What are you gonna say?

Day 3.

The funeral. Bells. LAERTES is mid-introduction – it feels a bit like the announcer at a wrestling match.

LAERTES: And now, HERE, to talk about his DAD, the man I know many of you have stood out here all night to see, back from school my friend, mon frere, Damerne og Manden, please give it up for Denmark's NUMBER ONE SON!

Thunderous applause that goes on for far too long. And then silence. HAMLET is a wreck.

HAMLET: *(Into mic.)* The dearth of a leader is something...

HORATIO hovers close, tense.

Sorry. Can I start again? Thank you.
No I'm fine. Thank you very much.

Getting out HORATIO's notes.

The death... of a leader is something this country wasn't prepared for. I wasn't prepared for.

How can we possibly, you may ask yourself, possibly be prepared for that.

When you find yourself in the thick of a fiasco, as we do now...

> *Totally breaking from the script. Frantic.*

You know, I would like to share some recollections about my dear dead dad. He used to sit me on his lap -

HORATIO: *(Hissing.)* Hamlet!

HAMLET: Okay, yes. *(Resuming script.)* Now. I favor as a practical policy the putting of first things first.

So, first, Hamlet.

My dear dead dad, Hamlet, loved his nation.

He took an interest in life.

Where?

Somewhere??

NO! HERE. Denmark!

Where everyone is fighting, I think.

And the end is hard to see.

But now is a time for change, my people.

Now is a time to look back, lean back, fall back, now is a time for revolution!

> *This begins to veer between the scripted speech, and new thoughts entirely.*

Don't blink.

And in order to achieve this we may suffer.

We must suffer.

Growing pains.

I love that show.

Now me personally, I am in it for the food.

Or, uh, the day off from work.

Yeah that's right, I heard you saying those things in the public urinals.

And I can understand, stress, obligation, a sense of anticipation of new national holidays.

A sense that there is a Denmark to which you belong, and there was a king, who is dead.

And HE was your king.

And now you have me.

You have me!

"Stand up, Hamlet."
"Hamlet is dead."

> *Knocking the lectern or floor. Banging, as if someone will open.*

HELLO?!
And if he doesn't come right now, he is never coming back.

> *HORATIO is trying to get HAMLET to stand, to collect himself. He begins whispering furiously into HAMLET's ear.*

> *HAMLET repeats, quickly, numbly.*

Damerne o manden.
We suffer youth like a serious sickness that is due to the time in which we have been thrown, a time that for all its strengths and its weaknesses opposes a spirit of youth.
A time of decay and disintegration.
Disintegration characterizes this time, and thus—
We are—
Uncertain.

HORATIO: *(Whispering, touch too loud.)* And they are looking to you.

HAMLET: *(Beat.)* And you look to me.

...

When you find yourself in the thick of a fiasco...
And I'm just somebody else's son.
Am I right?
Am I right?

> *He stares at the audience a long time.*

> *Finally looking at the notes again. Reading, almost a Kennedy.*

We dare not forget today that we are heirs.
We dare not tempt our enemies with weakness.
We are not here to curse the darkness.

> *Mic slam.*

> *Blackout.*

> *Flashback.*

> *The past. Before anything. Other than HORATIO, who is in the present, looking at his footage and watching the world fall apart.*

HAMLET: The end, the end of the world!
Past tense ASSHOLE!
Earthquakes.
Mailbombs.
Anthrax postcards–

OPHELIA: Tsunamis–

HAMLET: *(Breaking game.)* Shit wasn't that awful?

LAERTES: Did you make a donation?

HAMLET: Of course I made a donation.
ECLIPSES!
I wonder what people thought at the very first eclipse. "Du-ude! Check this out" or terrible fear, or singing, "Here comes the dark?" *(Continuing song...)*

OPHELIA: Maybe they weren't thinking at all. Maybe they were too busy looking for matches.

LAERTES: Bien! Tres bien!

OPHELIA: My brother is the David Hasselhoff of the French government!

HAMLET: We're all so proud of him.

LAERTES: How's school going Hamlet?

HORATIO: Hamlet?

HAMLET: How do you envision the end of the world Ophelia?

LAERTES: Don't upset her.

HAMLET: She's not a child Laertes.

HORATIO: *(Calling from the present.)* HAMLET!

OPHELIA: I imagine it all in the past tense. I fast-forward and I am an old and wrinkled woman, wearing adult diapers and hooked up to many many machines. At least twelve. Or seven.
And I've got tubes in my liver. And I'm telling my greatgreatgreatgreatgrandchildren, "The day the world ended."

HORATIO: The people are mad in the streets, Hamlet. They are screaming for a new king.

LAERTES: *(HORATIO overlapping.)* Atomic bomb.

70

HORATIO: They are screaming for a new vision. They are screaming for you. They've shut down the airport.

HAMLET: Obvious.

LAERTES: I hate this game.

HORATIO: They've cancelled all the flights out.

> *Day 3.*

> *The Funeral.*

HAMLET: Horatio?

> *A long silence as time comes back into focus for a moment.*

Who's playing at the funeral?

HORATIO: Billy Joel.

> *Music. The concert. Billy Joel's "We Didn't Start the Fire (Live)" plays through the house. There is a raucous childish awesome dance sequence to the first section of the song through the chorus. This then blossoms into a massive montage sequence.*

HAMLET: *(Shouting across the dance floor.)* OPHELIA!

> *HAMLET chases OPHELIA, and ALL follow, on a massive initially gleeful chase through the castle.*

> *At some point, the following dialogue/action begins:*

OPHELIA: *(Singing. Climbing on top of a table.)*
Save the children, save the whales, save the pigeons and the snails eat the children eat the children.

> *She is now standing on the table.*

> *Over the music, which is still pumping loud, the sound of a crowd erupts.*

> *She sees them, transfixed. They are shouting for her to lead them.*

> *She begins to shout at the crowd. Ophelia is transformed into a revolutionary. She pumps her fist, spilling everywhere the gallon of Poland Spring she holds in her hands. It is Evita. It is insane.*

We must rise up my people! We must stop these government pigs from thinking they can walk all over our freedoms!

I say freedom of the press!

I say freedom of speech! I say—

> *She suddenly begins shouting in Danish. It is long, ferocious. The crowd responds with enormous applause. She is glowing.*

(Quietly into the mic.) We must not forget today that we are heirs...

We dare not tempt our enemies with weakness.

> *Meanwhile HAMLET is in his room, looking everywhere for the ghost.*

HAMLET: Hello? HELLO?! CUE THE GHOST!

> *Meanwhile LAERTES is recording an on-camera interview.*

LAERTES: My father taught me to eat beef.

You watch these people in restaurants, cutting a burger into manageable bites.

Try eating the whole cow motherfucker!

> *LAERTES finds HAMLET.*

Boxing this afternoon?

> *LAERTES speaks into the mic to reporters as he and HAMLET, with help from HORATIO and OPHELIA, put on their boxing gloves.*

... They believe that solutions emerge from the judicious study of discernible reality. But that's not the way the world really works anymore.

We're an empire now, and when we act, we create our own reality. And while they're studying that reality – judiciously, as they will – we'll act again, creating other new realities, and that's how things will sort out.

We're history's actors and they, all of them, will be left to just study what we do.

And THAT, may I add, was a good question.

> *Screaming crowds.*

> *Into the boxing match. OPHELIA calls moves with accent into mic, not necessarily in time with the fight. ("Punch! Punch! Jab! Swing batter batter batter!" Etc.)*

> *LAERTES lays HAMLET flat.*

OPHELIA: BLACKOUT!!

Out of the match. HORATIO, OPHELIA and LAERTES at a press conference in an echo of the earlier image.

HORATIO: *(Into the mic.)* People ask me about my job. Is it hard being around that much money? Is it hard having to sleep with, you know, I mean you must have to sleep with one eye open.

Those kids.

You know the stories.

You know them.

Everyone knows the story. You know what happened.

Happens.

Is happening.

HAMLET?!

Do you understand that it is happening now?

HAMLET has arisen, still unsteady from the knockout, from the grief, from the accumulation of days.

OPHELIA: Well everybody uses some kind of recreational drug at some point or another!

LAERTES: No comment.

LAERTES has grabbed the mic and it is a direct segue into:

Day 3.

Bells. The funeral again.

LAERTES: *(At mic, OPHELIA weeping.)* We will miss him. I will miss him.
This tragic—

Tragedy.

But here we are.

HERE WE ARE!

Things are beginning to completely devolve. "We Didn't Start the Fire," which has been pummeling throughout, is now crumbling into blaring feedback. HAMLET is back at the airport.

HORATIO: *(To HAMLET.)* I'm so sorry H. You got my email, right?

Now back in the castle. He and LAERTES are sparring.

LAERTES: COME ON! COME ON! I don't get it! I don't get you man.
Sure. Grief. Fucking grief!

HAMLET punches LAERTES, whose hands had come down while trying to talk to him, in the stomach.

FUCK.

FUCKING.

You've been wearing black since you were 14 years old.

HAMLET: You s–s–stuttered until you were 12.

LAERTES: *(Throwing a violent feint from which HAMLET cowers. Laughing.)*
Don't BLINK, man, don't blink. Blinking insults your AUDIENCE!

LAERTES lands a hard punch, HAMLET doubled over.

The sounds of people screaming at the concert, blend with the sounds of a boxing match, blend with the sounds of a revolution or mob.

LAERTES has thrown HAMLET back onto the table, a hand on his throat. HAMLET laughing madly.

Say I look good in black.

HAMLET: You're crazy.

LAERTES: SAY IT. Do you believe it is happening now?

Say it!

SAY IT!

These are not small things!

Meanwhile OPHELIA is back on the table, in front of the people. HORATIO stands behind her like a revolutionary guard.

Slowly HAMLET and LAERTES stop fighting, becoming aware of what's happening. Impressed and terrified.

She speaks, slowly. In incredible control. The sound of blaring feedback is now just looping. Eerie.

NOTE: OPHELIA's speech is performed in Danish, punctuated by the English below. The translation of the original speech has been lost, and future interpretations are encouraged to come up with their own. OPHELIA is speaking as a political rebel exhorting the masses to rise up against those who hold power, to tear down the fascist, established systems that confine them as innately free individuals. She then goes on to say the form of this revolt should essentially be a suicide pact; that things have gotten so bad that they should drown themselves with water, as living embodiments of their freedoms being drowned. This devolves into chanting "Drink!"

OPHELIA: *[Original Text performed in Danish.]*
Ladies and gentlemen. Sisters and brothers.
DRINK.
DRINK.
My brother... And my father...
Hamlet...
DRINK. DRINK.

> *HORATIO begins to join her in the chant of "DRINK."*

> *Then, amidst the speech, she begins to cry out, in English for Hamlet. Panting with energy.*

Hamlet?
Hamlet?

HAMLET: Dude, you're sister's crazy.

LAERTES: I know, she cried harder than anyone else at the funeral.

HORATIO and OPHELIA: *(Like a song.)*
HAAAAAAAAAAAAAAAAAAAAAMMMMM-
LEEEEEEEEEEEEEEEETTTTTTTT!!!
Do you know what's going on up here?

> *A call back to the Abbot and Costello routine.*

LAERTES: What do you wanna say to the people, Hamlet?

HAMLET: *(Half playing.)* I don't know.
What do you wanna say to the people Laertes?

> *LAERTES is frozen at the mic for a moment.*

ALL: WE LOVE YOU DENMARK!!!

> *MORE DANCING. Jumping aggressively. There is no music. Just feedback and screaming.*

HAMLET: *(Exuberant.)* How do you envision the end of the world Ophelia?

ALL: Earthquakes.
Mailbombs.
Tsunamis.

A faster cycling through of images.

LAERTES: *(Pinning HAMLET.)* Say it! SAY IT! These are not small things!

HAMLET: *(To OPHELIA.)* Of course I made a donation! I love all our 432 children so so much I can't stand it.

HORATIO is leading OPHELIA by the shoulders.

OPHELIA: I had almost 10,000 people at my rally. Carrying signs that said "No War for Peace" and "Keep your hands off my bush!" This, people, is how movements are born.

Turning hard back onto HORATIO.

I believe it is happening now.

LAERTES: *(Sparring with HAMLET.)* Don't blink! Don't blink, blinking insults your audience.

The world spinning, HORATIO trying to regain control. Looking at all his footage.

HORATIO: Where are we!? I came into this blind with nothing but the best intentions. I am good at my job. I am a good person.

OPHELIA: Me too! Me too! I think babies with bloated bellies should be paraded through the streets so we can all see how wicked we are. I am a good person! I am a good—

Pouring a toast for herself and HORATIO who is horrified.

PERSON.

In Danish, into HORATIO's camera and the microphone:

I am a good person.

She begins to chug a gallon of water. This will continue and grow, until she is choking. Between gulps:

Names for babies! Abelone, Agnes... *(The list of Danish baby names continues.)*

HAMLET is in his room. Trying to hide from the chaos. Reading a copy of Shakespeare's Hamlet. *Looking for guidance.*

As HAMLET reads, HORATIO slowly approaches his door, and begins knocking.

HAMLET: What do you want to say to the people Hamlet? Hamlet?

"To be, or not to be. That is the question.
Whether 'tis nobler in the mind to suffer
The slings and arrows of outrageous fortune
Or to take arms against a sea of troubles,
And by opposing end them. To die – to sleep –
No more; and by a sleep to say we end
The heartache, and the thousand natural shocks
That flesh is heir to..."

HORATIO is banging.

HORATIO: HAMLET!

Hamlet!

Sudden silence and stillness across the stage.

Hamlet?

You may wanna sit down.

Day 6.

Everyone is vanquished. ALL stand in silence.

HAMLET: Am I supposed to–

They all look at him.

HORATIO: Hamlet?

Do you know what time it is?

ALL watch, expectantly.

HAMLET turns away, and slowly approaches the mic.

He inhales to speak.

BLACKOUT.

PARTICULARLY IN THE HEARTLAND

WRITTEN BY
JESSICA ALMASY, FRANK BOYD, RACHEL CHAVKIN,
JILL FRUTKIN, BRIAN HASTERT, MATT HUBBS, LIBBY KING,
JAKE MARGOLIN, and KRISTEN SIEH

WITH
STEPHANIE DOUGLASS, JAKE HEINRICHS,
CHANTAL PAVAGEAUX, and NICK VAUGHAN

Particularly in the Heartland was made possible with support from the Greenwall Foundation, and the Battersea Arts Centre.

It was developed at the Battersea Arts Centre in London, Soho Think Tank's 2006 Ice Factory Festival, and through a Chashama space grant.

The World Premiere of *Particularly in the Heartland* took place at the Traverse Theatre in Edinburgh, Scotland on August 3, 2006 with the following cast:

ROBERT F. KENNEDY/PILOT	Jake Margolin
DOROTHY	Jessica Almasy
TRACY JO	Jill Frutkin
SARAH SPRINGER	Libby King
TODD SPRINGER	Brian Hastert
ANNA SPRINGER	Kristen Sieh

The U.S. Premiere of *Particularly in the Heartland* took place in New York City on February 24, 2007 at Performance Space 122 with the following cast:

ROBERT F. KENNEDY/PILOT	Jake Margolin
DOROTHY	Jessica Almasy
TRACY JO	Jill Frutkin
SARAH SPRINGER	Libby King
TODD SPRINGER	Frank Boyd
ANNA SPRINGER	Kristen Sieh

Rachel Chavkin	*Director*
Nick Vaughan	*Set Design*
Kristen Sieh	*Costume Design*
Jake Heinrichs	*Lighting Design*
Matt Hubbs	*Sound Design*
Stephanie Douglass, Chantal Pavageaux	*Dramaturgs*
Jeremy Blocker	*Producer*
Dave Polato	*Stage Management*
Josh Hoglund	*Assistant Director*

Particularly in the Heartland was awarded a 2006 *Scotsman* Fringe First Award, and was named Best Production of the 2007 Dublin Fringe.

CAST OF CHARACTERS

ROBERT F. KENNEDY, American politician
and presidential candidate, assassinated in 1968

DOROTHY, businesswoman who falls from the sky

TRACY JO, dead pregnant teenager inhabited by alien spirit

SARAH SPRINGER, 16, oldest of Springer siblings

TODD SPRINGER, 13, middle sibling

ANNA SPRINGER, 10, youngest sibling

A NOTE ABOUT *PARTICULARLY IN THE HEARTLAND*

The process of creating *Particularly in the Heartland* involved a great deal of improvisation on the part of the actors. We spent hours in long-form improv sessions that not only generated the text that would ultimately become the play, but also defined and deepened the relationships between characters in very personal ways. We created backstories piece-meal, haphazardly, on the fly, but by the end of our process, our characters' games, secrets, stories and alliances had become the beating heart of the piece. It was a rich foundation to build a play on.

We spent a lot of development time in a sprawling, half-finished Chashama rehearsal space in Long Island City. The old Ohio Theatre on Wooster Street, where the show first previewed, used to be a factory and therefore felt like a playground with a very deep playing space. In rehearsal we filled every inch of these strange spaces with the intimate lives of our characters. For this reason, no actor in *Particularly in the Heartland* is ever off stage for more than a couple of minutes. When not directly involved in the primary scene being played, each actor (alone or in groups) is engaged in an activity that feeds the life of their character. Sometimes this means sleeping. Sometimes it means falling in love while playing doctor with masking tape. Sometimes it means enacting violent video-game fantasies. Sometimes it just means sitting in a chair feeling like shit. In short, the seams in this piece are to be filled with the vibrant life of the characters and the actors who play them.

– Kristen Sieh, Co-Author/Performer

The cast of *Particularly in the Heartland*, Ohio Theatre Ice Factory Festival, 2006
Photo: Nick Vaughan

As the audience enters the cast is onstage singing any song they can think of with the word "America" or any state name in the title or lyrics of the song. Requests should be taken from the audience. The spirit of this prologue is warm, inviting, absurdly patriotic, but also wry. We also recommend inviting the audience to sing anthems from wherever you might be performing the work.

At show time, this informal prologue can lead directly into the following:

JAKE/ROBERT: Well, everybody has the lyrics to the next song that we're going to sing in your programs. It's "The Battle Hymn of the Republic," which you guys'll all know the tune for when we start singing. It was the Northern anthem from the American Civil War and when everybody sings in here, it sounds really good.

> *The cast leads the singing of "The Battle Hymn of the Republic." This is the gateway into the play's fiction.*

1. *Mine eyes have seen the glory*
   Of the coming of the Lord;
   He is trampling out the vintage
   Where the grapes of wrath are stored;
   He hath loosed the fateful lightning
   Of His terrible swift sword;
   His truth is marching on.

    Chorus:
    Glory! Glory, Hallelujah!
    Glory! Glory, Hallelujah!
    Glory! Glory, Hallelujah!
    His truth is marching on.

2. *I have seen Him in the watchfires*
   Of a hundred circling camps;
   They have builded Him an altar
   In the evening dews and damps;
   I can read His righteous sentence
   By the dim and flaring lamps;
   His day is marching on.

    Chorus

3. *I have read a fiery gospel*
   Writ in burnished rows of steel;
   "As ye deal with my condemners,
   So with you my grace shall deal."

Let the hero born of woman
Crush the serpent with his heel,
Since god is marching on!

> *Chorus*
>
> *The cast fully transforms into character. Over the next verses we see flashes of Robert F. Kennedy's political ascent and assassination, but in reverse. A table becomes his coffin, being lifted off the train at Arlington National Cemetery. The performers become American citizens waving at the funeral train carrying his body to Arlington, and this then blends backwards in time into citizens across the country waving at his campaign train as it traverses the country in 1968.*
>
> *The actor playing ROBERT becomes invisible to them.*

ROBERT: He has sounded forth the trumpet!

4. *He has sounded forth the trumpet*
   That shall never sound retreat;
   He is sifting out the hearts of men
   Before His judgment seat;
   O be swift, my soul, to answer Him;
   Be jubilant, my feet!
   Our God is marching on.

> *Chorus*
>
> *We are now at Robert F. Kennedy's funeral.*

5. *(Softly.)* *In the beauty of the lilies,*
   Christ was born across the sea,
   With a glory in His bosom
   That transfigures you and me;
   As he died to make men holy,
   Let us live to make men free,
   While God is marching on.

> *A beat.*
>
> *And then a flashback. Sudden applause.*
>
> *We are in Los Angeles, June 4th, 1968, at the Ambassador Hotel.*

ROBERT: *(The applause settles.)* I am grateful for the votes that I received – that all of you have worked so hard for. I think it indicates quite clearly what we can do here in the United States. The vote here in the state of

California and the vote in the state of South Dakota: here we have the most urban state of our union, and South Dakota is the most rural state of our union. And we were able to win them both! *(Applause.)* I believe that we can end the divisions in the United States. What I think is quite clear is that we can work together in the last analysis. And that what has been going on for the past three years – the divisions, the violence, the disenchantment with our society, and the divisions, whether it's between the blacks and the whites, or between the poor and the more affluent, or between age groups, or over the war in Vietnam – that we can start to work together again. Because this is a great country. *(Applause.)* It is an unselfish country. *(Applause.)* And it is a generous country. *(Applause.)* And I intend to make that my basis for running over the period of the next few months… *(Quiet.)* So my thanks to all of you –

CAMPAIGN VOLUNTEER: You're welcome Bobby!

    Applause and celebration.

ROBERT: *(Preparing to leave.)* And now it's on to Chicago, and let's win there! Everybody!

    ROBERT conducts the group in song as he ascends the ladder, waving.

He is coming like the glory
Of the morning on the wave;
He is wisdom to the mighty,
He is honor to the brave;
So the world shall be His footstool,
And the soul of wrong His slave.

    A sudden gunshot.

    Screams.

    ROBERT grabs a dangling rope, holds on for dear life.

    A pause.

    The ensemble sings quietly, hushed. The nation as they pray and wait for news of his condition following the shooting.

Glory! Glory, Hallelujah!
Glory! Glory, Hallelujah!
Glory! Glory, Hallelujah!
His truth is marching—

ROBERT drops from the rope.

The funeral train whistles. The cast again become the mourners, watching the funeral train. ROBERT takes the ladder and exits.

The cast prepares for the next sequence.

SNAP to 2006.

1.

NOTE: Over the course of the next scene a flurry of activity happens. Think of it like a movie montage. The central events: A tornado strikes the SPRINGER family farm. DOROTHY's plane hits this storm, and she is the lone survivor when her plane goes down. An alien escaping from a dying planet inhabits the body of TRACY JO, a pregnant teenager who has died (likely violently, likely mixed up with drugs) and whose body has been left in a wheelbarrow.

SARAH: LET'S GO!

The SPRINGER kids run onstage chasing each other around the house. They stop suddenly, behaving as if they are meeting and welcoming the audience to Kansas.

SPRINGER CHILDREN: *(Singing playfully.)*
God Bless America. My home (woof) sweet (meow) home.

SARAH: *(To the audience.)* If you will look behind you – if you will please look behind you? You will see our great lady Kansas stretching out before your very eyes.

This is our house in June.

(Into the fiction.) Hey Anna, storm's comin'.

ANNA: I know. Do you think mom and dad will be back before it hits?

SARAH: S'yeah, they just went to Walmart, stupid.

ANNA: STUPID!!

ANNA goes to play in the grass. SARAH grabs her jump rope and begins physical training.

Meanwhile, in New York City:

DOROTHY: *(On the phone.)* No. No. I don't have an hour layover in Chicago. It's not enough time. I can't – *(To her taxi driver.)* This is great. *(Back on the phone.)* Look, I don't book the tickets, mother. I am trying to get home for Christmas.

Back in Kansas.

ANNA: *(To the audience.)* LADIES and GENTLEMEN! On a day like today, with the clouds brewing in the far Midwestern sky, you can see what Kansas must have looked like before God's eyes!

DOROTHY: *(To driver.)* Can I get a receipt? *(On phone.)* No I'm not talking to you I'm talking to the guy who drives the cab. *(To driver.)* Yeah I got it, thanks.

ANNA: *(To audience.)* First he separated the heavens from the earth and the waters from the waters, and he created Kansas!

TODD: *(In the house.)* Anna shut up, I'm writing!

ANNA: I am practicing! *(Back with audience, flustered.)* And – and – and He

DOROTHY: *(Into phone.)* I gotta go. I gotta go… *(This continues quietly.)*

ANNA: And ON THAT DAY, He said that a new day would come when He would return – with a flood of water and a burning flame!

SARAH: *(Overlapping quietly under ANNA's speech while she jumps rope. A jump rope rhyme.)* Mother went away and left us some fine day, some fine day, yeah, yeah. Packed up her bags and said she couldn't stay, can't stay bye bye, ooh can't stay – *(Now audible.)* Teeth were crumblin' like cheese from the moon –

ANNA joins her sister's jump rope rhyme.

ANNA/SARAH: SKY'S GETTING DARK AND RAPTURE'S COMING SOON!

DOROTHY: *(Overlapping.)*… I gotta go. I gotta go. I gotta go. *(Finally hanging up and speaking to the attendant at the airline ticket counter.)* MEXICO.

Thunder.

ANNA: *(Thrilled at this potential sign of the coming Rapture.)* Thunder thunder thunder thunder thunder thunder thunder thunder –

DOROTHY: *(Rehearsing for a major work speech, directed to the real audience.)* Ladies and Gentlemen, picture another day, like today, deep deep into our nation's past… A most *unfortunate* day for - NORTH *(Writing in the forgotten word.)* – North America 65 million years ago. A celestial chip shot strikes the earth at terrifying speed…

ANNA: LADIES and GENTLEMEN.

DOROTHY: *(Quietly to herself.)* They're not going to like 65 million…

DOROTHY boards the plane.

ANNA: I've been on the watch for a long time. "Keep ready, for at the hour you think least likely, the Son of Man is coming."

Crash of thunder and lightning.

Cut to the plane.

PILOT: *(Quietly over the plane intercom.)* Well Ladies and Gentlemen, we are currently flying over the former location of the Inland Sea, which used to cover the whole middle of this country, and if you look closely at the soil…

Cut back to Kansas.

ANNA: I've been charting and measuring the electrical outputs of storms for for for, like for years, and I really think the end times are coming. Soon Jesus will take the righteous and the sinners will be left behind! These are historical, biblical times. I have all my expert tools prepared. DO YOU WANT TO SEE?

Cut to plane.

DOROTHY: *(Working on her speech.)* A celestial chip shot… Something huge strikes the earth directly at the heart of the Inland Sea.

A momentary flash of Kansas – TODD's music blaring into his headphones.

Two continents converge.

PILOT: *(Over the intercom.)* Well Dorothy, we are currently flying over the former location of your beloved Inland Sea, and if you look closely at the soil…

The plane rocks with turbulence.

If you will look at the soil…
If you'll look out of the right side of the plane…

The plane rocks with turbulence.

If you'll look at the plains.
Uh… Dorothy –

A siren.

It is both on the plane and a tornado siren in Kansas.

SARAH stops jumping, panicked.

SARAH: There's something in the sky.

She begins to run to get a closer look.

TODD: Sarah, what is it?

ANNA: *(Terrified of the growing storm and her sister's state.)* Sarah? Where's Mom and Dad?

TODD: Do you see the car?

SARAH: Todd! Todd, take Anna inside!

SARAH runs to the roof. She is overwhelmed. A religious vision.

She sees the Rapture has come.

During the following vision, the cast becomes simultaneously the voice of the Book of Revelation, and also an alien race escaping from their dying world.

SARAH: Yes! I knew it! I knew you'd come for me. I knew it. I see you. I see you. I'm ready. I want to be filled with your light. I want to be filled with your light. Fill me! I'm ready for you. I'm so so ready for you. Take me. Please.

ALL: *(Overlapping whisper.)* And I saw when the lamb opened one of the seals. And I heard as it were the noise of thunder one of the four beasts saying, "Come and see."

And I saw and behold a white horse, and he that sat on him had a bow and he went forth conquering, and to conquer. And there went out another horse that was red and power was given to him that sat thereon to take peace from the earth, and there was given unto him a great sword. And I beheld and lo a black horse and he that sat on him had a pair of balances in his hand.

And I looked and behold a pale horse and his name that sat on him was Death, and Hell followed with him.

The alien race locates the dead body of TRACY JO, and possesses the pregnant teenager.

NOTE: In the original production, this was represented by a sound and light shift referencing iconic spaceship imagery, as well as by each of the actors circling the actress playing TRACY JO, holding an egg in an extended hand towards her. An actor in the center of the circle leaned over TRACY JO and "blew" an egg (previously punctured at both top and bottom of the shell), coating the face and head of TRACY JO with yolk. This image paralleled the look of a gooey newborn child, awakening for the first time.

In a cornfield, TRACY JO gasps to life.

Meanwhile on her roof, SARAH has sunk to her knees, awaiting instructions.

TODD waits for SARAH.

ANNA, always the scientist, flies her kite into the storm.

In the sky, DOROTHY's plane begins emergency landing procedures.

In her panic, she begins to hallucinate, imagining the PILOT speaking directly to her. In production, DOROTHY and the PILOT performed an elaborate and violent physical sequence during the following text.

PILOT: Well, Dorothy sit back and relax, looks like smooth sailing all the way to Mexico.

The sound of emergency.

Due to weather we are experiencing some unexpected turbulence.

You will notice that I have turned on the fastened seatbelt sign.

Dorothy, please return to your seat.

And fasten your seatbelt.

If you are in the lavatory, get out, return to your seat, and fasten your seatbelt.

Under your seat is an emergency guide.

Under your seat is the emergency guide.

ANNA: *(To the audience.)* I know things. I fear things. I fear that among this vast heap of signs mankind will have no significance.

TODD: *(Seeing what his sister is doing.)* Anna! Anna! Get your kite outta the storm!

ANNA: *(Realization.)* I will have no significance?? *(PANIC.)* SARAH!!!

> *The storm reaches full effect.*
>
> *SARAH is sprinting towards her siblings.*
>
> *ANNA and TODD race for her.*
>
> *DOROTHY's plane is crashing.*
>
> *TRACY JO is completely disoriented.*
>
> *The PILOT becomes ROBERT F. KENNEDY again, at the moment of assassination.*
>
> *The SPRINGERS take cover in the storm shelter.*
>
> *The three visitors prepare for arrival.*
>
> *Cacophony. Wind. The Rapture. Tearing metal.*

DOROTHY: *(Trying to calm herself as her airplane seat plummets through the sky.)* And then He planted Man in the center of a field. And Man was no more than a bump in a very flat space where God could find him. And then God said –

ROBERT: *(A vision.)* "Wait For Me Here."

DOROTHY: Okay! *(To herself.)* Dorothy, close your eyes!! And then God was gone. A vanishing point. *(She looks down.)* Oh my god.

> *An arrival.*
>
> *Quiet.*
>
> *ROBERT, DOROTHY, and TRACY JO are close. But nobody is ready yet. Disoriented, they slink into the cornfields.*
>
> *Quiet.*
>
> *SARAH emerges from the storm shelter. She sees their house is beaten but still standing.*
>
> *Their parents are nowhere to be seen.*

SARAH: *(Looking around.)* THE RAPTURE. IN STORES 06.06… oh.

2.

Thunder.

ANNA and TODD emerge. The three siblings look around at the destruction, and then at each other. Tentatively, then smiling. Relief. Delirious group laughter.

And then suddenly SARAH is weeping.

TODD and ANNA, alarmed at their older sibling's fear, look back out at the ruined landscape.

TODD: *(Quiet.)* They should've been back by now… Where's Mom and Dad? If there was a storm they should've… WHERE THE HELL ARE THEY?

SARAH: Todd!

ANNA: Oh no. Sarah, are we… Are they dead?

SARAH: *(Quiet. She is reporting the vision she had in the storm.)* They were Taken.

> *A beat as TODD and ANNA process the news.*

ANNA: *(Simultaneous.)* I missed it?!

TODD: *(Simultaneous.)* That's stupid!

SARAH: You watch your mouth or I'll wash it out with bleach! They are gone! And we are here! I saw it.

TODD: Sarah, please–

SARAH: I saw it Todd! I saw it… just be quiet. Please! Both of you just…

> *Thunder. They sit at the table and wait and wait and wait.*

ANNA: I have to pee.

TODD: May I be excused?

SARAH: Wait.

> *Thunder. More time passes. They wait. Maybe a week?*

> *TODD makes armpit jokes. Some laughter. TODD makes sex jokes.*

SARAH: Todd, so gross! So gross! *(He does more.)* TODD! GOSH! *(More giggling.)*

ANNA, now emboldened, begins putting her feet on the table.

SARAH: *(Quietly at first.)* Anna, get your feet off the table. Anna, please. ANNA, GET YOUR FEET OFF THE TABLE!!!

ANNA: *(Terrified.)* I'm not doing anything. I'm just going over here for a little while.

ANNA goes into the corner, like a frightened dog.

TODD: Sarah, I know this is hard but you do not have to yell.

(Time passes.) Sarah... Sarah, say something. *(Silence. SARAH is rocking.)* Why are you doing that? What are you thinking about? Sarah!

SARAH: Shhh.

TODD: Sarah, in the *Left Behind* books, aren't the kids always taken?

SARAH: Todd, be quiet.

TODD: *(A new tack.)* So, like, what was it that you think you saw? What did it look like?

SARAH: I don't know.

TODD: Sarah... do you really believe? I mean... how do you really know that Jesus is in your heart?

SARAH: Because He lives there Todd!

TODD: I know, I know, but... Like when someone tells you to think of nothing and you think that you're thinking of nothing. But you're still thinking, you know? So like, how how... how –

WHY ARE WE STILL HERE?

ANNA yelps. She is squatting in the wheelbarrow and peeing, panicked. SARAH and TODD respond, shocked. ANNA finishes, politely. Stands, wipes, gets out of the wheelbarrow, looks at her brother and sister.

ANNA: So. Should we tell somebody?

The siblings consider. They "Rock Paper Scissors" to see who might take the next course of action. Anna loses.

Fine.

ANNA goes and sits in the rocking chair.

She turns to the audience, desperate for someone to work this through with.

This is the scene! Sight unseen. This is what hitherto went therefore. No.

SARAH and TODD pull up close to their younger sister. Excited for a story. Anything to take their minds off what has happened. ANNA, always the clown, speaks in an old lady's voice.

I am here today at the Springer family homestead – *(Reporter voice.)* Reporting to you live! *(Back to old lady.)* A fantastical, phenominonical event has just occurred. Unlike anything our great lady Kansas has ever seen before. The clocks stopped at 6:06. A great wind swept the plains. An angelic squeal cried out from the heavens. And the vast Midwestern sky –

SARAH: Opened!

ANNA: *(A gasp, shocked her sister is finally sharing.)* Opened! Revealing our savior's hand, which reached down and Raptured up my folks like pigs in a blanket. I mean it. It took them!

And the car… *(They all consider this.)*
Huh.
(After a beat, resuming the reporter.) Thank you for joining me at the Springer family homestead where you have just been witness to a real live miracle.

Long silence.

TODD: We get a second chance, though, right?

SARAH: We weren't good enough. There was his army that was ready and he took them… And then there's his army that's half-ready. And we have to get stronger. We have to try harder. Cuz it's gonna get, like, a whole lot worse before it gets better.

TODD: What are we supposed to do?

SARAH: We have to help each other. I mean it. We wait. For the next message.

They wait. Looking out.

TODD: S'dark.

ANNA steps to the window and then slowly crosses outside.

SARAH: Anna—

ANNA: It's raining.

> *Rain. Music. The three kids rise and face the audience.*
>
> *A Baptism. A beautiful mourning dance is performed.*
>
> *It starts slow, contemplative. The SPRINGERS summoning a new strength.*
>
> *In the darkness, the ghost of ROBERT stirs:*

ROBERT: Some men see things as they are and say, "Why." I dream of things that never were and say, "Why not."

> *The distant sound of APPLAUSE at a campaign rally as ROBERT again goes dormant. The SPRINGERS' dance changes, and becomes whooping and hollering. Children unleashed and realizing for the first time that they are alone and can do anything.*
>
> *Into this cacophony stumbles a very disoriented TRACY JO out of the cornfield. She is covered in blood, very pregnant, and speaks no English.*
>
> *The kids see TRACY JO.*

3.

SARAH, ANNA and TODD: *(Shrieking at the terrifying stranger.)* AHHHHH!

TODD: Oh my gosh, it's the Antichrist!!

ANNA: She's inside out! She's inside out!

TODD: Anna get my gun!

ANNA: *(Holding out her fingers in the shape of a cross.)* I believe!

SARAH: Do I know you?

> *TRACY JO turns to the audience.*

TRACY JO: I am an alien. Shhhh.

> *TRACY JO turns back to kids, moans and collapses. TODD goes towards her lifeless body.*

ANNA: Watch out! She might have AIDS!

> *TODD reels back for a moment, but then gathers courage. He feels for breath.*

TODD: Sarah! Sarah she needs help.

> *This is a moral opportunity.*

> *TODD and SARAH pick TRACY JO up. ANNA crosses to them with a ladder.*

ANNA: Here, use this like, like a stretcher.

> *SARAH and TODD carry TRACY JO to the table on the makeshift stretcher. They speak during this move so that as soon as they land TRACY JO wakens and they run.*

ANNA: She looks familiar.

TODD: Oh! Sarah, it's that girl from your class who got knocked up and her tweaked out stepfather killed her!

SARAH: Shut up, Todd! S'not.

ANNA: It was in the *Observer*!

TRACY JO gasps suddenly and the children run screaming around the wall. They whisper "Rock Paper Scissors." ANNA loses. TODD and SARAH push ANNA toward TRACY JO.

ANNA: Shoot.

SARAH/TODD: Go Anna go./ Go go Anna.

ANNA: I hate democracy! *(To TRACY JO.)* What, what is your name?

TRACY JO honks. ANNA runs shrieking back to the other kids.

SARAH: Is she all right?

TODD: Yeah she's sitting up.

ANNA: Maybe we should clean her.

TODD: I know CPR.

ANNA: No, Todd... *(To SARAH.).* Ask if she's hungry.

TODD: Excuse me, are you—

ANNA: Not you.

SARAH: *(Creeping out.)* Are you hungry? Are you hungry?

ANNA: *(Creeping out.)* You're eating for two now you know.

TODD: Are you hungry? I'll make you a sandwich?

No response.

ANNA: Is she retarded?

TODD: Oh no, maybe she is!

SARAH: Maybe she's a sign. Who are you? Who are you?

TRACY JO seems to have something in her mouth. She gags once, twice. SARAH, frightened, puts her hands out to catch whatever TRACY JO is coughing up.

TRACY JO spits an egg into SARAH's hands.

TRACY JO: Tracy Jo.

Music. A montage in which TRACY JO is cleaned and welcomed into the SPRINGER family.

SARAH: *(Whispering. Stunned.)* Anna...

ANNA: Yeah?

SARAH hands ANNA the egg, who handles it like a holy relic.

SARAH: Todd, go get some water.

ANNA: Look

ANNA hands the egg to TODD.

Oh! Here.

ANNA and SARAH take off TRACY JO's shoes and socks.

SARAH: Um, right this way Madame.

ANNA: Careful, careful, careful, you're walking for two now you know. You don't have AIDS do you? Bet not.

TODD gets the tub. The children wash TRACY JO.

TODD: We are really good people Tracy Jo. We'll take care of you.

ANNA: One time when I was like six, I found three mossosaur teeth out here and got so much extra credit –

TRACY JO puts her newly discovered hand lovingly on ANNA's face and cuts her off.

TODD: You're really lucky we found you.

TRACY JO touches TODD's face.

SARAH meanwhile zooms up with a wheelbarrow.

SARAH: Hey Tracy Jo! Do you want to take a load off in my wagon?

TODD: Yeah Tracy Jo do it!

TRACY JO sits clumsily into SARAH's wheelbarrow.

SARAH: Oh my gosh. Anna, look at Tracy Jo. You guys! Look at Tracy Jo now!

SARAH is wheeling TRACY JO around. Suddenly, SARAH stops wheeling.

SARAH: Tracy Jo, look at the moon.

TRACY JO: S'small.

ANNA: Right?

SARAH dumps TRACY JO out of the wheelbarrow. Everybody jumps.

TRACY JO: *(A quiz.)* Christmas or your birthday?

ANNA: Birthday!

TODD: Christmas.

SARAH: Christmas.

TRACY JO: Birthday! Inside or outside?

ANNA: Outside.

SARAH: Outside.

TODD: Inside.

TRACY JO: Outside!

ANNA: *(Carried away.)* Mom or Dad?

SARAH: Anna!

TODD: Jesum crow, Anna!

TRACY JO/ ANNA: Mom!

ANNA gets her bag o'candy from behind the wall.

ANNA: Hey Tracy Jo do you want to eat the last of my Halloween candy?

TODD: Yes she does!

The candy is dumped on the table. TODD and ANNA sit at the table. TRACY JO sits in the rocker.

TODD: Smartees for your Snickers!

ANNA: No way!

TODD: Two Smartees for your Snickers!

ANNA: No, way, I'm not a little kid anymore. Snickers are like gold!

TODD: I'll punch you in the neck.

SARAH approaches TRACY JO while her two younger siblings bicker.

SARAH: Tracy Jo, would you like the last Pineapple Smuckers dum dum?

ANNA: Those are the gross kind, she's just being mean to you.

SARAH is horrified.

The music from the montage winds down.

ANNA and TODD fall suddenly to sleep.

Quietly, TRACY JO reaches for the dum dum. SARAH, heartened, crosses to the wheelbarrow next to TRACY JO and gives her the candy.

SARAH: *(In the silence.)* So do you like it here?

TRACY JO: It's alright.

SARAH: Yea... But, I mean, is it your favorite place?

TRACY JO: Is it yours?

SARAH: S'yeah... I mean I've never been anywhere else. It can get pretty scary out here sometimes at night. There's not a lot of stuff around—

TRACY JO: But you're in the middle of everything.

SARAH: That's true. Do you have a family?

TRACY JO: I don't know.

SARAH: This is my family. Now. Now that my parents are gone. I'm pretty much in charge of stuff. I'm glad you're here. I feel like I can tell you things, like stupid things, you know? Cause I don't know what to do if someone falls and gets hurt. Or if someone comes and tries to take the house. Or maybe if somebody comes that isn't *good*...

Do you pray? *(No response.)* That's okay. I can help you with that... Because we've got really dark times ahead. And my heart hurts sometimes, like when I get nervous or when I'm just out here looking out at all this space. Like I have this pressure... *(Gesturing to her chest.)* Like I need those paddles...

TRACY JO: Yeah, I know exactly what you mean.

SARAH suddenly springs up, excited.

SARAH: Do you want to take a walk?

TRACY JO: Can I stay here?

SARAH: *(Totally devastated.)* Sure you can Tracy Jo.

TRACY JO: Can I come with you?

SARAH: Yes! Come on.

SARAH and TRACY JO exit.

4.

Meanwhile, from another direction DOROTHY, still carrying her airplane seat (because it's all she has) approaches the house. She is clearly traumatized. Moaning, singed. Coughing. She has something in her mouth. She gags once, twice, spits up her keys. She sees the house and imagines perhaps this is the house the keys are for.

Inside ANNA has awakened and crept out to investigate the source of these strange noises.

ANNA: *(Trying to sound bigger, older, threatening, perhaps like a guard dog.)* GO HOME! RUFF! RUFF! GRRRRR! BAD! SHOO! GO HOME! BAD! GRRRRR! I'm not alone. My husband has a gun!

> *ANNA goes and wakes up TODD.*

ANNA: Todd, wake up, there is somebody outside.

TODD: Where's Sarah?

ANNA: I don't know.

> *TODD runs to the window. ANNA hands him the gun she has pulled from hiding.*

TODD: I don't see anybody.

ANNA: Here take your gun.

TODD: Careful, it's loaded!

ANNA: Sorry.

TODD: It's okay. It's okay, Anna. I'll take care of it—

> *TODD sneaks out to ambush DOROTHY.*

ANNA: Oh Jeez oh Jeez oh Jeez…

> *A panicked slapstick comedy routine. DOROTHY waves desperately at ANNA who she catches sight of through the window. ANNA freaks out and screams.*

AHHH!

> *TODD, now outside, runs to help his sister. DOROTHY, terrified by ANNA's screams, runs the other way back to her chair where she is spotted by TODD who aims his gun at her. DOROTHY screams.*

TODD: Freeze, right there dirt bag! Get on the ground! *(DOROTHY falls to the ground.)* No get up against the wall – *(DOROTHY stands.)* No, I was right the first time, get on the ground!

> *DOROTHY falls to the ground, moaning. TODD softens and approaches this weeping woman on the ground.*

Oh. Oh my gosh. Are you okay? I'm sorry. What's wrong? I know CPR...

> *Meanwhile, ANNA, not realizing her brother has it under control, is creeping out to come to his aid.*

ANNA: *(To the audience.)* One time, on *The Jenny Jones Show*, I saw how a young girl can take down a rapist four times her size just by using velocity.

TODD: What's your name?

ANNA: The effect would be like hurling a bowling ball at somebody.

TODD: Do you speak English? *(DOROTHY doesn't seem to understand.)* I'm going to call you Dorothy cause of your shoes, okay, Dorothy?

> *He points gently. They both look at her shoes. They look at each other.*

DOROTHY: *(Gasping, her hands raised in the air.)* S'kaaay.

TODD: Good. Dorothy. Good. What do you want? English?

ANNA: I may be small, but I am 75 pounds FULL OF SPEED!

> *From out of the darkness ANNA charges DOROTHY, jumps on her. DOROTHY screams, and then begins laughing. Perhaps there are memories of a daughter?*

> *TODD pulls ANNA off DOROTHY. ANNA, still panicked, grabs the gun from TODD and points it at DOROTHY.*

TODD: Anna, that gun's loaded.

ANNA: How did you get here?

TODD: Anna, ANNA! She doesn't understand you. She's a Mexican and she's in trouble!

ANNA: They are always in trouble.

TODD: How did you get all the way to Kansas without speaking Engli-

DOROTHY drops her pants and pees. SARAH and TRACY JO enter, blissfully, and come to a horrified halt.

SARAH: Oh my gosh, are you okay? TODD! Why is there a grown woman peeing on our lawn? Why didn't you let her inside? What kind of a Christian are you?

TODD: Sarah!

SARAH: *(Leaning in gently to DOROTHY.)* Where are you from?

TODD: She's a Mexican. I've named her Dorothy.

SARAH: *(Speaking now extremely slowly and loudly and with gestures.)* DOROTHY! WHERE? ARE? YOU? FROM?

TODD: Mexico.

DOROTHY, stunned, points upward.

SARAH: Oh my gosh. Maybe she's a sign!

ANNA: Like Jesus undercover.

SARAH: Are you here to test us? Because we are really good people. Dorothy I'd like you to meet somebody. This is Tracy Jo. Tracy Jo also needed our help. Tracy Jo, this is Dorothy. Do you want to come inside? Insid-o!

TODD: I'm sorry about the gun.

DOROTHY: *(Gasping.)* S'kaay.

The family goes inside. TRACY JO crosses to DOROTHY, who takes her wet pants off and tosses them into the grass.

TRACY JO: S'okay. I understand. I was poor, tired, and a huddled mass too. *(Suddenly threatening.)* But I was here first, Dorothy. Just remember that.

SARAH: *(Popping outside, super polite, imitating her mother.)* Yoohoo, ladies! Don't be lawn ornaments. Come inside the house.

TRACY JO: *(Grabbing DOROTHY ferociously by the shoulders.)* This is America!

TRACY JO thrusts DOROTHY inside. She turns to the audience.

In July.

5.

Time has passed.

A cake is brought out.

Everyone sings "Happy Birthday, Anna" except for TODD who sings "Happy Birthday, America."

ALL: Happy Birthday to you/me/Anna/America
Happy Birthday to you/me/Anna/America
Happy Birthday dear me/Anna/America

ANNA: TODD!!

TODD: Well it is!

ALL: Happy Birthday to youuuuu ANNNA/AMERRICAAA

ANNA: I hate you!

TODD: God heard that!

> *TODD blows out the candles and swipes part of the cake and runs. ANNA is horrified.*

TRACY JO: *(A quick attempt to distract.)* Ready or not, here I come!

> *TRACY JO begins counting Mississippi's, but her eyes are open. For some reason DOROTHY counts off on her fingers*

TRACY JO: One Mississippi, Two Mississippi–

SARAH: Tracy Jo. You're cheating!

TRACY JO: Cheating is fun Mississippi.

ANNA: No, Dorothy, you don't count. Tracy Jo count-o. *(ANNA grabs DOROTHY by the hand, leads her to hide.)* No–

SARAH: Seriously Tracy Jo, that's not what we talked about. You have to close your eyes.

> *TRACY JO does. Outside ANNA drags DOROTHY around like a doll.*

ANNA: Sometimes Dorothy, it's really hard to share your birthday with a national holiday. Because, for real, everybody knows that the birth of America is so much more important than the birth of one small nine-year old. *(Gasp.)* Ten year old! I'm into the double digits. I don't even know what I want to win my Nobel Prize for. *(Turning on DOROTHY, a teaching moment.)* NO-BELL-PRIZE. Oh you really have to learn English, Dorothy. C'mon, you're going to love this.

ANNA leads DOROTHY offstage.

TRACY JO: 29 Mississippi, 30 Mississippi, 31 Mississippi. 31 Mississippi. 31 Mississippi. *(A terrified honk. Everything is dark for some reason.)* Sarah?...

SARAH: *(Emerging, worried from her hiding place.)* What happened?

TRACY JO takes her hands off her eyes. Relieved.

SARAH: Oh gosh. What are you doing?

TRACY JO: Finding you.

SARAH: Look over there!

TRACY JO does. SARAH runs to the table and hits it.

SARAH: BASE! Yes! BASE! *(She cracks up.)* I said look over there!

TRACY JO: Yeah you did.

TRACY JO and SARAH high-five. Again. Suddenly TRACY JO grabs SARAH's hand and studies it. It is remarkably intimate.

TRACY JO: Look at all the colors in your hands. Your skin is pink from all the blood and blood is salt to the taste. The hands are two intricate, prehensile, multi-fingered body parts and the fingertips contain some of the densest areas of nerve endings in the human body, so they are our primary source of tactile feedback from our environment. Like other paired organs-

SARAH smacks TRACY JO's hand. She moves away quickly. TRACY JO is hurt, but also fascinated by her skin's reaction to the hit.

TRACY JO: After impact, capillaries are damaged, causing blood –

SARAH: S'gross.

TRACY JO: *(Stopping. Seeing she's upset SARAH.)* Yeah. S'gross! *(Trying to change the subject.)* Feet – feet – feet are just... brown...
Hands or feet?

SARAH: Hands. Tracy Jo... I wanna show you something. Please step into my office.

SARAH and TRACY JO exit.

SARAH, a hypochondriac, will show TRACY JO her pretend medical equipment over the next sequence.

Meanwhile, like a commando, TODD throws his pants over the wall.

TODD: DECOY! *(He sprints for and then pounds the table.)* BASE! Yeah!

He waits. Looks around.

Is anybody even still looking for me?!

He decides to hide again. ANNA and DOROTHY reappear, sneaking towards the table. They stop.

ANNA: Look, Dorothy. Dor-o-thy. I don't think anybody is even still looking for us. So, do you wanna watch me dig?? You so do! C'mon!

Meanwhile SARAH leads TRACY JO solemnly to a table for an "ultrasound."

Um, these are my expert tools and we are on an excavation expedition da-da-da. I once found three mossosaur teeth out here. Betcha didn't know that Kansas was used to be underwater. Betcha didn't know that Dorothy. S'true. The whole middle of America was used to be a... a Sea...

Just imagine...

The space becomes a bit transcendent. And somewhere, in the back of DOROTHY'S mind, a memory is stirred.

You are rocking at the bottom of a vast Inland Lake Ocean... that used to divide this great country of ours into two, two, two totally separate continents, east and west. I like to imagine I'm just like floating all day. Like some huge weightless creature... And I just imagine my bones are gone (poof) and my smallness is gone (poof). And I'm just being a part of so much space! Dinosaurs were so big and they were ALL OVER KANSAS! So there's fossils all over Kansas. And I figure if I can find a whole skeleton I will get extra credit for like for for for my WHOLE LIFE! A whole skeleton... I saw one once, at the Kansas City Natural History Museum.

(A confession.) I wasn't even supposed to be in that room. And that's when I really started to believe in God. Because... It was glorious. Truly RADIANT in its complexity. And that's when I knew that something – that He had to be making everything, Dorothy. Because it's just so

good! So just IMAGINE that something that miraculous is lying buried right here in MY OWN FRONT YARD!

That spot looks like a good one, that one there. Watch and learn.

ANNA begins to dig carefully. She finds something. Brushes it with her toothbrush.

Hey Todd! Hey Todd, I found your retainer again! That's so frickin' weird!

TODD: *(From somewhere.)* Anna, shut up! I'm hiding!

ANNA: God heard that! *(She returns to digging. Finds something else.)* Oh! I forgot I buried my memory box here. Here. *(She hands it to Dorothy who begins to open it.)* NO! NO! NO! I mean, please don't do that.

In the dirt ANNA finds something weird.

She digs deeper. Fingers. She is both creeped out and excited.

Fossil hand! JACKPOT DOROTHY!! I think we found an Okie. Or a homesteader. Or a union member! Or a cro-magnum man –

ANNA stops short as ROBERT F. KENNEDY emerges from the soil. He gags once, twice. He coughs up a chunk of dirt.

ROBERT: *(Caught in a violent dream, not really seeing ANNA and DOROTHY.)* No – no – no – no – no.

ROBERT is spasming through moments of his life.

Meanwhile SARAH, hearing the commotion, rushes to get TODD's gun.

And now it's on to Chicago and let's win there! *(His hand yanking upwards into an oath.)* I, Robert Francis Kennedy, I AM RUNNING, I am running for PRESIDENT of the United States of America.

ROBERT's hand shoots outward for a handshake. Uncontrollable political instincts. ANNA goes to shake it but DOROTHY throws her backwards. She looks up just in time to see SARAH taking aim at this man who seems to be attacking ANNA and DOROTHY.

DOROTHY: SARAH!

BANG! ROBERT is shot. He falls to the ground.

SARAH: Got him!

A stunned silence.

TRACY JO: Why did you do that?

ANNA: *(Terrified.)* Robert?

SARAH: You knew him?

ANNA: Robert Francis Kennedy–

> *DOROTHY goes to SARAH, who is now horrified. TODD runs out as well.*

SARAH: What did I do? I thought he was gonna–

TODD: Good shot Sarah.

> *All move towards the body.*

ANNA: Get away from him! Let him be dead like a great man.

TODD: *(After a few beats.)* Antichrist?

ANNA: He was JFK's little brother.

SARAH: What did I do?

TODD: That's a Kennedy?

SARAH: Oh Jesus forgive me.

ANNA: No, it's okay, he was dead already. He died in 1968.

TODD: So, you shot a zombie? *(Sudden panic.)* Sarah you can't kill a zombie with a regular bullet!

> *ROBERT gasps to life. Everyone screams.*

ROBERT: Was anybody else hurt?

> *An explosion in the sky. FIREWORKS!*

TRACY JO: FIRE IN THE SKY – FIRE IN THE SKY! Oh my gosh. Oh my gosh. *(Recognizing what she's read about in books.)* It's the Fourth of July and ANYTHING IS POSSIBLE IN AMERICA!! Happy birthday dear America! Ha… Happy Independence Day! Oh, thank you, Happy Independence Day to you, too! Sarah! The fireworks!

> *Meanwhile, ROBERT has arisen and seen SARAH with the gun.*

ROBERT: What are you thinking? This is the United States of America, you cannot just shoot people!

TODD: Like heck you can't!

ROBERT: Okay, you give me that!

DOROTHY: Give me that!

> *His head spinning as they all grab for the gun. DOROTHY, whose amnesia has suddenly disappeared, is also spinning as she tries to take control.*

ROBERT: You tried to kill me?

ANNA: Hey! You are a ghost!!

DOROTHY: You're dead. Already–

SARAH: Who are you?

TODD: Who is he?

ROBERT and DOROTHY: Where am I?

ANNA: I already told you. He's Robert Francis Kennedy.

TODD: Francis?!

ANNA and SARAH: Shut up Todd.

SARAH: I thought all the Kennedy's were dead.

DOROTHY: They are.

(Turning on ROBERT.) You're dead. You're dead, but you're here. But, JESUS Robert WHAT are you doing here? You've been dead since 1968.

ANNA: Sirhan Sirhan. He killed you. I had to do a report.

ROBERT: I don't know what you're talking about.

DOROTHY: Did you know that? He was a child. He was a child who watched a profuse amount of television. *(Warning the SPRINGERS.)* A profuse amount of television. Jesus Bobby, what are you doing here? *(Prompting.)* You had won California...

TRACY JO: Dorothy speaks English.

TODD: Yeah, for a former Mexican mute she can really talk.

ANNA: You lied to me.

SARAH: Why would anybody do that?

TRACY JO: It's a miracle! It's an Independence Day miracle! Nobody does America like the Fourth of July, and nobody does the fourth like the Heartland! Sarah, fireworks!

ROBERT: What year is it?

Nobody knows how to answer.

SARAH: It's the Fourth of July.

TODD: It's Independence Day.

DOROTHY: You've been dead since 1968. They put your body on a train, and they took you to Washington DC, like Lincoln, and they buried you on a hill, near your brother. Nixon won.

ROBERT: *(A slow dawning.)* Nixon? No. No. No. A kitchen. I was in a kitchen. We were walking back through the kitchen and now it's on to Chicago and…
And.
And…
Excuse me, what year is it?

TRACY JO: It's the Fourth of July! Happy Independence Day. *(She thrusts him a flag.)* Oh, thank you, thank you, SAY THANK YOU…

ROBERT: *(Quietly.)* Thank you.

TRACY JO: Oh, THANK YOU! Happy Independence Day to you, too.

ROBERT: Thank you.

TRACY JO: Yes, yes, yes! *(Trying to move them along to the fireworks.)*

DOROTHY: Robert, why have you come here?

ROBERT: What's that noise?

ANNA: They're just fireworks Robert.

TRACY JO: You haven't missed it! You didn't miss it! It's the Fourth of July and you still have time.

TRACY JO begins singing the national anthem loudly. The others fall in.

ALL: ***Were so gallantly streaming***
And the rocket's red glare
The bombs bursting in air
Gave proof through the night

ROBERT: Oh, c'mon!

> *ANNA jumps jubilantly onto ROBERT's back.*

ALL: ***That our flag was still there***
Oh say does that star spangled banner yet wave
O'er the land of the free!

> *Sudden silence. Flags down. ROBERT puts ANNA down.*

ROBERT: Wait, what state are we in?

ANNA: Kansas!

ROBERT: Oh. Shit.

ALL: ***And the home of the brave!!***

> *Night settles on the land. It is still the Fourth of July, the glow of fireworks still in the sky.*

> *Quiet. DOROTHY is alone. Her body remembers being on the phone, but all she holds is one of her red shoes.*

DOROTHY: Business class. I was seated in Business Class. And we were watching some idiotic film. And then there was heat. And then there was a blast. And then the floor opened up under me. And I fell. I fell out. And I landed. I landed in a field of corn. And I fell asleep and I couldn't wake up and there was corn all in my face. No, this was not a dream mother. No the corn was not cooked; it was like on the cob, mother. I was embedded in a business class seat for I don't know how long for for for... for uh days ... And Mother... mother...

> *The world pieces back together. SARAH and TODD and TRACY JO stare at her with tremendous suspicion.*

> *Meanwhile inside ANNA and ROBERT talk gently as she makes PB&J sandwiches.*

SARAH: Mothers are serious business huh?

DOROTHY: Yeah, yeah... where's yours? *(No response.)* Hello!

DOROTHY/ROBERT: *(Overlapping.)* When will your folks/mommy and daddy be back?

ANNA: They're not coming back.

TODD: They were Raptured.

ROBERT: Oh I am so sorry.

DOROTHY: Excuse me. What?

ROBERT: You know I lost my brother.

ANNA: Duh hickey. And they're not dead...

TODD: Christ came and claimed them. Have you read the *Left Behind* series? It's really helpful. Hey, do you want to be a part of our Tribulation Force?

TODD and SARAH and TRACY JO: "He lives there." *(TRACY JO, TODD and SARAH tap their chests in a secret Tribulation Force sign they've worked out.)*

DOROTHY: Okay... How long have I been here?

SARAH: Six years. *(DOROTHY panics.)* Haha. One month, Dorothy.

TRACY JO: It's the Fourth of July, Dorothy. You're in Kansas, the geographical center of the United States of America.

DOROTHY: Great. WHERE ARE MY PANTS.

TODD: No, no! They're gone! Don't tell her, Sarah!

SARAH: Dorothy, you're going to have to pay us for the corn you damaged.

DOROTHY: Excuse me?

SARAH: Yeah, that corn was for sale.

TODD: Sarah! That's not generous.

SARAH: She's been lying to us Todd, I bet Dorothy's not even her real name, is it, Dorothy.

DOROTHY: Actually, it is.

TODD: Really?

DOROTHY: Yes.

TODD: Awesome.

DOROTHY: PANTS!

TODD: Pants are dead. Just forget about the pants.

SARAH: Todd, pants.

TODD, disgruntled, goes inside and gets a pair of his mother's pants and presents them to DOROTHY. They are not fashionable.

DOROTHY: Oh no, no, no, no, no.

SARAH: No, Todd, those are mom's pants.

TODD: I know. I couldn't find Dorothy's pants.

DOROTHY: Ok! *(Looking to each teenager to figure out who is most trustworthy.)* Can you, can you, can YOU point me in the direction of the nearest shopping center? Hmm?
Gas station.
Walmart!

SARAH: Car was taken.

DOROTHY: I can walk.

Everyone laughs.

TODD: You can't walk anywhere in Kansas.

DOROTHY: I am walking.

TRACY JO: You can't leave-

DOROTHY: *(Shouting to ROBERT through window.)* Uh, best of luck to you!

ROBERT: Thank you.

DOROTHY: *(Muttering off.)* Fucking weird.

She exits. ROBERT, starving, grabs another sandwich (ANNA's) while ANNA puts the PB&J away and watches DOROTHY stalk off bemusedly.

SARAH: S'weird...

TRACY JO: Yeah. S'weird.

DOROTHY re-enters and vehemently grabs her airline chair. Everyone woofs.

DOROTHY: What?

She leaves, disgusted.

SARAH/TRACY JO: People come and go so quickly here.

SARAH: Jinx.

ANNA: *(Coming back out and seeing her sandwich gone.)* Hey! That's mine! *(Repressing anger.)* 10 9 8 7 6 5 4 3...

SARAH: *(Overlapping.)* 1 2 3 4 5 6 7 8 9 10 you can't talk till I say your name. Tracy Jo. Are you having a nice time?

TRACY JO: Yea. I love it.

SARAH: This is America on the Fourth of July. You're looking at the heart of a nation, Tracy Jo.

ANNA: *(Forced politeness.)* Of course you may have my sandwich, Robert. I'm happy to be sharing with you. I'm just going to go right over here for a little while.

> *ANNA runs out of the kitchen and sits between TODD's legs as he rocks on the rocking chair. They watch the fireworks together.*

SARAH: My hands are sweaty.

TRACY JO: There are glands in your hands.

> *Takes SARAH's hand. They hold hands and are still for a moment. Then SARAH slaps her hand.*

SARAH: S'gross. I mean, um, please don't do that. Tracy Jo... I have a shirt you could borrow if you want to change out of that dirty one. Come on.

> *SARAH and TRACY JO exit.*

TODD: So have you been good?

ANNA: Okay... I was just almost bad! I just almost didn't give my sandwich to Robert, but I fixed it. How bout you? Have you been good?

TODD: I don't know. It's really hard. I don't know how to tell.

ANNA: Yeah...

TODD: Hey, do you wanna go for an airplane ride?

ANNA: Yes!!!

TODD: *(ANNA jumps on his back.)* Whoa, you're getting big.

> *TODD begins to fly ANNA around.*

> *SARAH and TRACY JO stand on the roof.*

> *ROBERT emerges outside and looks at the cornfields. He looks at the stars.*

ROBERT: *(Quietly.)* Dear God, I uh…

Oh Jesus help me.

SARAH: Every time I see a shooting star, Anna says it's a broken satellite.

TRACY JO: They grow up so fast.

SARAH: Do you think there's anyone left?

TRACY JO: Yes.

> *TODD gently lands ANNA back on the ground. They salute each other.*

TODD: Did you have a nice flight?

ANNA: Yes.

TODD: Sweet.

> *She embraces him abruptly, and then almost immediately falls deep asleep. TODD lays her gently down on the stairs.*

TRACY JO: *(Notices ROBERT in the grass.)* Hey Robbit, have you ever seen a shooting star?

ROBERT: No… no I really don't think so.

> *TRACY JO sees a shooting star, gasps and points. ROBERT misses it.*

ROBERT: No…

> *Fireworks continue in the distance.*

> *TODD in the rocker. DOROTHY comes in, slowly, with her chair.*

DOROTHY: Jesus.

TODD: Todd. Two "d's"

DOROTHY: Right.

> *She sets her chair down, completely exhausted. They both sit, listening to the fireworks.*

> *Elsewhere, SARAH finds ROBERT in the darkness, pokes him in the back.*

SARAH: Look I'm sorry I shot you.

ROBERT: Yeah… I guess it's alright.

SARAH: Yeah…Whoops. *(This is awkward…)* Can you help me with something?

DOROTHY: Did you ever see that *Twilight Zone* episode with that couple in the weird town, and… Well, they try to get out. So they get on this train. And they go around and around and around and they get out and they're back exactly where they started. So they get BACK on the train –

TODD: Shhh. *(He points up at the fireworks.)*

> *SARAH has brought ROBERT to a light bulb, long burned out.*

DOROTHY: *(Misunderstanding, lowering her voice.)* So they get BACK on the train. And they go around and around and around and when they get out again, they're back exactly where they started! And then the camera pulls out, and like pans back and you hear the music – *do do do do* – and you see that they're actually trapped in this snow globe and these aliens are, like, playing with them… HOW LONG IS THE FOURTH OF JULY IN KANSAS?!

TODD: Do you have like trouble being quiet?!

> *Long pause. TODD ashamed of his rudeness. DOROTHY horrified with it all.*

Um, I mean, do you have a favorite? My favorites are bottle rockets. And, y'know, I still love those little black pellets that you light and they turn into long black ashy worms. I guess I'm still a kid at heart.

ROBERT: Hey do you know how many Harvard students it takes to screw in a light bulb?

SARAH: Um, 13.

ROBERT: No.

SARAH: 52.

ROBERT: Come on, Sarah.

SARAH: I don't know.

ROBERT: One. He just holds onto the light bulb and the whole world revolves around him.

> *TODD jumps up and goes into the grass. He emerges with DOROTHY's pants.*

DOROTHY: *(Grateful whisper.)* Pants.

> *DOROTHY changes in the grass. TODD covers his eyes with a flag.*

SARAH: I don't get it.

TODD: You know, I have a whole stash of illegal fireworks. My dad drove me to Missouri to get 'em. Not Robert. My real dad. I've got um, black cats and M-80's and M-100's and roman candles and this one that I've been saving for a really special occasion, like this one. It's called "ultimate climax." *(Light bulb illuminates.)*

SARAH: Hey!… So you were almost the President?

ROBERT: Yeah. I was almost President.

SARAH: Well, you know, Washington DC's pretty far away from here.

ROBERT: Yeah, you're telling me.

TODD: Do you want to see it?

SARAH: Robert, can you stay here for a little while?

ROBERT: Yes.

DOROTHY: Umm…Yes!

TODD: Awesome!

ROBERT: *(Newfound energy.)* Now you wait for me right here. I'm gonna be right back. *(ROBERT runs to ANNA, both get in starting race position.)* On your mark, get set…

6.

ANNA: *(To audience and the stage.)* August!

ROBERT: And they're off!

> *ROBERT and ANNA race. He shoves her and wins, exiting in a sprint.*

ANNA: *(Running after him.)* Hey, no fair!

> *TRACY JO douses herself and SARAH with a bucket and sponge. It is sweltering.*

> *TODD gives DOROTHY a jubilant tour of the house.*

TODD: So, this is the kitchen. We don't really do a lot of cooking in here anymore, but in here is where I listen to mostly classic rock. Bands like Nirvana, also Pearl Jam, also Metallica – oh! and also bands from your era. Like the Supremes.

DOROTHY: *(She hits him.)* Show me something else.

> *TODD and DOROTHY run around the wall.*

TODD: This is the – *kitchen*...

> *SARAH and TRACY JO role-play.*

SARAH: Ding Dong.

TODD AND DOROTHY: *(Looking at each other,* Twilight Zone *theme.)* **Do do do do, do do do do** ...

TRACY JO: Oh! Who is at the door?

SARAH: It's me, Tracy Jo. Please let me in.

TRACY JO: Oh I'm sorry. Sarah says I shouldn't talk to strangers.

SARAH: Tracy Jo! ... I want to play the other one.

> *ROBERT and ANNA enter running.*

> *Time jump. The SPRINGERS and TRACY JO all splay themselves on the floor to listen to ROBERT tell stories. DOROTHY observes from the side.*

ROBERT: Now, Anna, you have no idea how close. It was everything. New York, DC, Miami, San Francisco, Los Angeles...

SARAH: Kansas?

ROBERT: I suppose so. You see, once we discovered that the missiles were already *IN* Cuba, we realized that we had 2 options. Now the first option was just to bomb the hell out of Cuba – which Bob and I SUPPORTED–

ANNA: Bob?

DOROTHY: Robert McNamara.

ROBERT: Jack's Secretary of Defense.

No flicker of recognition.

ANNA: Oh…

ROBERT: So we are urging Jack to strike now. And, Jack, the one thing he's adamant about for the entire thirteen days is that the United States is not a country that preemptively strikes.

ANNA: Why not? *(TODD raises his hand.)*

ROBERT: Todd.

TODD: Because everybody would have been vaporized.

ROBERT: Yes, yes I guess that's true. However, Jack's point was that what was at stake was America's right to the moral leadership of the planet. Now, Anna, I am the smartest guy that you're ever gonna meet, but President Kennedy, my brother, he saved the world by deciding that I was wrong. You have no idea how close – Christ, *we* had no idea how close.

Time jump. Back to TODD and DOROTHY's tour.

TODD: This is the bathroom, obviously. In here is where I come to listen to sad music. Like Tori Amos.

ANNA: How do you *get* to be president? *(Everyone looks to ROBERT for the answer.)*

ROBERT: Anna, anyone who knows what I know about the presidency can never be certain that anyone mortal can fill that position.

ANNA: I could be President.

ROBERT: *(Getting an idea, excited.)* Anna, you wait for me right here. I'm gonna be right back.

> *ROBERT exits and returns with a trash bag (packed with leaves).*
> *A lesson.*

Now Anna, I love Autumn…

ANNA: I *ALSO* love Autumn!

7.

ANNA and ROBERT reach together into the bag and toss their handfuls upwards.

LEAVES EVERYWHERE!

ROBERT plays in them.

Time jump.

DOROTHY comes out onto the porch as the leaves settle. ROBERT nails her with a handful of leaves.

DOROTHY: Oh! Hey.

ROBERT: Hay is for Horses.

DOROTHY: You're good with them.

ROBERT: Well, I had some practice.

DOROTHY: May I? *(She moves closer to him. Long pause.)* You miss your kids?

ROBERT: Yes, of course I do.

DOROTHY: Of course... you know, my father hated you.

ROBERT: Really?

DOROTHY: He thought you were hugely manipulative. A real son-of-a-bitch. *(Bad joke.)*

ROBERT: Well, what do you think?

DOROTHY: Oh – you're my hero. *(He is moved.)* You were HUGELY manipulative!! I mean, look at that speech you gave in Indianapolis the night Martin Luther King was shot.

ROBERT: Bad night.

DOROTHY: Yeah...
I've seen the video.
You equated a white man killing King to a white man killing your brother.

ROBERT: Yeah.

DOROTHY: Yeah... It's NOT the same.

ROBERT: Well I know that Dorothy.

DOROTHY: No, but you made it the same! Just saying it. The entire country was a mess, but there were no riots in Indianapolis that night. Because you soothed people. I think it was great. It was a great thing. It was a brilliant speech. And it *worked*. You don't understand – politics don't *work* anymore–

TODD enters, his face covered with shaving cream.

TODD: Excuse me Robbit? Pardon the interruption. But do you know how to shave?

ROBERT: Yes… *(Sees TODD.)* Oh Jesus Todd, I'll be right there. *(Going to exit.)* I guess I never thought of that as politics. That was the only time I ever spoke of my brother's assassination, publicly. Did you know that?

SARAH runs on.

SARAH: Robbit think fast! *(She tosses the football. ROBERT catches it and runs off.)*

DOROTHY: *(Calling after him.)* Robert?! …I'm so sorry you're dead.

Time jump. Back into SARAH and TRACY JO role-playing.

SARAH: Ding Dong.

TRACY JO: Oh! Who is at the door?

SARAH: *(Very butch.)* S's George. I'm here to check your meter.

TRACY JO: Oh, I'm sorry. I don't know any men named George.

SARAH: No, no, no you know me. It's George from the electricity store.

TRACY JO: No – I don't want any candy.

SARAH: But I'm here to check your electricity–

TRACY JO: Sarah, why are we playing this?

SARAH doesn't answer.

Elsewhere, TODD sits in the rocking chair. Quiet.

DOROTHY: What are you doing?

TODD: Thinking.

DOROTHY: You sit here a lot?

TODD: My dad says that the porch is the throne of modern man.

DOROTHY: *(Laughing hysterically.)* Really? Your dad really said that?

TODD: Yup.

DOROTHY: *(Seeing TODD's not laughing.)* Well that's funny. I mean that's a funny thought. Because historically the *perch* is the throne of the modern man. Like back in the earliest literary images – like in the Bible – there are pillars of salt and towers of dirt...

TODD: The Bible isn't literature.

DOROTHY: *(Beat.)* Like, in the *Bible* there are pillars of salt and there are towers of dirt and...

TODD: The Bible is fact.

DOROTHY: *(Beat.)* Do you really believe that?

TODD: Yes I do. We do.

DOROTHY: *(Long beat.)* That's beautiful... Fuck.

TODD: F-bomb!

> *ROBERT and ANNA reenter running.*
>
> *Music re-surges.*
>
> *TRACY JO goes to get her eggs and takes them into the grass.*

ROBERT: *(Calling to ANNA.)* GO LONG JACK!

SARAH: *(Running in.)* Dorothy, stay right there. Close your eyes. I wanna show you something.

> *DOROTHY stays. SARAH blindfolds DOROTHY and then goes off to get her secret box.*

ROBERT: Go long Jack! Oh yes, that's the ticket! Oh Jack, once you've decided which way you're running, nobody can catch you. Hut! Hut! Hike! And go long! *(Shouting at his imagined family.)* Ted, you might as well stay exactly where you are, cause you're a no good goddamn teamster commie son of a bitch and you're getting clobbered by Bobby and Jack!

> *ROBERT throws the ball at ANNA. She drops it.*

ANNA: How come I can't catch the ball?!

ROBERT: I have no idea Anna. Probably because you don't really care whether or not you catch it.

ANNA: I do so care!

ROBERT: So what's going to happen if you don't catch the next ball I throw right at you?

ANNA: I dunno! It'll end up on the ground...

ROBERT: Right. And what does that say about you?

ANNA: That catch is not my forté?

ROBERT: No. No. It says that you've chosen not to excel, and that you've chosen not to hone your skills. Now Anna, if you want to be president, you have the opportunity right now to turn yourself into the type of person whose failures have consequences. Sometimes you just have to craft those consequences for yourself.

ANNA: But this is just a football.

ROBERT: No Anna – this is not a metaphor.

> *ROBERT exits, leaving her. ANNA stands stunned and then sees TRACY JO in the grass.*
>
> *SARAH re-enters, putting the box before DOROTHY and removing the blindfold.*

SARAH: Open sesame. Ta-da.

ANNA: Hey Tracy Jo. I'll trade you this great football for those stinky eggs.

TRACY JO: Okay.

ANNA: Great.

> *Giggling, ANNA turns to the audience. She begins to hand out eggs (i.e. consequences).*

Here, here, here. Here. You have to share. You have to share too.

> *ANNA, giggling, exits.*
>
> *In the box SARAH has brought is a woman's purse.*

SARAH: Is it yours? I found it in the bushes. It must've fallen from your plane.

DOROTHY: How long have you had this?

SARAH: Oh, not very long... *(DOROTHY looks at her.)* I mean awhile...

DOROTHY begins to rummage through the contents.

What is that?

DOROTHY: I don't know.

SARAH: What are those?

DOROTHY: I don't know.

SARAH: Dorothy what are those?

DOROTHY: *(Sharp.)* These are vitamins.

SARAH: Do you take them?

DOROTHY: Yes.

SARAH: Are you sick?

DOROTHY: I don't think so...

SARAH: I didn't take any!

DOROTHY: ...It's ok.

DOROTHY offers her the case.

SARAH: I get a pain in my heart sometimes...

DOROTHY: ...I don't think I have any vitamins for that.

SARAH: What's that one?

DOROTHY: Sea kelp.

SARAH: Sea Kelp.

DOROTHY: Seek Help. *(SARAH doesn't get it. She pulls out another pill.)* Choline inositol.

SARAH: Do you know what it does?

DOROTHY: Yes. A. B. C. Zinc.

SARAH: Can I just take them all at once?

DOROTHY: No.

SARAH: Are they chewable?

DOROTHY: No they are not chewable!

SARAH: Can I take them with Diet Coke??

SARAH downs all the pills with a swig.

DOROTHY: No! Wow. *(DOROTHY takes her bag.)* You know, Sarah, you really shouldn't drink Diet Coke. It's bad for your bones.

DOROTHY walks away from the stunned SARAH. She approaches the audience, giddily removing a pack of cigarettes she has found from her purse.

Does anybody have a light?

TRACY JO: Oh Dorothy, can I get a drag of that?

DOROTHY: It's not—

TRACY JO takes the cigarette and inhales.

Lit. Okay, okay. You're pregnant.

TRACY JO: *(So proud.)* I know.

DOROTHY: So when are you due?

TRACY JO: I'm not doing anything.

DOROTHY: No, I mean when are you having the baby?

TRACY JO: Oh… *(Caught off guard.)* I don't know. I haven't really been keeping, keeping, trackin' it. Keepin count. *(To ROBERT.)* Have you ever been pregnant?

DOROTHY: *(After a weird beat.)* I have.

TRACY JO: Well where's your baby?

DOROTHY: I don't know. Where's your husband?

TRACY JO: I don't know.

DOROTHY: Well, that's a really nice ring.

TRACY JO: It's yours! Sarah gave it to me.

DOROTHY: Oh my God.

TRACY JO: Do you want it back?

DOROTHY: *(Overwhelmed.)* …No. Thank you.

TRACY JO: Suit yourself.

Suddenly and with great fanfare, ANNA enters. She is wearing a poncho and carries a huge plastic tarp, and huge drop cloth. She drops them all center stage.

ANNA: *(To audience.)* Ladies and Gentlemen!!! The time has come for a recipe for disaster! I need helpers.

The cast springs into action, preparing the space for the mess.

This next section should feel improvisational, and should strongly encourage the audience that it's okay to throw the egg.

I am about to do something that you have never seen before. I am going to jump a jump rope for fifteen minutes without stopping. *(SARAH hands ANNA her jump rope.)* Thank you, Bob. And if I mess up, you have to throw your eggs at me. For real! For real. Because we're learning about consequences. Anyway, if you don't throw them, then you just have to hold onto them for the whole rest of the play. I'm gonna put on my super extra, anti-ovular gear. Made for me in the Himalayas. How are my helpers doing? Oh good. Okay, I'm gonna set the timer for 15 minutes.
For real, I'm not kidding with you.
Okay. Ready, go.

ANNA jumps rope and chants rhyme.

Mother went away and left us some fine day, some fine day, yea, yea.

She messes up. Ducks. Hopefully some audience members throw their eggs.

No, no, no, stop, stop, stop, stop, stop, time out, doesn't count!!!!!
THAT DID NOT COUNT. That was a, that was a test run.

For real.
I'm... I'm resetting.

She resets the egg timer.

Okay, okay. This time, this time for real. *(If the stage is raised above the audience, or if the audience seems to need extra urging to throw.)* You can, if you need to you can stand up to throw them too. It's hard from like... okay, for real.

ANNA jumps rope and sings song again.

Mother went away and left us some fine day, some fine day, yea, yea.
Packed up her bags and said she couldn't stay. Can't stay, bye bye OOH
CAN'T –

> *She messes up. Ducks and immediately begins screaming at the audience,*
> *who hopefully have thrown their eggs at her.*

NO, no, no, no. Stop, stop. Stop! Stop! Stop stop! That is not fair!
I – I have a football injury!!
That didn't, that did not count. Okay, for real. For real. I'm setting the
timer again.

> *Very serious, she resets the egg timer and tries again. She does much*
> *better. But messes up, ducks.*

> *Audience throws their eggs, or are all out of eggs. ANNA is disgusted.*

> *If anyone still has an egg, she grabs it from them, or she goes to her box*
> *of eggs angrily. She holds the egg aloft, glaring at the audience, as if she*
> *is going to pelt them with it. Then suddenly and violently she smashes*
> *the egg on her head. It oozes…*

8.

The adults begin to clean the stage.

The weather grows cold and dark. A heavy mood settles on Kansas.

TODD: Hey Anna—

ANNA: Leave me alone.

> *ANNA goes inside. She stares in the mirror.*
>
> *TODD looks into a mirror, separate.*
>
> *SARAH looks into a mirror, separate.*
>
> *The three visitors talk outside as the children each fall apart inside in their own way.*
>
> *ANNA cleans herself from the eggs and begins to dress as her mother, quietly speaking to herself as she does so.*
>
> *SARAH plays doctor on herself, imagining she is very sick.*
>
> *TODD role-plays violently, imagining himself a soldier in military movies, including* Top Gun *and* Deerhunter.

ROBERT: Jesus Christ, it's terrifying out here.

DOROTHY: Yea, well, we're in the middle of nowhere.

ROBERT: So, Dorothy, do you have kids?

TRACY JO: She doesn't know where they are.

TODD: *(Role playing quietly.)* I'll give you your dream shot. I'm sending you up against the best. You two characters are going to Top Gun.

DOROTHY: What have you been telling Anna?

ROBERT: She's quite a little dynamo, isn't she?

SARAH: Hi Dr. Fletcher...

ROBERT: You know, we've just been talking about certain... qualities. About responsibility and integrity... because she cheats at everything.

DOROTHY: You cheat at everything.

ROBERT: ...Point taken.

SARAH: *(As doctor.)* Hello Sarah, how are you?

TODD: Sir, yes sir!

ROBERT: You know, at her age I was an altar boy.

DOROTHY: Is that what you've come here to do?

ROBERT: What? To be an altar boy again?

SARAH: Well, I'm okay. I've got some soreness.

ROBERT: She has potential.

DOROTHY: Obviously. She wants to be a scientist.

ROBERT: Yes, but she could do anything.

DOROTHY: What have you been telling her?

ROBERT: You know, you keep implying that I know something about this great cosmic plan that brought me here.

SARAH: My right eye's blurry.

TRACY JO: Do you know something?

ROBERT: Look the last thing I remember is thinking what the hell was going to happen in Chicago.

TRACY JO: It's so dark.

DOROTHY: Yeah well we're in the middle of nowhere.

TRACY JO: I love this place.

DOROTHY: I bet you do.

TRACY JO: Why are you here Dorothy?

DOROTHY: I don't know!

SARAH: *(As doctor.)* We're going to have to check the pressures and the vitals.

DOROTHY: They're children.

TODD: You know, I flew with your old man.

DOROTHY: You, Tracy Jo, the four of you—

TRACY JO: I'm not a child.

DOROTHY: And Sarah needs to grow up. The four of you were living like the lost boys—

TRACY JO: *Peter Pan.*

DOROTHY: Are you from Mars?

TRACY JO: Yes. *(They absorb this.)*

SARAH: So just go ahead and get undressed and I'll be back in a few minutes.

ANNA: Hi Mom. What are you doing?

DOROTHY: ... Twilight Zone.

TRACY JO: We didn't need you to take care of us DONNA REED. *(Whispering to ROBERT.)* She was an American mother in the 1950's –

ROBERT: I know who Donna Reed was, thank you very much. I wasn't apparently shot until 1968 –

TRACY JO: Why'd they shoot you then?

DOROTHY: Some crazy kid wanted to be on television.

TRACY JO: I love television.

DOROTHY: They don't even have a television.

TRACY JO: S'broken.

DOROTHY: FYI. This isn't 1968.

ROBERT: No, but there's always towns. / There are always farmers. The smallest stop – planned, unplanned. The train slows down and there are folks who want to shake your hand and tell you they're proud of you and that they're praying for you. I mean, where is everybody? Where is anybody?

DOROTHY: *(Overlapping.)* No, there are no downtowns or hometowns. The schools don't survive. Everybody's old or too young to drive away. There's no community... and that is also totally not true. *(Cutting through.)* No - NO it's BULLSHIT ROBERT. There's *church* things and *church* malls and *church*, mega, sprawling, all this space—

ROBERT: Dorothy—

DOROTHY: I'm standing in the grass with an alien and a dead man.

SARAH: There's something wrong with me.

DOROTHY: You know this entire space used to be an ocean. A sea. 65 million years ago.

ANNA: You look really nice.

ROBERT: You cannot just write off the entire middle of the country Dorothy.

ANNA: You look really nice too.

DOROTHY: Thank you Robert. You know I'm not a reporter.

ROBERT: I don't think that I'm here to run for President again actually Dorothy.

DOROTHY: Oh no, of course that's Anna's job. Please stop using my name so much.

TRACY JO: Why don't you like it here? You have a family.

DOROTHY: I *had* a family! They probably think I'm dead.

TRACY JO: Maybe they were taken-

DOROTHY: Oh shut UP Tracy!

TRACY JO: Jo!

DOROTHY and TRACY JO: Tracy Jo!

ROBERT: I don't – / Just STOP asking me why I'm here. I don't know, I don't know, I DON'T KNOW WHY I'M HERE. I'M TRYING! SOMETHING'S WRONG BUT I CAN'T – WHAT AM I SUPPOSED TO DO? I'M TRYING GODDAMMIT – YOU MOVE FORWARD DOROTHY. YOU MOVE!!

DOROTHY: *(Overlapping.)* YOU ARE A DEAD HERO! YOU'RE A FICTION OF A DREAM THAT THIS COUNTRY ONCE HAD. I'VE FUCKING LOST IT. I'VE JUST – SOMEONE JUST GIVE ME MORE MEDICATION CAUSE THIS IS INSANE.

TRACY JO: *(Overlapping.)* Stop shouting please. Stop, stop, stop shouting STOP IT!!

DOROTHY: Fine! Fine. I'm leaving!

DOROTHY begins to storm off.

TRACY JO: I'm going to find Sarah.

TRACY JO storms off.

DOROTHY: *(Firing back at ROBERT.)* You cannot possibly understand this country. *(She exits.)*

ROBERT: *(Quiet.)* That's not what I meant by move.

TODD enters at the height of a fevered role play, with gun in hand.

ROBERT: Not now Todd.

TODD: I've never shot anybody before Robert.

ROBERT: *(Slowly, looking down the barrel which TODD is holding in his face.)* No. No... Todd, please - DON'T!

TODD shoots ROBERT, who falls to the ground, limp.

9

ROBERT lays on the ground. TODD, breathless, stands over him. The others come running in from all over.

ROBERT gasps to life.

ROBERT: Was anybody else hurt?

> *ROBERT locks eyes on TODD.*

TRACY JO: Why did you do that?

ROBERT: *(Rising slowly. White-hot fury. He grabs TODD by the shoulders. Quiet at first.)* What are you thinking? What, what are you thinking? What are you thinking?

> *TODD has curled into himself like a young child. ROBERT yanks him back up.*

You stand up, boy. What are you thinking?! WHAT ARE YOU THINKING? WHAT ARE YOU THINKING?!

> *ROBERT repeats the line, shaking TODD to the point of exhaustion.*

ANNA: *(Quietly, attempting to channel her mother, whose clothes she is still wearing.)* I think I've got it under control...

> *ROBERT continues. "What are you thinking?"*

Let him go Robert – I've got it under control!

ROBERT: Like hell you do. Kids with guns. YOU ARE A CHILD!

TODD: Sarah!

SARAH: Robert let him go!

ANNA: I think we are having a conflict of ideals.

DOROTHY: Robert let him go.

> *ROBERT finally does. TODD runs to SARAH's and ANNA's feet, collapsing.*

ANNA: We are getting really far away from something important.

ROBERT: What are you wearing? We are not playing house! *(Charging.)* You, get up boy!

SARAH: He's not your boy!

ANNA: YOU KEEP AWAY FROM HIM. You keep away from us!
We would like you to leave. Now.

ROBERT: I would like nothing better.

ANNA: ALL OF YOU!

TRACY JO: Me?

ANNA: Yes.

DOROTHY: WHAT?!

TRACY JO: I LIVE HERE.

ANNA: *(Transformed.)* Todd, get up. Everybody out! You're all a wicked
temptation. Todd. Sarah.

TRACY JO: Sarah?

> *SARAH looks at TRACY JO.*

ANNA: Sarah, it's time for grace now.

> *SARAH slowly walks to her siblings. She takes ANNA's hand, and TODD
> takes the other.*
>
> *ANNA stands center, dressed in their mother's clothing.*
>
> *TRACY JO, ROBERT, and DOROTHY watch.*

ANNA: *(To ROBERT.)* What?

TODD: *(To DOROTHY.)* What are you looking at?

SARAH: *(To TRACY JO.)* What do you want from me?

ROBERT: I may not avert my sight... This is like a goddamned train wreck.

> *The SPRINGER children face out, holding each other's hands.*

ANNA: Dear Jesus: On this day of thanks. On Thanksgiving Day. I am
thankful for my family, Sarah and Todd Springer. I am thankful
for their strength in you oh Lord especially in the face of of... of
OUTSIDERS.

TRACY JO: People turn on each other so quickly here.

DOROTHY: Okay Anna, look, calm down –

ANNA: This is a day of thanks. On this day, I am thankful that I know you, Jesus.

DOROTHY: Anna, you're being ridiculous–

ANNA: You are not mom.
I am thankful that my family has been raised properly, and that we are forgiven. I am thankful for this country. And for what we are trying to do and be.

DOROTHY: (*After a stunned moment, overlapping.*) No. No, I'm not your mother. Your mother is probably OFF somewhere doing WHO KNOWS WHAT–

ANNA: You shut up – you don't know anything about – DEAR JESUS.

TRACY JO: Sarah talk to me!

ANNA: You are – we don't NEED ANY OF YOU! We're getting back on track Jesus.

TRACY JO: I don't understand any of this.

ROBERT: I am trying to help you! Something has gone terribly wrong here–

ANNA: You are a GHOST! You don't exist any more. (*Turning on DOROTHY.*) And you –

DOROTHY: I got carried away. It's just, you're all alone here –

ANNA: (*Frighteningly composed.*) We're fine. We know exactly who we are and we know exactly what we are doing here. Do you know why you're here? Do you have any idea? You're a tourist. You write all these books about us, and you look at us like – like –
I know why I'm here! I know why I'm here. (*Beginning to fall apart.*) I know. I know…
Dear Jesus…

> She has absolutely no idea what to pray for and becomes a child again, overwhelmed.

ROBERT: (*After a long time.*) Amen.

ANNA: FUCK YOU!

> A terrible beat. SARAH walks slowly to the audience…

10.

House lights rise.

SARAH: *(Quiet. And slow.)* If you have any questions, I'm prepared to answer them now.

> *NOTE: Typically it took a long time for the audience to understand the performer was not being rhetorical. She ad-libbed small jokes, such as impersonating Elvis, or tapping the end of her jump rope like a microphone, "Is this thing on?" Enough to allow the audience to soften.*

I mean it. If you have any questions about anything, you can ask.

> *The audience begins to ask questions. Sometimes they are about the play. Sometimes they are directed at the characters. Sometimes they are directed at the actors. Only the SPRINGER children should answer unless it would be especially rude for DOROTHY, TRACY JO, or ROBERT not to do so. SARAH should be the primary speaker. Answers are given in character, while not pretending that there isn't a play happening.*

> *Finally, after at least 3 questions, TRACY JO quietly raises her hand.*

TRACY JO: Sarah, what was your favorite day?

SARAH: If you didn't hear the pregnant girl in the "I Love Jesus" hat, she just asked me what was my favorite day. That's a hard one.

> *Everyone in the cast turns to an audience member close to them, makes intimate eye contact, and answers this question as themselves, just loud enough for that audience member to hear them. This moment should not feel performative in any way.*

> *After all the cast has finished:*

SARAH: My favorite day hasn't happened yet.

> *House lights fade.*

> *ANNA, SARAH and TODD inside the house, looking out. After a long period of time.*

ANNA: I don't know what to do. There's so much space. I can't see anything. There's too many options.

DOROTHY: There are a lot of options.

ANNA: I feel bad. I like it here. I'm a really big fish.

DOROTHY: And it's a really small pond. Maybe there's not enough–

ANNA: Kelp?

DOROTHY: Kelp... I was gonna say oxygen, but she said kelp, we'll go with kelp. ...kelp. May I come in?

ANNA: Yes.

DOROTHY: Thank you. Thank you.

> *Happy to come in from the cold, walking exceedingly delicately so as not to inflame things again.*

So, okay. Which one of you is going to go to college? *(SARAH and TODD immediately point at ANNA, who has simply rolled her eyes at this question.)* Okay. And what do you want to be when you grow up?

ANNA: I want to be president.

DOROTHY: Wants to be the president. Okay. So. Um. And what do you need to do that?

SARAH: You need money.

DOROTHY: Money... Yes, what else?

ANNA: A car...

DOROTHY: A car, yeah, what else?

ANNA: Helpers?

DOROTHY: Helpers, yes.

ANNA: What do you do? I mean... what do you do?

DOROTHY: I work... It's not that interesting.

ANNA: I'm interested.

DOROTHY: I work, um, with money.

ANNA: Like, hedge funds?

DOROTHY: Anna, do you know what a hedge fund is?

ANNA: No. But I would like to learn.

DOROTHY: Okay.

SARAH: Dorothy, could I be excused?

DOROTHY: Okay. *(SARAH exits.)* Anna. Hedge funds are really boring so let's talk about markets.

ANNA: Markets?

DOROTHY: Yeah, markets. Markets are like... evolution.

> *TODD gasps and buries his head in his hands.*

DOROTHY: Oh no, no no no. Okay, uh, markets are amoral.

ANNA: What?!

DOROTHY: No, not *immoral*. Amoral. The market doesn't value good or bad. It values scarcity. *(Extending her hand.)* C'mon Anna. You're gonna love this.

> *DOROTHY and ANNA exit.*

TODD: *(After a long beat.)* Robert, I was just... practicing. I was afraid that I wouldn't be able – I signed up to join the Army yesterday. I mean. I sent in that application. I said I was 18, and I figure that since I'm big for my age and cuz my folks are gone and cuz they really need guys right now that they probably won't ask me too many questions. And I'm not delusional. I know that there's a really good chance that I could be killed or maimed. And that if I were, that Sarah and Anna would be really sad. But I've got to get right with God. And I love my country, and we're under attack right now.

> *DOROTHY and ANNA re-enter.*

DOROTHY: So I say to you, Anna, that it would be wise for you to remember that two of the most beautifully adapted species on the planet are the cockroach and the rat, okay? This was just an overview. Any questions?
(ANNA raises her hand. DOROTHY points at her.) Yes?

ANNA: Um did you learn this in school?

DOROTHY: Yes.

ANNA: *(Sudden and total grasping panic.)* Will you write me my recommendation letter? I want to be the president! Where do I go?

DOROTHY: Well, you need to go to a place where people know who you are.

ANNA: Oh, I know! I know. I, I know it starts when I'm young. But I don't know any presidents' kids! I only ever play with Todd.

SARAH enters in a dress.

SARAH: Dorothy, um how do I look?

DOROTHY: Wow! Um…

ANNA: Okay, so for a Vice President, is a dead Kennedy preferable to somebody more alive but much less charismatic?

DOROTHY: Oh geez honey, I don't know.

ANNA: I'm going to make myself *scarce.*

ANNA exits.

SARAH: Dorothy is there anything missing??

DOROTHY: Do a spin. (*SARAH does.*)

ANNA re-enters and exits across the stage.

ANNA: My bedroom is that way!

DOROTHY: *(Having pulled out a lipstick when SARAH's back was turned.)* Lipstick?

SARAH: Thank you Dorothy! Ciao, ciao. (*SARAH exits.*)

DOROTHY: Ciao, ciao.

TODD: Do you think I'm doing the right thing?

DOROTHY is caught off guard, thinking he too is talking to her. But after a few beats:

ROBERT: *(Who has been listening outside all this time.)* Todd, I have absolutely no idea. Maybe. Perhaps. Dorothy will you come and speak with me in my office for just one minute? (*DOROTHY and ROBERT stand in the grass.*) Dorothy, that kid's entirely underage.

DOROTHY: *(Having no idea what they're discussing.)* Yes, he is entirely underage. There is not one bit of him that is of age.

He re-enters, fortified, leading DOROTHY and believing they are totally on the same page.

ROBERT: Todd why do you want to join the military?

DOROTHY: Woah –

TODD: Well, why did you join the Navy?

DOROTHY: Uh! Okay, uh, it's different being a Kennedy.

ROBERT: Thank you, Dorothy.

DOROTHY: You don't have to try as hard.

ROBERT: Hey.

TODD: Is that true?

ROBERT: We are going to get back to that. Now I asked you a question. Why do you want to join the military?

TODD: Uh… Okay – See the world. Money for college!

ROBERT: Okay! And what do you want to study while you're in college?

TODD: I don't know. I'm not really interested in anything.

> *TODD crumbles.*

DOROTHY: *(Putting her arms around him.)* It's ok. Hey. We are so proud of you.

TODD: Oh, crap.

DOROTHY: We are figuring this out.

> *DOROTHY looks to ROBERT, prodding him with her eyes to come and hug TODD. ROBERT leads TODD offstage. DOROTHY delicately picks up the gun and turns to follow. She turns back to the audience.*

We are figuring this out.

> *They exit. SARAH enters the empty stage and lays out a picnic blanket and snacks. After the picnic is set, TRACY JO whistles. SARAH tries to whistle back and can't. She makes a bird noise.*

> *TRACY JO enters the stage quickly. She is also changed, a dress she has found somewhere.*

SARAH: You look nice.

TRACY JO: You look nice.

SARAH: I've prepared a snack.

TRACY JO: It looks delicious.

SARAH: I put you on the left.

> *TRACY JO hands SARAH flowers. They sit.*

TRACY JO: It's nice weather.

SARAH: How are you?

TRACY JO: Nauseous. I like it.

SARAH: You like to feel nauseous?

TRACY JO: Yeah. You never know what's going to happen.

SARAH: Those are butterflies, Tracy Jo. I have them too... You seem distant.

TRACY JO: I'm sorry. I've never been on a date before. I'm sorry.

SARAH: You don't have to be sorry.

TRACY JO: *(Overlapping.)* I like you. I think you're beautiful. Did you ever read that book? *The Diary of Anne Frank?* Well, in it she says that she believes that people really are good at heart. And you, Sarah Springer, make me believe in that.

SARAH: She sounds like a nice person.

TRACY JO: She was.

SARAH: Do I have a temperature?

> *TRACY JO feels SARAH's forehead. Suddenly SARAH grabs TRACY JO and kisses her.*
>
> *Eventually SARAH pulls back. Shy. Stunned.*

11.

Uptempo Christmas music.

TRACY JO: Do you want to dance?!

SARAH: *(Burying her head in the picnic blanket.)* I'm going under here for a little while!

TRACY JO: I do!

> *TRACY JO grabs SARAH by the hand. They are the center of the HUGE CHRISTMAS WINTER DANCE, while all around them the house is set up for Christmas. In the original production, this was performed to Sufjan Stevens' "Come On! Let's Boogey to the Elf Dance!"*

> *NOTE: Much of this section was ad-libbed and future productions are encouraged to improvise. The important event in this section is the kiss between DOROTHY and ROBERT.*

ROBERT: So the Canadians, in all of their northern ingenuity, decided to name a goddamn mountain after my brother. I have to climb the stupid thing... There you go Anna, you can make it. It's not too steep. Is it windy? Is it cold?

ANNA: *(Climbing on the table.)* I claim this mountain for America-erica-erica.

> *Everyone strings the house with Christmas lights and celebrates when the lights work. All don winter coats and accessories. Snow is thrown in the air, much like leaves earlier.*

ROBERT: Dorothy, will you come and see me in my Oval Office for one minute?

> *They step into the snow-covered grass.*

Dorothy what is on the wall?

DOROTHY: That's a flag.

ROBERT: No Dorothy, what is on the wall?

DOROTHY: That's mistletoe.

> *They kiss.*

DOROTHY: *(To the audience.)* Merry Christmas.

The dance finishes. The SPRINGERS have set up for their pageant. The visitors sit with the audience, eating popcorn. DOROTHY might share some with the audience.

SARAH: *(To TRACY JO.)* See you after the show. You're going to love this.

TRACY JO: I know I'm going to love this.

ROBERT: *(After confirming the SPRINGERS are ready, to the audience and DOROTHY and TRACY JO.)* Ladies and gentlemen, *A Christmas Carol.* Did you know that my kids used to do this?

DOROTHY: No.

ROBERT: Every year.

SARAH/TODD/ANNA: *(Singing, poorly)*
God rest you merry gentlemen

> *ANNA violently shakes her head in disagreement with the pitch they've found. They adjust and try again.*

SARAH/TODD/ANNA:
God rest you merry gentlemen
May nothing you dismay
Remember Christ our Savior
Was born on Christmas Day
To save us all from Satan's pow'r *(Todd yells this)* **when**
We have gone astray
Oh-oh tidings of comfort and joy
Comfort and Joy
Oh-oh tidings of comfort and joy

TODD: *(Beginning the story proper.)* Marley was dead as a door-nail. There is no doubt that Marley was dead to begin with.

ANNA: SCROOGE! *(She plays violently with SARAH in front of her, who plays Scrooge in the pageant.)* A squeezing, wrenching, grasping, scraping, clutching, covetous old sinner. Hard and sharp and secret and solitary as an oyster! Once upon a time!

SARAH: *(As Scrooge.)* What right have you to be merry? What reason? You're poor enough!

> *Silence. It is the nephew's turn to speak, which TODD is supposed to play. However he has missed his cue. ANNA starts again.*

ANNA: Once upon a time!

SARAH: What right have you to be merry? What reason – you're poor enough?

ANNA: Todd s'your cue!

TODD: I'm playing Marley.

ANNA: No you're not. I'm Marley! *(He shoves her violently and chaos ensues. ANNA is weeping. SARAH yelling at TODD.)*

SARAH: *(Shouting over the din.)* What right have you to be merry? You're poor enough. TODD!

ROBERT: *(ROBERT holds the weeping ANNA and shoves popcorn in her mouth.)* Now buck up.

TODD: *(Frustrated, relenting.)* What right – *(More frustrated. He begins again, assuming a "British" accent.)* What right have you to be dismal? You're rich enough!

SARAH: What else can I be when I live in such a world of fools as this? Merry Christmas! Out upon Merry Christmas! *(Seeing her pouting sister.)* Anna, please.

ANNA: *(Playing back.)* Bah humbug!

TODD: Uncle!

SARAH: Nephew!

TODD: Christmas is the only time I know of in the long calendar of the year when men and women seem by one consent to open their shut-up hearts freely, and to think of people below them as if they really were fellow-passengers to the grave, and not another race of creatures bound on other journeys. So Merry Christmas!

SARAH: Good Afternoon!

TODD: And Happy New Year!

SARAH: Good Afternoon!

> *TODD and SARAH high five at his excellent accent and performance.*
>
> *SARAH now mimes walking home through the snowy streets, with ANNA using popcorn to enact the snow and wind around her, and rather violently too. TODD plays "Silent Night" on his harmonica.*

ANNA: Now let it be known that there was nothing at all particular about the knocker on the door except that it was very large. Let it also be known that Scrooge had as little of what is called fancy about him as any man in the City of London.

ROBERT: This is my favorite part in the book.

ANNA: Then can anyone tell me how it was that Scrooge saw in the knocker – not a knocker, but Marley's face!

> *ANNA becomes Marley – straddling two chairs and shouting – and walks forward toward the now screaming SARAH/SCROOGE. TODD plays a jig and fun chaos ensues.*

SARAH: How now! What do you want with me?

ANNA: *(Waving her arms and body in a goofy "ghostly" way.)* Much!

SARAH: Who are you?

ANNA: Ask me who I *was!*

SARAH: Who *were* you, then?

ANNA: In life I was your partner, Jacob Marley!

SARAH: Can you sit down?

ANNA: I can.

SARAH: Sit down then.

ANNA: Okay. *(She sits carefully, and then immediately resumes her ghost impression.)* You don't believe in me.

SARAH: I don't.

ANNA: Why do you doubt your senses?

ROBERT: *(Joyfully frustrated with ANNA's goofy portrayal of Marley, he swings her out of the chair and takes over.)* Man of the worldly mind, do you believe in me or not?

SARAH: *(After a beat.)* Uh, I do.

ANNA: Hey–

ROBERT: I'm gonna play Marley now. I can't believe I remember this!

ANNA: *(Whispering as she joins the watchers.)* Dad used to play this part.

ROBERT: Man of the worldly mind, do you believe in me or not?

SARAH: I do, but why do spirits walk the earth and why do they come to me?

ROBERT climbs onto the chairs.

ROBERT: It is required of every man that the spirit within him should walk abroad among his fellow men, and travel far and wide; and if he goes not forth in life, he is condemned to do so after death. He is doomed to wander through the world - *(This begins to settle with him.)* – Oh woe is me – and witness what he cannot share, but might have shared in life, and turned to happiness.

SARAH: You are fettered. Tell me why.

ROBERT: I wear the chain I forged in life…

DOROTHY: *(In the quiet.)* Robert? We don't have to do this—

ROBERT: No, I'm fine—

ROBERT grabs the ladder and holds it to his body like shackles.

ROBERT: I wear the chain I forged in life. I made it link by link, and yard by yard; I girded them on my own free will and of my own free will I wore them. Is its pattern strange to *you?* Or would you know the weight and length of the strong coil that you bear yourself? It's a ponderous chain.

ROBERT puts the ladder onto the kids.

ANNA/TODD/SARAH: Speak comfort to me, Jacob!

ROBERT: I don't have any to give you. That comes from other regions, Ebenezer Scrooge, and is conveyed by other ministers to other kinds of men. A very little more is all that's left to me. I cannot rest. I cannot stay. I cannot linger anywhere. *(Becoming desperate.)* Oh, hear me!

DOROTHY: They will.

ANNA/TODD/SARAH: We will.

ROBERT: I believe…

For a moment it seems ROBERT is flashing back, like he might even launch into a speech.

DOROTHY: Robert!

ROBERT: How it is that I appear before you in a shape that you can see, I may not tell. For, I have sat invisible beside you for many and many a day…

I believe that I am here tonight to warn you that you have yet a chance of hope… *(Dropping Marley's voice entirely.)* I don't remember what comes next.

The spell is broken. DOROTHY slowly rises.

DOROTHY: Well… In the story, Scrooge wakes up, and laughs it off, and says it was a dream.

ROBERT looks at the kids to see.

ALL are rising, a bit dazed.

TRACY JO: And then Scrooge is visited by three Spirits.

And he wept.

And he was saved.

DOROTHY: *(Can't resist.)* Or he saved himself.

A long beat. ANNA faces out.

ANNA: Are we good people?

A plunge into the final dance.

During the course of this dance, a year passes. It should recall the year we have just seen. But it might be the year that comes next. It is a dream with both private moments and moments of full company.

In the original production, this was performed to Sufjan Stevens' "The Predatory Wasps of the Palisades Are Out to Get Us."

Individual moments of the dance are denoted in the following text. Future productions are encouraged to interpret or flesh-out these beats with additional improvisation to communicate the passing of time.

A. ANNA gets an idea and runs offstage where she grabs a half dozen eggs. She enters giggling wickedly at the audience.

TODD: Do we get to throw these?

ANNA: Yes!

Each cast member gets an egg and runs forward. They pump their arms and hold the eggs up, as if they are going to pelt the audience with them. The eggs are smashed, revealing a shower of glitter.

ALL: Happy New Year!

> *B. Spring. Everyone pulls off their winter coats and piles them on TRACY JO.*

> *C. ROBERT gives ANNA a history lesson.*

ROBERT: We the People of the United States of America do hereby declare ourselves sovereign and independent of your goddamn tea taxes! Basically.

> *D. Summer. Firecrackers. ANNA's birthday is celebrated properly.*

> *E. Autumn. Leaves fall. DOROTHY and ROBERT walk together through them.*

ROBERT: Even in our sleep, a pain which cannot forget falls drop by drop upon the heart until, through our despair, and against our will, comes wisdom through the awful grace of God...

> *DOROTHY stops him suddenly, remembering.*

DOROTHY: Robert... TURKEY!!!

> *The cast springs into action. They set up the dining room table for Thanksgiving.*

> *DOROTHY pulls a severely burned turkey out of the oven.*

DOROTHY: *(To audience.)* It's a little crisp. *(To all.)* IT'S A LITTLE CRISP!!

> *The cast all take hands around the table.*

> *JAKE/ROBERT (as actor) shouts up to the director or stage manager.*

JAKE: Hey [Chavkin], should we put a grace in here?

CHAVKIN: *(From back of house.)* YES!

ALL: Grace.

> *ALL but ROBERT fall promptly to sleep.*

> *F. Winter. It begins to snow.*

> *ROBERT wakes DOROTHY and they go out into the snow.*

> *The kids all wake and play in it.*

> *In production, this was represented with flour, which eventually covered the heads of ROBERT and DOROTHY, who appeared to age significantly, even as the children and TRACY JO remained the same.*

> *G. Spring. ANNA and ROBERT look at stars.*

She leaves him and joins her siblings who watch the sky.

DOROTHY rocks and listens to ROBERT.

ROBERT: When I think of President Kennedy, I think of what Shakespeare used to say in *Romeo and Juliet*:
"When he shall die, take him and cut him out in little stars,
And he will make the face of heaven so fine
That all the world will be in love with night
And pay no worship to the garish sun."

DOROTHY touches ROBERT tenderly.

The sound of thunder in the distance.

ANNA: *(Not thinking much of it.)* Storm's comin.

SARAH rises slowly and comes forward, as she did at the beginning of the play. TRACY JO follows closely behind.

SARAH: *(Weeping, quiet at first.)* Anna... Todd... HE'S COMING BACK!! HE'S COMING!!

SARAH sprints to gather her siblings. The stage is in chaos. ROBERT is preparing for a tornado, trying to get TODD into the storm cellar. DOROTHY is desperately hugging ANNA who is screaming.

ANNA: I'm not ready yet! I'm not ready!

DOROTHY: It's okay sweetie! You gotta go!

SARAH, running, suddenly stops when she sees TRACY JO, who is still.

TRACY JO: *(After a long beat.)* Go!

SARAH runs. TODD runs to her. DOROTHY hands them ANNA.

The three SPRINGER children stand gripping each others' hands. Staring into an incredibly bright light.

DOROTHY watches them. TRACY JO departs the teenager's body, who again lies dead. ROBERT prays.

The theatre shakes with the noise.

BLACKOUT.

ARCHITECTING

WRITTEN BY
JESSICA ALMASY, DAVEY ANDERSON, FRANK BOYD,
RACHEL CHAVKIN, JILL FRUTKIN, MATT HUBBS, LIBBY KING,
JAKE MARGOLIN, DAVE POLATO, KRISTEN SIEH,
LUCY KENDRICK SMITH, NATHAN WRIGHT, and NICK VAUGHAN

WITH
JAKE HEINRICHS, BRIAN SCOTT, and STEPHANIE DOUGLASS

Architecting was co-produced by the National Theatre of Scotland and Performance Space 122.

It was made possible with support from the National Theatre of Scotland, the British Arts Council, the Battersea Arts Centre (BAC Scratch Commission), the Greenwall Foundation and the Panta Rhea Foundation.

It was developed at 3LD Art & Technology Center, the Battersea Arts Centre, the Arches, the Orchard Project, and the 2007 Prelude Festival.

The World Premiere of *Architecting* took place at the Traverse Theatre in Edinburgh, Scotland on August 4, 2008 with the following cast:

CARRIE CAMPBELL/BRADY	Libby King
HENRY ADAMS/MAMMY/ JOHN ST. JEAN ASHLEY/UNCLE PETER/MALE SCARLETT FRANKLIN DELMORE MCKINLEY	Jake Margolin
MELLY/MELANIE/CAROL/JO	Jill Frutkin
MARGARET MITCHELL/LUCY WATERS	Jessica Almasy
SCARLETT O'HARA/CAROLINE	Kristen Sieh
SCOTT STAPHF/RHETT BUTLER/JOSH	Frank Boyd

Rachel Chavkin	*Director*
Nick Vaughan	*Scenic and Costume Design*
Jake Heinrichs	*Lighting Design*
Matt Hubbs	*Sound Design*
Brian Scott	*Video Design*
Dave Polato	*Production Stage Manager*
Renee Blinkwolt	*General Manager*
Davey Anderson	*Associate Director*
Emily Lippolis	*Assistant Set Design*
Kate Rusek	*Assistant Costume Design*
Terry Girard	*Director of Photography*
Ashima Jain	*Graphic Design*
Paz Hilfinger-Pardo, Josh Hoglund	*Assistant Director*
Judy Bowman Casting	*Casting Consultant*

The U.S. Premiere of *Architecting* took place in New York City on January 9, 2009 at the Public Theater, co-presented by PS122's COIL Festival and the Under the Radar Festival, with the original cast.

Architecting was awarded a 2008 *Scotsman* Fringe First Award and Edinburgh Fringe Total Theatre Award.

CAST OF CHARACTERS

CARRIE CAMPBELL, an architect

LUCY WATERS, employee of the Campbell family's architecture firm

HENRY ADAMS, historian; grandson of president John Quincy Adams; great-grandson of president John Adams

MELLY, bar owner in New Orleans

JOSH, gas station attendant

CAROLINE, beauty pageant contestant

SCOTT STAPHF, movie producer

JOHN ST. JEAN, movie director

CAROL, assistant to Scott

MARGARET MITCHELL, author, *Gone With the Wind*

SCARLETT O'HARA, heroine, *Gone With the Wind*

RHETT BUTLER, leading man, *Gone With the Wind*

MELANIE, Scarlett's sister-in-law, *Gone With the Wind*

ASHLEY, Husband to Melanie, *Gone With the Wind*

MAMMY, slave owned by O'Hara family, servant following emancipation, raised Scarlett, *Gone With the Wind*

UNCLE PETER, slave owned by O'Hara family, servant following emancipation, *Gone With the Wind*

BRADY, a horse

FRANKLIN DELMORE MCKINLEY, a character imagined by our Margaret Mitchell

MALE SCARLETT, played by male actor

JO, a customer at the gas station

With the exception of "I Wish I Was in Dixie" and "The Bonny Blue Flag," all songs referred to in the text are original to the production. Future productions may contact the TEAM for chord charts and/or recordings of the music as originally performed, or compose new music.

This work was originally imagined as four separate chapters:

1. The Education of Henry Adams

2. The Re-Education of Margaret Mitchell

3. The Ballad of Caroline and Josh

4. Thanks for Coming Home, Carrie Campbell

At that time, Mitchell's *Gone With the Wind* was our primary inspiration. We knew we were interested in making a work about reconstruction. Then several of us read Naomi Klein's book, *The Shock Doctrine*, and were blown away by the fact that Klein (we think unknowingly) almost directly quoted Mitchell's war profiteer Rhett Butler when describing "disaster capitalism." During an early flirtation with Scarlett, he informs her that there are two times for making money: slow money on the up-build, fast money on the destruction.

But the strands didn't come together until after John Tiffany, then Associate Artistic Director at the National Theatre of Scotland, saw the show in workshop form and pointed out what we hadn't quite yet seen ourselves: that New Orleans was the play's emotional center. We worked to bring the strands of the failed Reconstruction Era following the Civil War into focus alongside the failures to protect and rebuild vast sections of New Orleans, largely low income and predominantly African American neighborhoods, disproportionately damaged or destroyed by Hurricane Katrina.

Architecting is a sprawling play, and one we may return to at some point for further reworking. Related to this desire is the following: at the time of the World/U.S. premieres, we were still only casting from the core ensemble, and thus presented the show with an entirely white cast. This was a controversial and complicated decision within the company in 2008/2009, and remains so today. There still isn't consensus amongst us, but we would strongly encourage a thoroughly multiracial cast in future productions. And we would encourage artists to be aggressive in challenging the stereotypes (both racial and gender stereotypes) inherited from *Gone With the Wind*, and other melodramas.

– Rachel Chavkin, Director/Co-Creator

Jessica Almasy as Margaret Mitchell in *Architecting*, **Traverse Theatre,
Edinburgh Fringe, 2008**
Photo: Eamonn McGoldrick

Preshow. The Oasis, a hole in the wall bar in New Orleans. Sometime after August 2005.

MELLY sings accompanied by JOSH on guitar and greets audience members as they enter. In the corner HENRY, a regular, works on a complex paper model of the Cathedral of Chartres at a bar table.

At start of show:

MELLY: *(Singing.)*
> **Yes I'm here**
> **Every single night**
> **Doesn't mean I'm just passing my time**
>
> **Just because I always say I'm fine**
> **Doesn't mean I got nothing on my mind**
> **Why has it been**
> **Fifty fucking years**
> **Since I heard a good patriotic song**
>
> **A man who has nothing for which he would die**
> **Is not fit to live**
> **At all**
>
> **Boys, now it's time**
> **To have a drink**
> **On the House**

JOSH: Go on then.

MELLY: *(A whistling interlude.)*
> **I know, New Orleans bars usually close by four**
> **But boys, tonight we're gonna hunker down**
> **And boys, this I know, for sure**
> **Our time is gonna come**
> **Again**

> *MELLY exits.*

HENRY: *(To the Audience.)* A Dynamic Theory of History. OK, stick with me, I'm gonna go slow anyway, for Josh. Thermodynamics.

It's a physics term. Concerning heat and energy. I like it because it has laws. So clean, simple.

Ergo: The Thermodynamics of History. Concerning heat. And progress. Heat. Energy. And progress. In which Energy equals the ability to bring about change or to do WORK.

I wrote my dissertation on this, essentially…

JOSH exits, trying to do so unobtrusively.

Goodbye Josh. Anyway… Energy … it exists in so many forms, and thermodynamics is the study of energy. Of force.

Now, <u>man</u> is a force, but so is the <u>sun</u>.

Historians are generally more concerned with the former, with the force of man.

But I, uh – did she mention? – Henry. Hi. I, a thermodynamic historian, I am more concerned with the latter.

With the sun.

Uh, wind.

Force.

Suddenly focus shifts.

VIDEO: CARRIE travels to New Orleans via train and car.

CARRIE: *(In VIDEO, on cell phone.)* Probably another 30 minutes…

HENRY: Or I suppose how man responds to…

Lives with…

Deals with forces outside of his control.

Perhaps backing up one step.

Historians undertake to arrange sequences, called stories.

Histories. We write histories as an attempt to bring sense or…narrative to our past. Now I teach at Harvard. And each year when a new crop of students comes, arrives at Harvard, waves of new eighteen year olds ready to assume control – picture a tweedy faculty of geniuses and sub-geniuses preparing for the new mob, over coffee. The faculty… Secure…

Formerly secure. Formerly Faculty. I *taught* at Harvard. I live down here.

Now…

Anyway, I want you to picture a faculty room.

We begin each fall by commiserating over what year the incoming class was born.

1987.

After the Challenger explodes.

1975.

Post Nixon.

1946.

Children of a post-atomic world.

So how do I – what am I supposed to do? ...I, who understands that there was in fact a *TIME* before the bomb. *(Getting slightly lost.)* 1900. The era of the dynamos...

Dynamo. An engine. For creating energy. Anyway.

Apologies!

> *He falls silent, looking at the paper model.*

This is Chartres.

It is the most perfect piece of architecture in the world.

Yes – nothing in education is so astonishing as the amount of ignorance it accumulates in the form of inert facts.

Chartes... Progress... Anyway.

A law of progress... a law of acceleration – like *any* LAW of mechanics – cannot relax its energy simply for the convenience of man.

> *Getting idea, a teaching tool. He grabs the model. Pointing.*

And this... uh, tension?

Between force. And man.

This is history.

> *VIDEO and sound cue of "The Dynamo" – an image that will recur multiple times throughout the show. In the original production, this was represented by a 360-degree panoramic view from the top of the spire at Chartres, which then began to spin at dizzying speed.*
>
> *Out of which comes MARGARET's singing of "Admirable Things."*

MARGARET: *(Singing.)*
  Admirable things.
  Admirable things.
  Admirable things.
  Yeah I am interested in
  Some honest enterprises...

> *CARRIE comes onto stage for the first time. She is talking to LUCY on the phone. LUCY is not seen, but her voice is panicked.*

CARRIE: Lucy, hi. Sorry I lost you, I'm in the sticks.

LUCY: Yeah, I'm not sure where I got cut off. I've got Brad Pitt's people on the phone – I've got this swarm of students protesting outside with his face on their t-shirts... GO TO SCHOOL!

CARRIE: ...Lucy, okay. We don't need Brad Pitt and his "do the right whatever" –

LUCY: Yes, I'm telling them this.

CARRIE: Ok let's just focus on the basics alright? We have to ask them and then tell them... you know. Ask them – Who is the architect? And then we tell them who the architect is. You know, something like Steve Campbell started it, but I am going to finish. Then we ask them – Who are the investors? And we tell them THEY are the investors. Big round of applause. And we ask them who the buyers are. And then we tell them there are PLENTY of buyers. You have to spell it out for these people...

LUCY: Should I be smiling and handing out lollipops when I say this?

CARRIE: Uh, sure smiling's great. You have a great smile.

LUCY: Thanks. You know, I haven't had to do one of these in a really long time, Carrie.

CARRIE: Well, Lucy, have you ever heard of notecards?

LUCY: Actually, someone just handed me one with "the chocolate city" written on it. How do you explain this?

CARRIE: No Response, table that, moving forward. Tell them I am here – now –

LUCY: WHERE ARE YOU?

CARRIE: Ok, I'm not there yet. I'm on the road. Tell them nobody needs to worry, and nobody needs to panic.

LUCY: Carrie, hate to break it to you, but it's little too late for that.

CARRIE: Okay, we're on the same team, we need to be on the same page.

LUCY: We need to be in the same room!

CARRIE: *(Beat.)* Okay. The point is – yes – the architect... died. And that I'm going to...

LEFT: Jessica Almasy performs *Give Up! Start Over!* in the window of 208 W. 37th Street as part of Chashama's Not For Sale Window Series, 2004

Photo: Rachel Chavkin

BELOW: "Babies, given up for dead, who struggle towards national life and make it. For just a minute." *Give Up! Start Over!* Chashama's Not For Sale Window Series, 2004

Photo: Rachel Chavkin

LEFT: "Five minutes is smart. One minute is smarter." *Give Up! Start Over!* at C Venues, Edinburgh Fringe, 2005

Photo: Rachel Chavkin

ABOVE: "And we walk away together…into the Technicolor, hyperreal, plasma screen sunset."
Give Up! Start Over! at C Venues, Edinburgh Fringe, 2005

Photo: Rachel Chavkin

ABOVE: "How do you picture the end of the world?" Brian Hastert as Laertes, Kristen Sieh as Ophelia, and Jessica Almasy as Hamlet in *A Thousand Natural Shocks* at C Venues, Edinburgh Fringe, 2005

Photo: Rachel Chavkin

LEFT: "King Claudius welcomes you to the fairytale land of Hans Christian Anderson, and the existential playground of Kierkegaard!" Kristen Sieh as Ophelia in *A Thousand Natural Shocks* at C Venues, Edinburgh Fringe, 2005

Photo: Rachel Chavkin

ABOVE: **"There's no one in the place 'cept you and me."** Kristen Sieh as Ophelia and Jessica Almasy as Hamlet in *A Thousand Natural Shocks* at C Venues, Edinburgh Fringe, 2005
Photo: Rachel Chavkin

BELOW: **"When you find yourself in the thick of a fiasco—"** Jessica Almasy as Hamlet and Jill Frutkin as Horatio in *A Thousand Natural Shocks* at C Venues, Edinburgh Fringe, 2005
Photo: Rachel Chavkin

LEFT: "We love you Denmark!" Brian Hastert as Laertes and Jessica Almasy as Hamlet in *A Thousand Natural Shocks* at C Venues, Edinburgh Fringe, 2005

Photo: Rachel Chavkin

BELOW: "We didn't start the fire." The cast of *A Thousand Natural Shocks* at C Venues, Edinburgh Fringe, 2005

Photo: Rachel Chavkin

ABOVE: "Battle Hymn of the Republic." Jessica Almasy as Dorothy, Jill Frutkin as Tracy Jo, Brian Hastert as Todd, and Jake Margolin as Robert in *Particularly in the Heartland*, Ohio Theatre Ice Factory Festival, 2006

Photo: Nick Vaughan

RIGHT: "And then he planted man in the center of a field and Man was no more than a bump in a very flat place where God could find him." Jill Frutkin as Tracy Jo, Jessica Almasy as Dorothy, and Jake Margolin as Robert in *Particularly in the Heartland*, Performance Space 122, 2007

Photo: Rachel Roberts

ABOVE: "No. No...Todd, please—DON'T!" Frank Boyd as Todd, Jake Margolin as Robert, and Kristen Sieh as Anna in *Particularly in the Heartland*, Performance Space 122, 2007

Photo: Rachel Roberts

LEFT: "What state are we in?" "Kansas!" Jake Margolin as Robert and Kristen Sieh as Anna in *Particularly in the Heartland*, Traverse Theatre, Edinburgh Fringe, 2006

Photo: Nick Vaughan

RIGHT: "Are we good people?" The cast of *Particularly in the Heartland*, Ohio Theatre Ice Factory Festival, 2006

Photo: Nick Vaughan

LEFT: The cast of *Particularly in the Heartland*, Ohio Theatre Ice Factory Festival, 2006

Photo: Nick Vaughan

LEFT: "Yes I'm here / every single night…" Jill Frutkin as Melly in *Architecting*, 3LD Art & Technology Center, 2008

Photo: Yi Zhao

RIGHT: "I am unimpeachable! Isn't it delicious!" Kristen Sieh as Scarlett in *Architecting*, 3LD Art & Technology Center, 2008

Photo: Yi Zhao

BELOW: "You is gwine eat eve'y beite of dis." Jake Margolin as Mammy, Jessica Almasy as Margaret, Kristen Sieh as Scarlett in *Architecting*, Traverse Theatre, Edinburgh Fringe, 2008

Photo: Eamonn McGoldrick

ABOVE: "Never mind Peggy, Mr. Staphf… She doesn't decide where I stop." Libby King as Brady, Jessica Almasy as Margaret, Heather Christian as Scarlett, Frank Boyd as Scott Staphf in *Architecting*, Performance Space 122, 2009

Photo: Nick Vaughan

LEFT: "But, business being business, Scarlett managed to control herself…" Libby King as Brady, Kristen Sieh as Scarlett, Jake Margolin as Uncle Peter in *Architecting*, Traverse Theatre, Edinburgh Fringe, 2008

Photo: Eamonn McGoldrick

LEFT: The company of *Architecting*, Traverse Theatre, Edinburgh Fringe, 2008

Photo: Eamonn McGoldrick

ABOVE: Jake Margolin as Franklin in *Architecting*, 3LD Art & Technology Center, 2008
Photo: Yi Zhao

RIGHT: The company of
Architecting, The Public Theater,
Under The Radar Festival, 2009
Photo: Nick Vaughan

ᴀʙᴏᴠᴇ: "I'm taking the necessary steps to make sure I can't ever go back to being the way I was. Thank you." Frank Boyd as Josh, Libby King as Carrie, *Architecting*, The Public Theater, Under The Radar Festival, 2009

Photo: Nick Vaughan

ABOVE: The company in an early workshop of *Mission Drift* at BRICLab, 2008
Photo: Peter Dressel

BELOW: "The sound of sand under tires. The sound of sand under boots." Libby King as Catalina, Ian Lassiter as Chris, Brian Hastert as Joris in *Mission Drift*, Performance Space 122, 2012
Photo: Ves Pitts

ABOVE: "I kinda got a thing about lizards." Amber Gray as Joan, Ian Lassiter as Chris in *Mission Drift*, Performance Space 122, 2012

Photo: Ves Pitts

BELOW: "There is something nuclear about their adolescence! And it shines in the dark." Libby King as Catalina, Brian Hastert as Joris in *Mission Drift*, ArtsEmerson, 2011

Photo: Rachel Chavkin

ABOVE: "Viva Las Vegas!" The company of *Mission Drift*, National Theatre Shed, 2013
Photo: Nick Vaughan

BELOW: "I am an anchor in the desert." Brian Hastert as Joris, Heather Christian as Miss Atomic in
Mission Drift, Culturgest, 2011
Photo: Rachel Chavkin.

ABOVE: **Amber Gray in *Mission Drift*, Performance Space 122, 2012**
Photo: Ves Pitts

A long beat.

LUCY: I'm sorry Carrie. Are you okay?

CARRIE: The job is in good hands. The perfect hands. Can you say that with me?

CARRIE and LUCY: The job is in good hands.

CARRIE: That's right Lucy. You need to reassure people. That is your job. You need to get them all together. We need to fly them all in – we have to put them up in the Quarter, the French Quarter, some decent un – we have to feed them – feed them some crawfish étouffée and chicory coffee and...

LUCY: Oh my gosh, now they're throwing lettuce at the house!

CARRIE: I'll call you back.

> *In an interstate rest area. CAROLINE and JOSH are at a McDonald's counter. CARRIE enters and stands behind them on line. Long silence.*

CAROLINE: You gonna get anything?

JOSH: No.

CAROLINE: You should get somethin', we're gonna be driving awhile.

JOSH: I'm good.

CAROLINE: Okay, but do not start eating my fries when we get in the car.

JOSH: I won't.

CAROLINE: *(Looking around.)* Wow this place is huge. Lot bigger than the rest stop you worked at, huh?

CARRIE: *(Eavesdropping.)* Rest... stop. I've always thought that was kind of redundant.

> *An awkward moment between the worlds.*

JOSH: *(Quietly, helpfully.)* Um, actually, they call these, uh, 'Travel Centers'... so...

> *Awkwardness...*

CARRIE: Oh. Um, are you on line?

CAROLINE: (*Overlapping.*) Yes.

JOSH: *(Overlapping.)* No.

> *Back on VIDEO, CARRIE on the phone with LUCY. CARRIE onstage observes the moment, disembodied.*

CARRIE: *(On VIDEO.)* I am fine. Don't worry about me.

I am sure that they are freaking out, I'm sure they are – the fucking architect died. Everybody's freaking out, ok?

Well I'm... Well it's... maybe you could just tell them that it wasn't his idea in the first fucking place. That it was his ten-year-old genius daughter came up with the whole G.D. thing...

No, Lucy I don't actually want you to tell them that. And I definitely don't want you to tell them that that's why the whole fucking thing looks like Disneyland.

Are you crying?

Lucy. Lucy. Oh boy. Lost her.

CARRIE: *(Onstage, spoken simultaneously with VIDEO.)* Lucy. Lucy. Oh boy. Lost her.

> *Hanging up.*

Ladies and gentlemen,

Ladies and gentlemen:

Ladies AND gentlemen.

It is going slower than we anticipated. We did not anticipate the hold outs. There are hold outs. They're holding out.

Steve Campbell said, "Make no small plans." Ladies and gentlemen I want to assure you: Make no small plans.

> *On VIDEO: a sign for New Orleans coming into view.*

(Quieter.) A promise was not fulfilled here.

It's raining.

> *On VIDEO: rain on CARRIE's windshield.*

HENRY: *(Singing, distant in the background.)*
Build your house on a rock, boy.
Build your house on a stone.

CARRIE: Night drive to New Orleans. Chase the birds south across America.

> *Thunder.*

CARRIE: Jesus

MARGARET: *(Singing.)*
Admirable things...
Admirable things.

> *VIDEO: CARRIE is back in her car in the rain.*
>
> *The image/sound of the Dynamo again.*
>
> *On stage in the darkness, SCARLETT in mourning clothes enters and exits. A ghostly vision.*
>
> *Lights rise again on "normalcy." In The Oasis, where something is being nailed to the outside of the front door. MELLY enters, bringing HENRY a drink.*

HENRY: *(Has been talking to JOSH about Chartres.)* ...being struck by lightning and burnt to the ground.

MELLY: *(Referring to the hammering on the door.)* What is that, Henry...

> *MELLY opens the front door to find CARRIE nailing an eviction notice to the door.*
>
> *(Bursting into tears.)* Oh Jesus.
>
> *MELLY exits, leaving CARRIE in the doorway, embarrassed.*

CARRIE: What a night, huh? *(Not much response. Pointing at HENRY's model.)* Your clocher vieux is crooked.

HENRY: The irony is not lost on me. The most perfect piece of architecture in the world and I glued it on wrong. Options: The glue was bad. The air was damp. The Anonymous Architect was drunk.
You recognize it?

CARRIE: Architecture 101. Listen, do you know that you're not supposed to be here?

HENRY: You remind me of a cathedral I was once in.

CARRIE: You an architect?

HENRY: What did one architect say to the other architect?

CARRIE: Gosh I don't know. What?

HENRY: ...Well, you're the architect. I'm an historian.

CARRIE: You're not from around here.

HENRY: Negative.

CARRIE: You don't have an accent. Everybody down here has –

Gesturing to the eviction notice, which he is inspecting.

HENRY: Do you know what they're building?

CARRIE: Who?

HENRY: You.
(He smells blood.) The Yankees is comin'.

CARRIE: It's a TND.

HENRY: A what?

CARRIE: Nothing, it's uh, housing. So… you're from up North then?

HENRY: I'm from Cambridge.

CARRIE: Nice. How much for a soda?

MELLY: *(Enters, new composure.)* Why don't you tell us something about yourself first Ms…

CARRIE: Campbell. What is this place?

HENRY: Down here Ms. Campbell it is considered very poor etiquette to put up a demolition notice and ask for a beverage without first *(Mockery of a Southern drawl.)* tellin' us a little something about yourself.

CARRIE: My name is Carrie Campbell. Uh…This is the first time I've been below the Mason Dixon line. Can I please have a Coke?

MELLY: What kind of Coke you want?

CARRIE: …A *Coke.*

MELLY: *(MELLY gets CARRIE a Coke.)* How long do we have before you raze this joint to the ground?

CARRIE: Not long.

HENRY: Days? Hours? Minutes?

CARRIE: Ok, it is not that soon, you know. It's all tied up in City Council Hearings… Historical Society ladies with nothing to do but drink sweet tea and wrap everything in red tape… that kind of thing.

MELLY: *(To HENRY.)* What's *this* one building?

HENRY: It's not entirely clear yet. What are you building?

CARRIE: I'm not a builder. We're *developing* –

MELLY: What are you selling then?

CARRIE: I'm not in sales – *(MELLY exits.)* So what brings you down here?

HENRY: I had my historical neck broken.

CARRIE: Painful.

HENRY: Hmm.

CARRIE: *(Sensing opportunity.)* You know what? We're trying to put together a neighborhood history. Do you know what used to be here?

HENRY: I have no idea. Slaves probably. Swamps before that. You should really ask Melly. She *is* the local heritage society.

CARRIE: I thought you were the historian?

HENRY: I *was* an historian.

CARRIE: You're retired?

HENRY: You could say that.

CARRIE: Well what are you doing here? I mean, do you have a research project or a… a… So what was your, like, specialty? Area of focus?

HENRY: America.

CARRIE: Wow. I bet you were a really popular lecturer.

HENRY: Thermodynamics.

CARRIE: What?

HENRY: I wrote about force, Ms. Campbell.

CARRIE: Like gravity?

HENRY: No. Like the forces that determine human movement. For instance: how did you get here?

CARRIE: Plane. To Little Rock. And then I had to drive from there.

HENRY: No, a plane is an excellent example of force – because planes carry people and bombs. I took a bus.

Now I would like you to picture that we are driving in your rental car at a terrific speed toward *(Invoking the model.)* a 12th century cathedral. Now this, a cathedral and an automobile. This is a dynamic theory of history.

CARRIE: Okay, I'm not really following you...

HENRY: ...I'm a man. I live in constant tension with forces outside of my control. And I find myself, with a demolition notice in my hand. Don't know where the floors went. Don't know where the walls went. I'm just there, staring up at the ceiling. Waiting for some sign to emerge from the plaster that's going to tell me who and what and where I am.

CARRIE: You're in New Orleans.

HENRY: Right you are! History does lead somewhere.

CARRIE: Who are you?

HENRY: Call me Henry.

> *THUNDERCLAP.*
>
> *MARGARET enters, with great fanfare, completely soaked, and with provisions.*

MARGARET: Thunderclap! And he forgot the best part – that he's an Adams! From a very very great line of presidential Adamseseses. *(To CARRIE.)* Who are you? *(Pointing at eviction notice.)* What is this? *(Referring to Chartres.)* Your steeple is crooked.

CARRIE: *(Whispering.)* Is that your wife?

MARGARET: *(Referring to the hurricane.)* Oooh it's gonna be a good one!

HENRY: *(To CARRIE.)* I present to you the inimitable MARGARET MITCHELL.

CARRIE: *(Stunned.)* Tara...

HENRY: Peggy, this is Carrie Campbell. This is her first time below the Mason Dixon line.

MARGARET: Nooooo.

HENRY: Yeeeeess.

> *CARRIE spots a copy of* Gone With the Wind.

MARGARET: Well how do you do Miss Campbell. Welcome to America.

HENRY: So what do you think of it?

CARRIE: It's hot, sticky. People are nice. Slower pace.

MARGARET: *(Putting on an absurdly slow drawl, over her already thick drawl.)*
Well…
What
Are
You
Doing
Down
Here?

HENRY: She's building a TND.

CARRIE: I'm building a TND.

MARGARET: What is that?

CARRIE: It's a thing, that's the terminology. It's called a traditional neighborhood development.

MARGARET: What is that?

CARRIE: That is housing. It's a housing development.

HENRY: What does it *do*?

CARRIE: Do? It's houses.

HENRY: But what will it *do*? For example, a cathedral / does worship.

MARGARET: *(Overlapping.)* / Always a cathedral, always a damn cathedral. Has he talked to you about **FORCE** yet? THE FORCES OF HISTORY!! *(Holding up the copy of the book.)* My book is a force.

HENRY: A cathedral *for instance* does worship by making people look up.

CARRIE: You're talking about programming.

MARGARET: What is *that*?!

CARRIE: Programming? Ok, uh, so an architect designs a space and she also designs how people will *behave* in that space. For instance, there was an architect and he was designing this airport, and he hired a ballet choreographer because he wanted the people to swirl.

MARGARET: "Swirl?"

CARRIE: Yes. Anyway, a Traditional Neighborhood Development will foster an old sense of real American community. It's something my father came up with.

MARGARET: Well, I do like an old sense.

CARRIE: Really? Wow. This is actually a pretty remarkable coincidence. Did you know that one of the home styles we're offering is a mansionplex which is modeled after the original Tara from the 1939 film. We will have a total of three of these, each commanding a picturesque view of the Phoenix Meadows wetlands.

MARGARET: *(Beat.)* Uh-huh. *(Beat.)* Will it have columns?

CARRIE: Absolutely.

MARGARET: Over my dead body.

CARRIE: Excuse me?

MARGARET: *(Putting the polite back on.)* So this is your project?

CARRIE: Uh, yeah, it was my father's…

HENRY: But it's yours now.

CARRIE: Yup.

HENRY: How old are you?

CARRIE: Twenty-eight.

MARGARET: Wow. That is not a vast age to have gained the world and lost your soul.

> *The Oasis TV starts playing a Hurricane Emergency Warning. MELLY emerges from the back with a tray full of hurricanes. JOSH crosses the stage and exits through the front door with a large piece of plywood.*

MELLY: Oh it's gonna be a bad one.

MARGARET: *(Referring to provisions brought in earlier, Ho Hos.)* That was all they had left at the store Melly.

MELLY: Damn. Hello. My name is Melanie Hamilton Wilkes, and I'm the Proprietor of this Establishment. Welcome to the Oasis. *(Holding out a drink to CARRIE, who does not take it.)* This is a hurricane party. You hunkering down here?

CARRIE: Actually no thank you. I have to get going.

MELLY: You've never been through a hurricane before have you darlin'? Well don't you worry. We'll be gentle. *(Beat.)*

MARGARET and MELLY: Take the drink darling.

A loud hammering sound from outside the front door.

MELLY: So. Who are your parents?

MARGARET: *(Under breath, to MELLY.)* Who taught you how to hunt?

MELLY: *(Under breath, to MARGARET.)* My daddy.

CARRIE: My father was Steve Campbell.

MELLY: And you've never been to New Orleans before? Isn't that a shame. As you can see there's not much left. You been down to the French Quarter though?

CARRIE: Yeah.

MELLY: Heard some jazz?

CARRIE: Yeah.

MELLY: That's nice.

CARRIE: Yeah.

MELLY: Yeah. *(Sharp.)* They don't have much weather up north do they?

CARRIE: Uh, actually…

MELLY: We sat through Betsey and ___. *(Rather than finishing the thought, they all pour a bit of their drink on the floor for who and what's been lost.)* I guess the third time's the charm…

HENRY: Whoa Melly –

MARGARET: Do you like to play cards Carrie?

Things beginning to spin a bit more rapidly, taking on a manic air.

HENRY: Yes Peggy!

CARRIE: I guess.

MARGARET: Well I do. I love games Carrie, and I love cards most of all. Men may have their poker, but I do believe cards are a lady's pastime. Don't you agree? I used to play this game called "Hearts." The object of this game was to give all of your Hearts away. And you won the game

if you were left with none. But there was this additional rule, this…
exceptional rule, that you could trump the other players by collecting
all the Hearts instead. But you had to get them all. Every single one.
They called this move "Shooting The Moon." D'you know why?

HENRY: Tell us Peggy!

MARGARET: Because it was practically impossible to do. *(Mood beginning to
sink and twist.)* It was SUICIDE.

> *CARRIE tries to exit but upon opening the bar door finds that it has been
> boarded over.*

Essentially. Well.
Not in my 49 years of playing Hearts did I ever meet someone who had
managed to Shoot The Moon.

HENRY: That's a lie, Peggy! I shoot the moon almost every time we play.

MARGARET: It's a story, Henry Adams, and it's a better story the way I told
it.

HENRY: *(Slowly beginning to sing.)*
Oh I wish I was in the land of Cotton,
Old times they are not forgotten
Look away, look away, look away,
Dixie Land…

MARGARET: *(Overlapping.)* He knows I love it when he sings this song!

> *MARGARET has begun happily clapping along with singing HENRY
> when:*
>
> *Suddenly the power surges. THUNDER.*
>
> *Lights dim once.*
>
> *Twice.*
>
> *They return, strange.*
>
> *In the darkness, SCARLETT in mourning veil has entered, and appears –
> ghostly – at a mic.*

SCARLETT: We now return to our regularly scheduled programming.

> *A surge. The image/sound of a Dynamo growing.*

HENRY: *(Singing.)*

> *Oh I wish I was in the land of Cotton,*
> *Old times they are not forgotten*
> *Look away, look away, look away,*
> *Dixie Land.*
>
> *Oh I wish...* (Continuing.)

MARGARET: He doesn't know any of the other verses!

> *MARGARET and the other women gather at the mic, like the Andrews Sisters.*

MARGARET and MELANIE and SCARLETT:
> *In Dixie land where I was born in,*
> *Early on one frosty morning,*
> *Look away, look away, look away,*
> *Dixie Land.*
>
> *HENRY joins in, and whisks MARGARET into a spirited dance to the song.*

WOMEN and HENRY:
> *Oh I wish I was in Dixie, Hurray, Hurray,*
> *In Dixie land I'll take my stand to live and die in Dixie.*
> *Away, away, away down south in Dixie!*
>
> *HENRY spins away from MARGARET, grabbing his cathedral.*

HENRY: Miss Campbell, if you find yourself getting dizzy, try to find a fixed point, and keep your eyes on that.

> *HENRY exits through the bar door which is no longer boarded up. Light pours through it. It slams shut behind him.*

MARGARET: Have you ever read my book Carrie? *(Tossing her a copy.)*

CARRIE: *(Reading aloud.)* "It was a savagely red land..."

CARRIE and MARGARET: *(With CARRIE dropping out after a bit.)* "Brick dust in droughts, blood-colored after rains. It was the best cotton land in the world!"

MARGARET: Get out or sing!

> *During the song MELANIE and SCARLETT launch at CARRIE, throwing her over a chair and forcibly lacing her into a corset.*

MELLY, SCARLETT and MARGARET:

Oh Southerns! Hear your country call you, Up!
Lest worse than death befall you!
Look away, look away, look away,
Dixie land.

Oh Hear the Northern thunders mutter!
Northern flags in South wind flutter,
Look away, look away, look away,
Dixie Land.

MARGARET: And the woods... At the edge of the fields rose virgin forests, dark and cool even in the hottest noons, mysterious, a little sinister, the soughing pines seeming to wait with an age-old patience, to threaten with soft-sighs: Be careful.

MELLY, SCARLETT and MARGARET: Be careful. We had you once. We can take you back again...

MARGARET: She loved this land so much, without even knowing she loved it...

> *Sudden silence and stillness as SCOTT STAPHF, a contemporary Hollywood producer, bursts through the door of the bar. He is dressed for the storm.*

SCOTT: Hi! I'm looking for Margaret Mitchell?

> *The four women, all in corsets now, feign calm. After a long beat:*

MARGARET: Never heard of her.

> *SCOTT exits uncomfortably. CARRIE runs and grabs her things and tries to follow out after him. The ladies watch.*

MELANIE: Ms. Campbell? Why don't you take a load off?

CARRIE: I have to go.

> *CARRIE opens the bar door to find that it is again boarded up.*

MARGARET: Let me rephrase that. Take a load off, Ms. Campbell.

MELANIE: Let's visit Margaret Mitchell's Atlanta.

> *Long awkward stillness. MARGARET at her typewriter. Frozen, and seeking inspiration.*

She begins typing, first one key at a time.

She is startled to discover that as she types, SCARLETT begins to come to life and take shape.

She removes her veil and moves jerkily, like a puppet. Eventually SCARLETT speaks what she types.

SCARLETT: Mee-oh-my… me-oh-my… oh my goodness graciousfulliciousness. Meow. Cracker barrel! Fiddle faddle! Fiddle dee dee! Fiddle fa… fuck! Fuck! Fuck you Dee Dee, you never were a sister to me.

Dauocovnaoeuihaldj-snack.

Noapoidfhaperhfaouhnjkfa.

(A single final key.) Nigger!

> *SCARLETT and MARGARET's hands fly to their mouths simultaneously, shocked with the utterance.*

MARGARET: There.

She thought…

I've said "nigger."

And Mother wouldn't like that at all.

SCARLETT: Nothing her mother had taught her was of any value whatsoever now!

MARGARET: It did not occur to her that her Mother could not have foreseen the collapse of the civilization in which she had raised her daughters.

SCARLETT: Nothing, no nothing she taught me is of any help to me! What good will kindness do me? What value is gentleness? Better that I'd learned to plow or chop cotton like a darky.

MARGARET: She did not stop to think that the old ordered world was gone and a brutal new world had taken its place, a world wherein every standard, every value had changed. She only saw that her mother had been wrong, and Scarlett changed swiftly to meet this new world for which she was not prepared.

SCARLETT: *(Vicious.)* I don't want to be hungry again.

> *SCARLETT grabs MELANIE and the two exit – the door is no longer boarded up.*

MARGARET: *(Calling after her.)* Scarlett!

But SCARLETT and MELANIE have slammed the door behind them. Silence. MARGARET and CARRIE are now alone.

Do you have fear in your heart Carrie Campbell?

CARRIE: What?

MARGARET: Have you faced the worst that can happen to you?

CARRIE: I don't have any idea.

MARGARET: Where are you from?

CARRIE: New York.

MARGARET: Well. Welcome to America.

Momentarily aware of the repetition…

Do you think you'll make it? What is it that makes some people able to come through catastrophes and others, apparently just as able, strong and brave, go under? *(This is a real question for MARGARET.)* It happens in every upheaval. Some people survive; others don't.

SCARLETT/ASHLEY/RHETT/MELANIE: *(Suddenly appear, singing quietly.)*
Oh I wish I was in Dixie, hurray, hurray!
In Dixie Land I'll take my stand to live and die in Dixie!
Away, away, away down south in Dixie

MARGARET: Ms. Campbell, what qualities are in those who fight their way through triumphantly that are lacking in those who go under?

CARRIE: Uh… maybe they lost something.

MARGARET: That's a good guess.

CARRIE: Rage.

MARGARET: Maybe. I only know that the survivors used to call that quality "gumption." So I wrote about the people who had gumption. And the people who didn't.

Sudden loud knocking. Silence. More knocking.

MAMMY: *(Offstage, knocking.)* Miss Mitchell. Miss Mitchell, I know yous in there.

MARGARET: *(Thrilled.)* Mammy?

CARRIE: What?

MARGARET: Say "Mammy."

CARRIE: Mammy.

MARGARET: Say it sweeter.

CARRIE: Mammy?

MAMMY: *(Offstage.)* Miss Mitchell, ders two gempums here to see you, dey say dere expected by you.

MARGARET: I'm gonna go out the back door.

MAMMY: *(Offstage.)* Oh no you ain't!

Movie set noises begin.

SCOTT: Can I get a strawberry banana protein shake in studio 4. NOW.

CAROL: Miss Mitchell, would you like a beverage?

MARGARET: I'll have a Coke.

CAROL: You got it. *(Exits.)*

The space devolves in to chaos/Hollywood rhythm.

MARGARET: *(Grabbing CARRIE.)* Nevermind. C'mon, last time I went to Hollywood I went blind.

CARRIE: What???

MARGARET: C'mon!

CARRIE and MARGARET exit.

SCOTT STAPHF and JOHN ST. JEAN appear. JOHN ST. JEAN is in an opulent library. Ludacris blares in SCOTT's office. SCOTT is in his underwear. Throughout the scene CAROL dresses him.

JOHN: *(Answering the phone.)* Hello.

SCOTT: John babe, konnichiwa motherfucker.

JOHN: Scott Staphf! How the hell are you doing? Hey Scott! What's all that noise?

SCOTT: Oh, come on, son! Luda! *(Signals to CAROL to turn down music.)*

JOHN: I can't hear you! *(Music lowers.)* I forgot to call you – congrats on everything over at Fox...

SCOTT: Fuck Fox! Congrats on the fucking OSCAR dude!

JOHN: Oh... Thank you!

SCOTT: It's so deserv-ed.

JOHN: Well... A role like that...and the writing was *so* –

SCOTT: Oh, Come on, second black man to win Best Actor, not bad.

JOHN: Well actually Denzel was second.

>*Silence.*

Sidney Poitier was first. *(Silence.)* Scott. *Lillies of the Field,* 19–

SCOTT: Denzel is a fucking god.

JOHN: Yes, we're all aware, and he was also the second black man to win a Best Actor Academy –

SCOTT: *(Totally overlapping, to CAROL.)* No, no, the lavender! The lavender!

JOHN: What?

SCOTT: Hello?

JOHN: Hello?

SCOTT: I'm just saying, the second or third black man to win Best Actor – pretty good. How bout being the first to win Best Director?

JOHN: That would be really swell, Scott.

SCOTT: Right. I've got a project for you.

JOHN: With all due respect, I'm not interested in reality television.

SCOTT: Fuck reality television, I'm dabbling in fiction now.

JOHN: Honestly, I'm not interested in TV at all.

SCOTT: No no. This is a feature dude. Blockbuster. Budget's like 250 or 3.

JOHN: So, what's the script?

SCOTT: *Gone With the Wind.*

JOHN: What? Yeah right.

SCOTT: Serious dude.

JOHN: Okay, Scott. How did you get the rights?

SCOTT: I can't tell you that. Let's just say I was in Atlanta for this thing and the next thing I know I'm ploughing into Margaret Mitchell's third cousin or something and the next thing I know, well, you know. So what do you say, man? Let me fly you out? We'll get you set up at the Chateau. Come on out, you can bang Carol and we'll talk it over.

JOHN: Scott, I don't think I'm the right candida– I've never directed on that scale before –

SCOTT: NOBODY has ever directed on this scale before, dude. I need somebody with balls.

JOHN: I wouldn't be able to show my face at Christmas if I directed *Gone With the Wind*. I hate *Gone With the Wind*.

SCOTT: Good. So do I. You ever read the book?

JOHN: No, I wasn't allowed to–

SCOTT: It's even more offensive than the movie. We're gonna give this thing a makeover so it can fly ['09] babe. *(Pause, waiting for response.)* It's just a lunch, John…
Kiss Angela and the kids goodbye for me. You gotta be at the West Side Heliport for the JFK link at 6:15. See ya in the morning.

> *Movie set chaos again. SCOTT spots CARRIE, whom MARGARET is dragging by the hand as the two try desperately to hide.*

SCOTT: *(To CARRIE.)* You. Girl? Woman. Whatever. You ever seen *Gone With the Wind?*

CARRIE: Um, actually I'm reading it right now –

SCOTT: Not the book, not the book. The book doesn't. The movie. The movie. How does it open?

> *Suddenly across the stage flash the opening credits of* Gone With the Wind *which CARRIE reads aloud.*

CARRIE: "There was a land of cavaliers and cottonfields called the old South."

MARGARET: Did they see me?

CARRIE: I don't think –

SCOTT: Keep reading!

CARRIE: "Here in this pretty world gallantry took its last bow. Here was the last ever to be seen of knights and their ladies fair, of master and slave."

SCOTT: *(Re-entering.)* Downplay the slave thing.

CARRIE: For –

SCOTT: *(Seeing CARRIE really for the first time.)* Who are you?! CATHY!!!!

CAROL: Carol. You've got the contract?

SCOTT: *(Referring to CARRIE.)* Get her on tape!

> *CAROL whips CARRIE offstage. MARGARET is left alone, reading the grand opening lines of the opening credits – and increasingly dismayed.*

KEEP READING!

MARGARET: "For it was more than a dream remembered, a civilization gone."

MARGARET, SCOTT and CAROL: *Gone With the Wind!*

MARGARET: That's not how it starts! Selznik wrote that for the MOVIE!!

> *Credits/music abruptly cut out. We are in SCOTT's office.*
>
> *MARGARET hides from SCOTT and CAROL. Badly.*

SCOTT: Okay...we see you...cool cool. Wow!! Margaret Mitchell. You are really short. I like that. Mousy little Peggy Mitchell, author of the most famous novel ever which became the most famous movie ever, not counting all that *Harry Potter* bullshit, right here in my office trailer. In the flesh. Wow. Let's get Peggy some cake. Have a seat.

> *CAROL brings cake to MARGARET.*

MARGARET: Thank you. I'm sorry, you are...which one are you?

SCOTT: I'm Scott. Scott Staphf. I'm the producer. I mean, there are a lot of us. You've been communicating mostly with the director/actor, John St. Jean! And let me say the studio is so thrilled to have such an incredible African American voice at the helm of this project. But this whole thing started with me. So.

MARGARET: Yes of course, Mr. Staphf.

SCOTT: So you know why you're here.

MARGARET: Yes, I suppose I do.

SCOTT: Gotta finish the paperwork. I trust you've read the re-writes?

CAROL puts script on MARGARET's lap.

MARGARET: *(She is very concerned with the re-writes.)* —Yes.

SCOTT: *(To MARGARET.)* Judging from your tone there, is there a problem?

MARGARET: Yes.

SCOTT: Okay, do you have a question?

MARGARET: Yes –

SCOTT: Okay, I'm going to stop you there. *(To CAROL.)* Get out. *(To MARGARET.)* I should tell you this. My time is worth a lot of money. So I'm gonna talk fast and this meeting is gonna be short, okay? Okay lady, listen. I'm sure you never meant to piss anybody off and that the way the book is, is the just the way it flowed out of that brilliant, mousy little head of yours and we're all grateful for that anonymous scholarship fund you set up at Morehead State, etc., etc., and that all just kind of worked for Selznick because he could get away with not really talking about all the racist...

Freezing momentarily as he sees this comment surprises MARGARET.

Stuff in the book. And the movie made like a zillion dollars and the rest as they say is American history–

MARGARET: That's unfair. I was writing from a particular place at a particular time.

Suddenly MAMMY and SCARLETT burst onto stage.

MAMMY: Some folks thinks as how Ah kin fly.

SCARLETT: It's no use Mammy. I won't eat it. You can just take it back to the kitchen. I'm not gonna eat a bite.

Music begins. MAMMY and SCARLETT launch into a shockingly patriotic dance as they argue. MARGARET claps along.

MAMMY: Yas'm you is! Ah ain' figgerin' on havin' happen whut happen at dat las' barbecue w'en Ah wuz too sick frum dem chittlins. Ah et ter fetch you no tray befo' you went. You is gwine eat eve'y beite of dis.

The dance ends as abruptly as it started, and MAMMY and SCARLETT settle into the scene, though only MARGARET can see them.

SCOTT: Woah. Over here! Earth to Peggy. *(Exaggerated southern accent.)* He he he, I know all these here laghts and funny lookin' picture machines can be real confusing there Ms. Mitchell…

MARGARET: A word to the wise, Mr. Staphf – if you plan on staying in Atlanta, the essence of our dialectal nature is not made manifest in uneducated grammar.

SCOTT: What?

MARGARET: You do not have to use "ain't" with a limp to be Southern.

SCOTT: Cool cool. Okay, Peggy, here you go. Take a load off. *(Gets her a chair.)* Okay. You don't need to get defensive. This isn't personal. Really I don't care what you wrote. I believe all that stuff that's put out about the research you did on the slave dialects. I really don't care, but the studio–

MARGARET: If you don't care why did you bother writing entirely new characters for this film?! *(Opening and reading from the draft screenplay.)* For example, a one "James King, born in 1844, great-grandfather to civil rights leader Martin Luther King, Jr. Mr. James King works as a gardener for Rhett and Scarlett and moonlights as a local civil rights leader, who is successful in convincing his employers and their high-society counterparts to pay their black employees better wages!?"

SCOTT: Yes.

MARGARET: That is very unrealistic for the time and place in which this story lives.

SCOTT: Yea, we know. Peggy, I know. It's shit. It's rubbish.

MAMMY ties MARGARET into a corset.

MARGARET: Isn't that a problem for you?

SCOTT: No. No, Peggy. People don't care. Now that we have MLK's great-grandfather in here freedom fighting, it's safer for us to resurrect *Gone With the Wind* as a brand name. And we can even afford to have more of the happy slave types that you wrote so wonderfully. We just need a disclaimer.

MARGARET: I'm not afraid of people seeing my book the exact way that it was written.

SCOTT: Yea but it's not going to make any money.

MARGARET: I don't care about money. I have money—

SCOTT: I care Peggy. I care. We are gonna make so much fucking money. It's totally unprecedented.

MARGARET: I don't understand why you don't just get some other writer. Another writer who doesn't write the kind of characters that I write and make your own little money-making movie about your Civil War or some car that talks.

SCOTT: We've done that. I've done that. This is *Gone With the Wind.* This is Nike. This is Coca-Cola. This is *Gone With The Fucking Wind.* We need your name on this.

MARGARET: To do what, to give my blessing?

SCOTT: To sign over that you wrote the rewrites.

MARGARET: But I did not write these rewrites.

SCOTT: Just sign over that you did.

MARGARET: I am not a liar.

SCOTT: Yeah, but you're a nobody now. You're a TV movie of the week from 1996 with Shannon Doherty that nobody saw.

MARGARET: Mr. Staphf is it?

SCOTT: You're also a racist now.

> *Silence.*

I'm sorry. *(He taps his ear. Begins whispering.)* Yeah. I talked to him on Tuesday. *(He backs up slowly and it becomes clear he is talking on his Bluetooth.)*

Well, tell him to go fuck himself!

> *SCOTT exits.*
>
> *SCARLETT stares at the door where he has exited.*
>
> *A long pause.*
>
> *She then turns giddily to MARGARET.*

SCARLETT: I WANT HIM.

MARGARET: You can't have him.

SCARLETT: I *want* him.

MARGARET: You can't *have* him.

SCARLETT: I'm gonna have whatever I want today.

MAMMY: Oh no, you ain't.

MARGARET: Here Scarlett. Have a little bit of this cake.

SCARLETT: *(SCARLETT grabs cake and shoves it in her mouth, frustrated, as she exits.)* I'm gonna have a good time.

> *Silence in the wake of pouting SCARLETT, who has slammed the door in her face.*

MARGARET: Mammy?

MAMMY: Yas'm Ms. Mitchell?

MARGARET: Did you ever read my… Oh… nevermind! What's your real name anyway?

MAMMY: Peaches. Peaches Robillard.

MARGARET: Not your slave name. Your given name.

MAMMY: Harriet Tubman.

MARGARET: Oh, go to hell.

MAMMY: Terror.

MARGARET: Excuse me?

MAMMY: My father named me Terror.

MARGARET: Tara?

MAMMY: Terror. Like the emotion. Like what you feel when things break down.

MARGARET: Nice name.

MAMMY: Yeah, well. Daddy used to ride with the Angels. Promised a buddy that he'd name his first-born "Terror." Daddy went by Michael. Handsomest man you ever saw. With a pair of angel's wings tattooed across his back. Daddy and his friends used to call each other by their father's names. It's an affectionate thing, a way to keep their memories alive. You can call me Michael if you want to.

MARGARET: Wait, where're you going?

MAMMY: I'm gonna go away now…

>   *MAMMY begins to exit.*

MARGARET: Won't you stay?
I so like having you right there.
I SAID STAY!

MAMMY: The thing is Ms. Mitchell, that in addition to our many disagreements, I don't like you very much.

>   *MAMMY throws a copy of* Gone With the Wind *at MARGARET and vanishes.*
>
>   *MARGARET, disturbed by this turn of events, slowly opens the book.*
>
>   *MELANIE enters quietly in mourning clothes.*
>
>   *SCARLETT enters with CARRIE who is drunk, alternately exercising, practicing her pitch, and in a nightmare in which she is SCARLETT's horse, BRADY. SCARLETT maneuvers her by the strings of her corset.*

MELANIE: *(Under veil.)* It was a savagely red land, blood-colored after rains, brick dust in droughts, the best cotton land in the world.

SCARLETT: Frightened Peggy? It's very bad for a woman not to be afraid of something.

CARRIE: *(Amidst being groomed and galloping.)* This is the first take. Phoenix Meadows. First. Fuck. Second take.

MELANIE: Now, where's your patriotism? Does the Confederacy mean nothing to you at all?

CARRIE: My name is Caroline Campbell, ladies and gentlemen. Caroline – Caroline – most of you know me as Carrie. This is a new vision of classic American community. But a return to something lost. Because, ladies and gentlemen, something has been lost.

MARGARET: *(To CARRIE.)* You're reading my book? What is your favorite part?

CARRIE: There has BEEN A FUCKING LOSS HERE people!!!!

MELANIE: The South will show that she is leaving the Union not by the Union's kindness, but by her own strength.

MARGARET: It's good to read it slow. Take your time.

CARRIE: How to sell loss.

> *SCOTT enters. The world segues immediately into a tour of poster drafts for the movie. SCARLETT, as well as MARGARET, is now visible to him.*

SCOTT: This is a sample marketing scheme for grandma in Scarsdale. Notice the original typeface (that only cost me 8 million dollars, ha ha), it's sort…of a techni-color vibe. Think of it as *Saving Private Ryan* meets *Steel Magnolias*.

> *Beatboxes over to the next poster.*

Jamone! And this poster is for our most important target: fifteen-year-old girls everywhere. Notice the horses, dancing, lots of sex. It's *Titanic* meets *8 Mile*.

SCARLETT: It's so exciting Mr. Staphf!

SCOTT: This is Hollywood magic. Welcome to the show.

MARGARET: What is this?

SCOTT: That is a sample of our educational packet. You know, for schools.

MARGARET: Are students even still reading my book?

> *JOHN enters.*

JOHN: Yes, in their American history classes! Ms. Mitchell this is what Scott has been trying to explain to you. I'm John St. Jean. I'm so sorry I'm late.

SCOTT: Five-0 man.

> *SCOTT reaches out a "bro" handshake. JOHN is put off. MARGARET and SCARLETT are both taken aback and quietly processing the African American director, who MARGARET had not yet met in person. SCOTT and JOHN don't clock this.*

JOHN: *(At SCOTT.)* Jesus.

SCOTT: I met a bunch of 20 year olds in the Midwest.

JOHN: Really? Where?

SCOTT: Bar. And they had all read it. And they were virgins. *(ALL stare.)* Anyways… the point – the point IS – THAT – these girls, these generations, I've got like 3, 4 generations of soft little minds in my pocket. And I am going to capitalize.

MARGARET: Do you really think you can wield so much power with just one little movie?

SCOTT: If you didn't do you really think we would still be having this conversation?

SCARLETT: *(To CARRIE/BRADY.)* C'Mon!!!

> *Abrupt shift. SCARLETT begins to take BRADY for full gallop. The reigns are the strings from CARRIE/BRADY's corset, which have grown impossibly long.*

MELANIE: They want war? We'll make 'em sick of war.

JOHN: Ms. Mitchell the reality is that some details are going to have to change. This is [2009].

> *A blurry shift. SCOTT is alone for a moment.*

SCOTT: *(Trying to cast SCARLETT for the movie. Rolling the word on his tongue.)* Scarlett.

MARGARET: *(To JOHN.)* Vivienne Leigh was much too pretty…

SCOTT: Scarlett's going to be…

JOHN: We need a young Angela Bassett… but white.

SCOTT: Scarlett's going to be hard. We're back in ten people.

JOHN: Thank you, Carol.

> *SCOTT and CAROL exit. MARGARET and JOHN are left alone – both figuring out how to navigate each other.*

MARGARET: Scarlett's not supposed to be beautiful.

JOHN: I know, Ms. Mitchell, I read your book. When I took this job I hadn't. My parents wouldn't allow it in the house. I had seen the movie.

MARGARET: The movie was different.

JOHN: The movie was *very* – this is obvious , but – *very* different –

MARGARET: Yes. Selznik added columns. I said over my dead body would Tara have columns.

JOHN: How did you let that happen?

MARGARET: I did not enjoy Hollywood Mr. Saint Jean.

JOHN: You know what I was struck by the first time I read your book? The film is a romance. Grand. Epic. Sure. Two Discs. But your book Ms. Mitchell. I am – *(Choosing the word carefully.)* Overwhelmed.

MARGARET: It took me nine years to write it. I kept the pages in envelopes, in my refrigerator. Under my mattress. In stacks in closets. Hidden.

JOHN: I can't stop reading it. I keep reading it. I read it when I'm eating. I forget to eat because I'm reading it. This was supposed to be a sexy war film. But it's like there's this *beast* up there on the shelf. And most people don't even know what's inside of it.

MARGARET: Why are you making this film?

JOHN: They needed a black artist on the creative team. I actually thought – this was before I read the book – I thought I was going to be able to just re-imagine – re-create – fill in the characters – the perspectives – I am revolted. I am enchanted. I have no idea how to move forward.

MARGARET: It is a force. The only theme in this book is survival. How some people come through catastrophes... and others don't. Do you think people will want to see this movie?

JOHN: Yes, Ms. Mitchell. I do.

MARGARET: Do you think... everybody will want to see this movie?

JOHN: Everybody.

MARGARET: Black people?

JOHN: I said everybody.

MARGARET: May I call you John?

JOHN: Yes.

MARGARET: This is a white woman's story. It is a story about surrender. It is a story about the Confederacy. This is a story about coming home to find that home isn't where we left it. I just want people to hear my story.

JOHN: *(Getting an idea, suddenly brimming with excitement.)* Okay, Ms. Mitchell... This time? This time you are going to see *your novel* onscreen. You are going to see a film that is just as complicated and contradictory as your book really is. I'm gonna make it. I'm going to make it if it kills me. And I'm going to play Uncle Peter.

SCOTT re-enters. SCARLETT enters with CARRIE/BRADY.

Blurry. Nighttime.

SCARLETT talks to him as a vision in a dream/nightmare.

SCOTT: Huh? Who am I talking to?

SCARLETT: Never mind Peggy, Mr. Staphf.

MARGARET: Scarlett –

SCARLETT: She doesn't decide where I stop. *(To BRADY.)* Hyah!

> *BRADY runs in several full circles around the stage, panting and snorting. Suddenly, SCOTT grabs BRADY as she gallops past. She rears and then settles in his arms. He caresses her like both a horse and a woman.*

SCOTT: Ass. She should have an ass, you know. But a little, little waist. You can't fake that. Real small, like when you put your hands around it your fingertips touch.

SCARLETT: She started it, but I get to finish. I'm a symbol, you see, with a voice like a mission bell. Charisma beats the shit out of morality any day of the week, don't you think?

SCOTT: Everything important is on top or bottom, right? Nothing in between. Nice tits. Not too big, but tits, you know.

SCARLETT: I can't go to hell any more than a tank, a turbine, an outbreak, an atom bomb can! I am unimpeachable! Isn't it delicious! Her reputation suffers, hell, her house has been burned down a half-dozen times hasn't it? But I'm still America's sweetheart. Oppenheimer may have tossed and turned at night, but his baby just does what it does best, and everybody goes, "Ahhhhhhhh!"

SCOTT: A body like that chick who married Marilyn Manson but with a better face.

SCARLETT: So from here on out you just come to me if Peggy poses a problem. Bring all your ideas to me, and we will make sure that everybody's piggy bank gets pudgy. I'll deal with Peggy.

You wanna know how?

I'm a survivor Mr. Staphf.

I will be here tomorrow. And tomorrow. And tomorrow. Peggy knows better than anyone that you have to get out of the road if you can't lend a hand. *(Suddenly turning directly to MARGARET.)* You're standing right in the middle of this gentleman's new road honey!

SCOTT: Scarlett fucking O'fucking Hara. Hot. Hot!

SCARLETT: Mr. Staphf! I'm ready for my close-up.

> *Suddenly sweeping music.*

> *SCOTT and SCARLETT kiss, emphatically, during which SCARLETT steals SCOTT's Bluetooth without him noticing.*

> *She releases him – he is almost possessed.*

SCOTT: Who am I talking – Where's my headset?

SCARLETT: *(On SCOTT's Bluetooth.)* Hello? No, this is Ms. O'Hara… Well I can help you with that!

> *SCARLETT slips away.*

> *Meanwhile MELANIE and MARGARET take us into the fiction of the book by reading to/playing with/fucking with CARRIE who becomes the unsuspecting SCARLETT.*

MELANIE: Ms. Campbell, why don't you take a load off.

CARRIE: I have to get out of here.

MARGARET: Take a load off Ms. Campbell.

MELANIE: *(Reading.)* "They want war…we'll make them sick of war."

CARRIE: What war?

MELANIE: "The war, Goose! The war's going to start any day, and you don't suppose any of us would stay in college with a war going on do you?"

> *MELANIE hands her the book to read.*

CARRIE: *(Reading, unenthused.)* "You know – "

MARGARET: Say it sweeter –

CARRIE: "You know there's not going to be any war!"

MELANIE and MARGARET: Not gonna be any war?!

MARGARET: Look honey. Of course there's gonna be a war.

MELANIE: The South is aflame with it!

MARGARET: It's going to start any day now.

MELANIE: *(Singing.)*
And when our rights were threatened,
The cry rose near and far

MELANIE and MARGARET:
Hurrah for the Bonnie Blue Flag,
That bears a single star!

ALL: *(Other than CARRIE.)*
Hurrah! Hurrah! For Southern Rights, hurrah!

MARGARET: Sing Carrie. *(She does, with MELANIE's help. Over the song:)* Tara made her charming, but the war made her Scarlett O'Hara!

CARRIE: If you say "war" –

SCARLETT: *(Bursting onto stage.)* If you say 'war' just once more, I'll go in the house and shut the door.

ALL: *(But SCARLETT.)* WAR! *(War cry.)* AYEEEEEE!

MARGARET: And for the first time without knowing, it Scarlett heard the rebel yell.

> *Suddenly music blasts through.*

> *THE WALTZ. Everyone dances an elaborate waltz. Dancing continues as:*

MELANIE: I'm so happy and so proud of the soldiers that I just can't help crying about it.

MARGARET: There was a deep, almost fanatic glow in the eyes of the women. How could disaster ever come to women such as they when their stalwart gray line stood between them and the Yankees? Had there ever been such men as these since the first dawn of the world? How could anything but overwhelming victory come to a Cause as just and right as theirs? They expected death. They did not expect defeat.

> *RHETT clears his throat and bumps into CARRIE. The Waltz ends.*

CARRIE: Sorry.

> *Silence.*

RHETT: Permit a stranger to offer the comfort of saying that to die for one's country is to live forever.

> *Awkward pause as RHETT slowly stalks the stage. MARGARET looks on admiringly.*

MARGARET: He was dressed in black broadcloth. A tall man, towering over the officers who stood near him, bulky in the shoulders but tapering to a small waist and absurdly small feet in varnished boots. The clothes of a dandy on a body that was powerful and latently dangerous in its lazy grace. He looked, and was, a man of lusty and unashamed appetites with an air of displeasing insolence about him, and there was a twinkle of malice in his bold eyes.

SCARLETT: *(Staring at the approaching RHETT.)* I think you are horrid.

MARGARET: *(To CARRIE, as RHETT approaches SCARLETT.)* People tell me I didn't explain Rhett Butler. Well, I knew his mind so well, it did not occur to me that I had to.

CARRIE: Is this a romance or a war story?

MARGARET: It is a very, very, very long book, Carrie Campbell.

> *SCARLETT and RHETT dance through the following scene. An athletic waltz: two large cats wrestling.*

SCARLETT: How dare you make me so conspicuous, Captain Butler?

RHETT: When you've been talked about as much as I have, you'll realize how little it matters.

SCARLETT: How dreadful!

RHETT: Oh, not at all. Until you've lost your reputation, you never realize what a burden it was or –

RHETT and MARGARET: What freedom really is!

SCARLETT: You do talk so scandalous!

RHETT: Scandalously and truly. Always providing you have enough courage – or money – you can do without a reputation.

SCARLETT: Money can't buy everything.

RHETT: Someone must have told you that.

MARGARET: *(At the meta joke.)* Oh ha, ha, ha.

RHETT: You'd never think of such a platitude all by yourself. What can't it buy?

SCARLETT: Oh, well, I don't know – not happiness or love, anyway.

RHETT: Generally, it can. And when it can't, it can buy some of the most remarkable substitutes.

SCARLETT: And have you so much money, Captain Butler?

> *Suddenly RHETT slaps SCARLETT hard across the face, and the dance grinds to a halt, as does the music.*
>
> *Silence.*
>
> *She slaps him back, and he responds with another slap – immediately, almost before she is done. She moves quickly into a full crouching/ defensive position. He smiles. They stare at each other.*

RHETT: What an ill-bred question, Ms. O'Hara. I'm surprised. But, yes.

> *New music begins. Contemporary – and good – hip hop.*

MARGARET: This is a lesson in force.

RHETT: For a young man cut off without a shilling in early youth, I've done very well. And I'm sure I'll clean up a million on the blockade.

SCARLETT: Oh, no!

RHETT and MARGARET: Oh, yes!

RHETT: What most people don't seem to realize is that there is just as much money to be made out of the wreckage of a civilization as from the up-building of one.

CARRIE: And what does all that mean?

RHETT: Your family and my family and everyone here tonight made their money out of changing a wilderness into civilization. That's empire building. But there's more in empire wrecking.

CARRIE: What empire are you talking about?

RHETT: The empire we are living in –

MARGARET: The South –

RHETT: The Confederacy –

RHETT and MARGARET: THE COTTON KINGDOM–

RHETT: It's breaking up right under our feet. Only most fools won't see it and take advantage of the situation caused by the collapse.

RHETT, SCARLETT and MARGARET: *(To the audience and CARRIE.)* I'm making my fortune out of the wreckage.

> *RHETT begins changing in to SCOTT onstage, talking as he does so, into his Bluetooth.*

SCOTT: Ya. We're going in a different direction with Rhett. Diddy. I don't know Carol, Bling? Is that… ? Yeah, think about it. Rhett's a dandy. Who's a dandy these days? Who's your dandy!?! Write that down.

SCARLETT: *(Viciously to CARRIE/audience.)* Welcome to Atlanta. Welcome to a suburban metropolis.

CARRIE: Ladies and gentlemen, I am so thrilled to meet you at this historic moment. Phoenix Meadows stands on the brink of… We are met at the brink of… A… a new vision of… American democracy… I mean American community… I mean, shit.

MELANIE: *(To CARRIE.)* Southern manners: you must do your business while also thinking of others.

SCARLETT: Welcome to a rural region, welcome to a transportation center!

CARRIE: I think people are wondering what I am going to do here – how I am going to respond – what I am going to do with this… opportunity. There is a question of blame. I think we are looking for someone to blame. Something. Someone. But keep in mind, my father said MAKE NO SMALL plans. A massive gesture is required ladies and gentlemen, and I want to assure you: the job is in good hands.

MARGARET: She and Atlanta are exactly the same age.

CARRIE: Who?

MARGARET: *(Pointing at SCARLETT.)* That one.

SCARLETT: Welcome to a commercial city.

CARRIE: Okay, it's not like I'm gonna build uh… a cathedral instead of… you know? I just think that it is very important that we save something for these people.

MARGARET: Has he talked to you about force yet?

CARRIE: What?

MELANIE: The symbol of Atlanta is the phoenix.

MARGARET: Planes! Trains! Automobiles.

MELANIE: The phoenix was a mythical bird that burned itself every seven years to regenerate from the ashes.

MARGARET: *(To CARRIE.)* What did one architect say to the other architect?

SCARLETT: Today's Atlanta is home to national and regional corporate headquarters.

MARGARET: If I were you I would invest in wood. Phone call for you.

> *MARGARET hands CARRIE a phone. CARRIE suddenly comes to her senses, remembering her responsibilities here. Everyone drops quiet while CARRIE takes the call.*

CARRIE: Lucy! Hi. Yeah. Yeah. No I've been fine. I'm sorry I haven't been in touch. No I'm sorry I haven't been in touch. Everything's moving along fine. No you definitely don't need to come down to the site. No it's clear. I have been taking care of – demolition's done. Totally done. Listen, Lucy? Lucy? I'm losing you. Yes I will be there. Yes I will be in a dress.

> *SCOTT and JOHN enter.*

SCARLETT: *(To CARRIE.)* You can start your visit in the era of your choice. Let's visit Margaret Mitchell's Atlanta.

> *SCOTT and JOHN are driving around, location scouting.*

JOHN: Well Atlanta's a shithole.

SCOTT: Depends on the neighborhood.

JOHN: Really?

SCOTT: *(Laughing.)* BUCKhead. It's nice. It's like Soho. You know where we should shoot this thing?

JOHN: I have no idea Scott.

SCOTT: New Orleans.

JOHN: What?

SCOTT: They've already got the rubble.

JOHN: Oh my God, you cannot–

SCOTT: And SEE! It's EMOTIONAL... and it's CHEAP. Write that down.

JOHN and SCOTT exit.

SCARLETT: Atlanta has redefined itself time and time again.

MELANIE: We have been burned down, burned ourselves down and bulldozed our buildings to the ground, but it takes more than Yankees or a burning to keep Atlanta down.

MARGARET: Are you building a memorial?

CARRIE: No, it's houses. People need *houses.* And then we can start – maybe to move forward. And then the people are going to come.

MARGARET: Are you in mourning, Carrie Campbell? I'm sorry. That was a leading question.

CARRIE: I am just trying to – DO something – because *something* has to HAPPEN, be done – be done TO – People need homes before memorials.

ASHLEY appears. Total shift of space into romantic melodrama.

ASHLEY: Dear Wife –

SCARLETT and MELANIE: *(SCARLETT and MELANIE both weaken at the knees.)* Oh Ashley!

ASHLEY: If I have concealed aught from you it is because I did not wish to lay a burden on your shoulders. But Melanie, heavy thoughts lie on my heart and I will open my heart to you. When I lie on my blanket and look up at the stars and say 'Ashley, what are you fighting for?' I think of States' rights and cotton and the darkies and the Yankees whom we've been bred to hate, but that is not why I am here. I, who have no love of death or misery or glory and no hatred for anyone.

CARRIE: *(As if speaking to his ghost, on a phone, at MELLY's bar.)* Dad! Hi. I mean. Hi.

ASHLEY: Perhaps this is what is called patriotism, love of home and country.

CARRIE: I'm... OKAY. Uhm... Things are... moving. It's, it's a... things are a lot messier than I thought.

ASHLEY: But it goes deeper than that for I am fighting for the old ways I love so much but which, I fear, are now gone forever, no matter how the die may fall.

CARRIE: People are still living in FEMA trailers – The city is a ghost town.

ASHLEY: For, win or lose, we lose just the same.

CARRIE: There's some sort of massive gesture needed here. Yes people need houses. Yes, I know, people need houses, people need porches, people –

ASHLEY: If we win this war and have the Cotton Kingdom of our dreams we still have lost, for we will become a different people and the old quiet ways will go.

CARRIE: There is a question of blame. And everything feels like an artifact. And I don't know what to save. And I am feeling very lost.

ASHLEY: The world will be at our doors clamoring for cotton and we can command our own price.

CARRIE: But there is some sort of shifting. And waiting. People are waiting – there's a quiet –

ASHLEY: Then I fear, we will become like the Yankees, at whose money-making activities, acquisitiveness and commercialism we now sneer.

CARRIE: I don't know, Dad. I don't know what's happened here. It's like something just opened up…

ASHLEY: And if we lose, oh Melanie, if we lose…

MELANIE: *(Singing – a quiet, a capella song.)*
It would be better to have a son,
Even if he got killed,
Than to never have one –
Oh-one…

CARRIE: It's like they're still fighting a war down here or something.

MELLY: Who you talking to honey? That phone hasn't worked for years.

> *Reality shifts. We are now back to the contemporary present in New Orleans.*

> *(Singing as MELLY.)*

All my life I've prayed,
All night and all day.
He will carry on after I've gone away,
And when my son comes,

I know we have won,
One more chance for the cause.

(Speaking.) So. Sell me on this place.

CARRIE: I can't.

MELLY: Well, you're developing my neighborhood, right?

CARRIE: Yes I just – I'm not really prepared –

MELLY: Well, this was your daddy's plan right?

CARRIE: Yeah.

MELLY: So tell me about him.

CARRIE: Steve Campbell. Steve Campbell is Phoenix Meadows. He was… uh, he was really smart. He was basically – he wasn't *basically* anything, he was a genius.

I mean, he's the one that came up with this whole thing, he led a group of architects to come up with this theory, you know, how to get people of different classes and backgrounds living together. New approaches, new possibilities. A new vision of classic American community. And Phoenix Meadows is an example of this –

MELLY: Of this TND.

CARRIE: That's right, Melly, and there's going to be new schools and new houses–

MELLY: New bars?

CARRIE: No.

MELLY: Yeah.

CARRIE: Yes, eventually yes. It's going to take a long time for the whole thing to – Because it takes a long time to develop home. But…space was made. *(An awkward moment.)* You know that thing that Henry's working on?

MELLY: The cathedral.

CARRIE: Yeah. The Cathedral of Chartres –

MELLY: *(Overlapping.)* Chartres.

CARRIE: That's right.

MELLY: I know.

CARRIE: Okay, well there's this story that...a long time ago Chartes was struck by lightning and it burned to the ground. And then out of nowhere people started coming. They started coming from everywhere. From all points of the compass, like a procession of ants, they came, and together they rebuilt the cathedral on its old site. I mean everybody from the nobles to the poverty stricken, everyone. And they worked until it was completed. But they all remained anonymous. The most perfect piece of architecture in the world and to this day no one even knows who built it. You see Melly, this could happen here.

MELLY: Phoenix Meadows?

CARRIE: That's just the beginning! Units are already being purchased, and people are coming from everywhere –

MELLY: Before it's even built?

CARRIE: Have you looked outside Melly? We're nearly halfway there.

> *MARGARET enters with a petition.*

MARGARET: Did you know the South lost the war?

CARRIE: *(Overlapping.)* Yeah.

MELLY: *(Overlapping.)* Tell me about it.

MARGARET: I didn't know the South lost till I was ten years old.

> *She marches up to CARRIE and slams the petition down before her.*

CARRIE: What is that?

MARGARET: That's our secession petition.

CARRIE: You're going to try and secede again?

MELLY: If Louisiana was independent we'd get all the revenue from our offshore oil drilling. You know, right now a quarter of this nation's domestic oil comes off our shores and the Feds take it all. As you can imagine we don't see too much return.

MARGARET: So we decided this time we would just pay for our own Reconstruction.

CARRIE: Well, you don't have a very good track record.

MARGARET: Well, we've never had the chance.

CARRIE: Come on, are you kidding? This is absurd.

MARGARET: We were the last bastion of American grace and dignity.

CARRIE: Yeah, built on an economy built on the backs of slaves.

MARGARET: Whose cotton you bought! / Let me remind you, this was a union that we tried to leave peacefully.

CARRIE: *(Overlapping.)* I didn't buy any—

MELLY: Hell, we did leave peacefully. We were an independent nation that you invaded.

CARRIE: This is not an invasion. We're here to help rebuild.

MARGARET: That's what you said last time.

CARRIE: There's no last time! We're building houses—

MELLY: You're bringing people, you're not bringing people back.

CARRIE: Ok, Melly, there are a variety of home styles, which means there are plenty of low-income housing options available.

MARGARET: We want what we had back.

CARRIE: That's not going to happen.

MELLY: I want New Orleans back.

> *MELLY exits.*

MARGARET: Look outside. What do you see? *(Pause.)* Well… history really does lead somewhere. Are you in mourning?

CARRIE: That's different.

MARGARET: Was your father a good person?

CARRIE: Yes. He was.

MARGARET: And if he wasn't, would you still miss him?

> *(Reading from* Gone With the Wind.*)* "The men and women of Atlanta looked the same but they were different. Something had gone out of them, out of their world. RECONSTRUCTION."

> *SCARLETT enters with a door slam.*

> *(With spite.)* An act to provide for the more efficient government of the rebel states.

SCARLETT thrusts her hand angrily into the air.

SCARLETT: I – Katie Scarlett O'Hara Hamilton Kennedy Butler, do solemnly swear that I have never voluntarily borne arms against the United States. That I have never voluntarily given aid, countenance, council, or encouragement to persons engaged in armed hostility against the United States. That I have not yielded voluntary support to any pretended government, authority, power, or constitution within the United States, and I do further swear that to the best of my knowledge and ability I will support and defend the Constitution of the United States against all enemies foreign and domestic. So help me God.

MARGARET: I'd have taken their damned oath if they'd behaved decent. I can be restored into the union, but I can't be reconstructed into it.

SCARLETT: *(To CARRIE, sharply.)* I don't know why we fought and I don't care. I'm not interested. I never was interested. War's a man's business. Not a woman's. All I'm interested in now is a good cotton crop.

> *Shrill "filming" bell.*
>
> *On the film set: SCARLETT and UNCLE PETER are in a carriage drawn by CARRIE/BRADY. They will enact the narration as MARGARET reads.*
>
> *At this point in the production we referenced and quoted a scene from Chapter 38 in* Gone With the Wind, *in which SCARLETT and UNCLE PETER are riding in a carriage and are stopped by a "YANKEE WOMAN" seeking advice on finding a nanny. The scene is a chilling one, which we aimed to present as "straight" as possible, as part of the larger critique of the book.*
>
> *In the original production, the actress playing MARGARET played the YANKEE WOMAN.*
>
> *At the conclusion of the scene, the carriage rolls on in silence for a long beat.*

JOHN: And cut.

> *Bell.*

Magnificent, thank you. *(Deeply moved, both as actor and director.)* Thank you, so much.

SCOTT: *(SCOTT has entered quietly during the previous scene, observing.)* Hey.

JOHN: Hi Scott.

SCOTT: What's going on?

JOHN: We're re-shooting the Uncle Peter scene.

SCOTT: It sounds like you re-wrote the Uncle Peter scene, too.

JOHN: Yes, I just wanted to put back in that magnificent language that Margaret wrote.

SCOTT: Interesting. *(To SCARLETT and CARRIE/BRADY.)* Get out.

SCARLETT: Scott–

SCOTT: *(To SCARLETT.)* Get out.

JOHN: Thank you. Thank you so much.

SCARLETT and CARRIE/BRADY exit.

SCOTT: What are you talking about?! We cannot have white people saying... that word.

JOHN: Margaret, did white people say "nigger" in 1867?

SCOTT: I don't care.

JOHN: *(To MARGARET.)* I need some help. Right now.

MARGARET: Well it was a different time.

SCOTT: I don't care. What are you doing, man? This is a war story. This is a love story. This is a corset story!

JOHN: I know... but Scott, listen to me – we have an opportunity here... I keep reading this book and – you have got to listen to me, this project could be magnificent.

SCOTT: What?

JOHN: We can actually do *Gone With the Wind*.

SCOTT: You are on contract. This is hijacking – you cannot just commandeer – you know, this is my fucking money!

MARGARET: This is my book! It's a eulogy Mr. Staphf –

SCOTT: You cannot mourn this shit. If I didn't think I could make a dime off of this thing I wouldn't even have it in my house.

MARGARET: It is a story about human beings doing the best they can as the world changes under their feet. Human beings, Mr. Staphf. You remember being one of those.

SCOTT: *(Beat.)* Okay, well, why don't you take your cavaliers and cotton fields and your Dixie shot glasses and your Scarlett O'Hara pageants and shove them up your ass sideways. And then why don't you take all of that back to 1930 when they tolerated this shit. You don't need to be here.

MARGARET: Am I being dismissed?

SCOTT: Yeah, my expensive lawyers will be in touch.

MARGARET: Is that all?

SCOTT: Yeah, yeah, yeah. *(To JOHN.)* Fucking writers.

> *MARGARET fades to the back.*

JOHN: Scott, that Uncle Peter scene goes in or I walk.

SCOTT: Where you gonna go, man? Come on, Saint, you gonna go back to New York? You gonna go make a play?

JOHN: I never should have taken this job. It's just getting way too complicated.

SCOTT: Look, this is a patch and paint job man. If there's a crack in the foundation you cover it up. You don't put a frame around it. And you sure as hell don't knock the whole house down.

> *SCOTT exits.*

MARGARET: *(Left standing stunned with JOHN. To SCOTT as he passes.)* Good afternoon.

MELLY: *(To MARGARET, having re-entered.)* We hold these truths to be self-evident. Government is by the people and for the people. And when that government starts, pardon my french, fucking those people, it is the right of the people to institute new governments, laying its foundations on the principles and organizing its powers in order to effect their safety, and happiness.

MARGARET: In a moment of weakness, I have written a book.

MELLY: *(To JOHN.)* The principles for which we contend are bound to reassert themselves, though it may be at another time, and in another form.

JOHN: What did you just say?

MELLY: *(To JOHN.)* Confederate car bomb? It's a shot of bourbon in a pint of sweet tea with a biscuit on the side.

JOHN: Yes please.

JOHN exits.

CARRIE enters running, breathless and excited.

CARRIE: Listen, we know there has been a lot of loss. I'm saving a house. There's this one house; it's a blue house. It's the only one still standing on the block and it has a little damage... a bunch of damage. Anyway, the point is we are keeping it. And it is going to be a reminder of what came before. It is going to be a memorial, and Phoenix Meadows is going to radiate outwards from this fixed point.

MARGARET: A reminder?

CARRIE: Yeah.

MARGARET: Where's the family that used to live in that house?

CARRIE: Um, we don't know...the records were very damaged – we think they were probably renting.

MELLY: St. Louis. They're in St. Louis. The father went missing. Whole family gone. And they owned their home.

MELLY exits.

MARGARET: What was the family name?

CARRIE: Uh, McKinley.

MARGARET: McKinley. McKinley. Like the President.

CARRIE: *(Grateful for the small joke.)* Yeah. Yeah, like the President.

MARGARET: But not. *(CARRIE stops smiling.)* Pardon me. I'm going to go watch the work outside.

MARGARET exits.

CARRIE stands alone, lost.

– INTERMISSION –

Libby King as Carrie in *Architecting*, Performance Space 122, 2009.
Photo: Nick Vaughan

ACT II

CARRIE has been onstage working during intermission. Blueprints, and lines of string – sculptures in space.

At some point, MARGARET and HENRY are glimpsed above, watching her.

CARRIE: *(To the audience.)* An architect and a money man are in a coffee shop... The architect says to the money man, "I want to build a cathedral." And the money man says, "Soon, but I need you to build a bank first."
Four months later. The bank is built. The architect and the money man are at the same coffee shop. Architect says to the money man, "I want to build a New American Cathedral." And the money man says, "Soon, soon, but I need you to build another bank first."
So four months later. Another bank is built. The architect, the money man, at their coffee shop, same coffees.
Architect says, "I want to build something beautiful. Something that people want to BE inside, something that WE have never seen before." And the money man says, "Okay! Sounds like we're on the same page. So a bank just like the last one, but with room for a parking lot."

> *Beat.*

Where do bricks come from?
Their mortars!

> *Long beat, perhaps in which the actress repeats the punch line multiple times in an attempt to finally land a laugh. Then, after awkward silence.*

Oh, I don't know... what do you call the design of a left-handed architect?

> *She shows her hand half-heartedly to the audience, which is now smeared with blue chalk from the blueprints.*

Blue handprints.
Okay. *(Setting up a camera with live feed on herself.)* This is the first take. What I propose to MWH Global Contractors and their... This is the second take. What I propose to MWH and their esteemed colleagues... This is the third take, this is the final take: What I propose to MWH Global Engineering and their superiors, the directors of the New Orleans Strategic Recovery and Rebuilding Plan is an act of architectural... is an act... is an act of architectural destruction. I want

to do it in CGI. I want to get the world's best engineers and designers to construct an entirely realistic plan of various available explosives to systematically destroy various parts of the nation's infrastructure. Like rings of a virus. First the suburban strip malls. Then all the domestic housing. Then the bowling alleys. Then all the multiplex. Multipli. And then I want to – We'll have to refugee all the people of course. The home dwellers. Maybe to Ireland. The Republic. Then I want – Oh! And I want to take aerial pictures, views from above of like, all of this. I want to blow up all of the schools. Then all of the government buildings. Like, the municipal ones. Not the historic. THEN, I want to blow up the historical buildings.

I think there probably will be another potato famine. When we all refugee to Ireland. Oh well. Then I want to blow up all the skating rinks, although that could probably get grouped along with the bowling alleys. So basically then what we'll be looking at is a ring of McDonald's Golden Arches, because we'll have blown up all of the other fast food chains and restaurants – and it will be like – the Lafayette Cemetery, the St. Louis Cathedral, all the Mississippi riverfront walkways, and McDonald's – and the concrete Harrah's Casino. 'Cause I like it. And Café Du Monde. And the Creole Queen. And Bourbon Street. Most of Bourbon Street, Disneyland and Disney World and the Lincoln Memorial. And Six Flags Great Adventure, Six Flags Across America, the green signs of Interstate 10 and various other highways. Because we'll still have the cars! People could sleep in the cars. The ones who didn't want to refugee. And then we could all drive to the major track for NASCAR and have one final race. It will be like Woodstock, people will have to park so far away that they can't even see it. But we can broadcast it on, like, CCTV in all the Texacos and bodegas and minimarts so anyone can watch the final race. Oh, I'm sure some reality show people will produce it. I bet Chuck Palahniuk could write me a really great opening speech –

Do I sound like a crazy person?

This is how I think.

This is how I think.

This is how I've thought since I was 10 years old. And then everybody who's still alive – we can make them build a – Do I sound like a crazy person? Do I sound like a crazy person? This is how I am thinking. I think the world doesn't give a young woman enough credit. So everyday she is performing. She is performing *(Southern accent.)* "The Act of Being a Well Behaved Young Woman." I want to be Henry Miller. I want to dot the world with Golden Arches – and then I want to build – then I want to build a…

Heavy knocking at the door. CARRIE hides.

MARGARET: *(From on top of the scenic structure.)* You're supposed to say, "Who is there?"

> *CARRIE suddenly and aggressively removes the entire door from its hinges, revealing an empty hallway. MARGARET leaves the two of them to talk.*

CARRIE: I can't see anything.

HENRY: *(Standing on top of the scenic structure.)* Maybe you need to get higher?

CARRIE: What are you doing up there? You shouldn't be up there.

HENRY: The Archangel loved heights.

CARRIE: Are you an angel, Henry?

HENRY: No. I'm a retiree. With way too much time on my hands.

CARRIE: How old are you?

HENRY: Too old to be climbing on roofs. Not too old to be climbing on roofs. Twenty-eight.

CARRIE: *(Imitating RHETT, plus accent.)* "That's not a vast age."

HENRY: You finished the book.

CARRIE: Yeah I finished it – "tomorrow is another" – I finished it.

HENRY: She *can* write.

CARRIE: I'm not sure anyone should ever read that book ever again.

HENRY: What do you think one generation has to say to another generation?

CARRIE: I don't know. I'm beginning to think not a lot.

HENRY: You're setting yourself up for disaster.

CARRIE: I've been set up for disaster.

> *HENRY chuckles.*

Don't laugh. Don't laugh!

HENRY: I'm sorry. You're in mourning.

CARRIE: I'm THINKING! I'm thinking about how to do this GD –

HENRY: Goddamned!

CARRIE: Goddamned!! Goddamned...

HENRY: GOD DAMN IT!

CARRIE: GOD DAMN IT!!!! God damn it this is a mess... this is a mess. This is such a fucking mess Henry.

HENRY: You know... I have no idea when this started, but now, all I think about is cathedrals. I don't remember why I ever used to think about anything less magnificent. There are things in the world, Carrie Campbell, and then there are magnificent things in the world. So just don't waste your time, y'know? Chartres.

HENRY and CARRIE: The most perfect piece of architecture in the world.

HENRY: Mont Saint-Michel.

CARRIE: Mont Saint-Michael in peril of the seas. "The archangel loved heights." Why did he love heights?

HENRY: Options: from a theological perspective: closer to God. But, from a military perspective, he could see across the water for miles and miles and miles and miles and miles. From a revisionist historian's perspective, maybe he was calling for help from higher ground.

> *HENRY sees something in the distance, which flies over his head. He waves at it for help, but it does not come. It flies away.*
>
> *A long beat.*

CARRIE: How is the view? Do you see anything different?

HENRY: Space.

CARRIE: Yeah.

HENRY: Space filled with an unbelievable amount of shit.

CARRIE: Yeah.

HENRY: *(Still looking out.)* Carrie? Have you always worked for your father?

CARRIE: Yes. Yes I have.

HENRY: I think it's time.

CARRIE: I think I'm waiting for something…

HENRY: And I think it's time for you to clear the slate. Carrie Campbell. So…what will be the first to go?

> *He cuts her string sculpture. The strings fall into a heap onstage.*

MARGARET: *(Singing offstage.)*
Admirable things…
Admirable things…

> *CARRIE and HENRY exit.*

> *CAROLINE enters driving alone, practicing her beauty pageant speech.*

CAROLINE: Well thank you for asking that question, Paul! I've got gumption. I've got a fire burnin'. I am the woman you are looking for, Paul. You see I'm from Hope! Hope, Arkansas! I drove 300 miles to be here! I'm from Hope, Arkansas, and I believe in hope! Hope!

> *Suddenly the sound of tires, glass crunching, metal smashing.*

> *CAROLINE's car crashes!*

> *After a long silence, she emerges, and looks at it. Completely in shock.*

My whole life was in that car. Oh God dammit. God dammit. God dammit. Goddamn the, goddamn car!

…
Okay.
Okay…
Okay.
Okay.
Okay.
Okay.

> *She repeats "okay" until she builds up her strength.*

Could be worse. Could be on the goddamned ocean. Okay.

> *CAROLINE exits with purpose.*

> *A transition to a Sunoco gas station.*

> *JOSH is at work.*

> *He reads to himself from* Gone With the Wind *(borrowed from the station's book rack).*

As he reads, MALE SCARLETT slowly enters in hoop skirt and corset.

JOSH: "Charles was not excited over the prospect of marrying her, for she stirred in him none of the emotions of wild romance that his beloved books had assured him were proper for a lover. He had always yearned to be loved by some beautiful, dashing creature full of fire and mischief. And here was Scarlett O'Hara teasing him about breaking her heart!"

MALE SCARLETT: *(Played by man, in a man's voice.)* Why you gonna break my heart?

JOSH: "He tried to think of something to say and couldn't, and silently he blessed her because she kept up a steady chatter which relieved him of any necessity for conversation. It was too good to be true. 'Now, you wait right here till I come back, – '"

MALE SCARLETT: Now, you wait right here till I come back,

JOSH: "'For I want to eat barbecue with you.'"

MALE SCARLETT: For I wanna eat some barbecue with you.

JOSH: "'And don't you go off philandering with those other girls, –'"

MALE SCARLETT: Don't you go off philandering with those other guys,

JOSH: "'Because I'm mighty jealous.'"

MALE SCARLETT: Because I am mighty jealous.

JOSH: "Came the incredible words from the red lips with a dimple on each side; and briskly black lashes swept demurely over green eyes. 'I won't,' he finally managed to breathe, never dreaming that she was thinking he looked like a calf waiting for the butcher..."

    MALE SCARLETT drifts back into the darkness.

    DING!

    JO enters store. JOSH quickly puts down the book.

JO: Hi Josh.

JOSH: Hey Jo.

JO: Brought you another box of yellow ribbons.

JOSH: Good. We's close to out.

JO: Could I get ten on two?

JOSH: Sure thing.

JO: Josh, so I just came by to let you know, but we're probably heading out soon.

JOSH: What do you mean?

JO: Going home. Arkansas's nice but it isn't home.

JOSH: Thought they was settin' you up pretty good.

JO: Oh yeah, me too. But I think I've been waiting for a check that isn't coming. You know?

JOSH: Yup.

JO: So we're gonna go home. Figure... start over.

JOSH: You be careful.

JO: You're sweet.

JOSH: How them boys doin?

JO: They're good. Yeah, got a letter. Said it's 125 degrees over there.

JOSH: Damn.

JO: Yeah, sure is cold in here, though.

JOSH: Yeah. Boss likes the AC on full blast for folks. Right at 62.

> *Silence. JO notices the copy of* Gone With the Wind.

JO: Hey, what are you reading?

> *JOSH quickly and uncomfortably hides the book.*

Okay... Well, you keep handing out those ribbons for me. Yeah, I'll see ya Josh.

> *JO exits. JOSH resumes reading. CAROLINE enters and peruses the snacks.*

CAROLINE: You got anything low fat?

JOSH: Water.

CAROLINE: Anything else?

JOSH: Wiper fluid... I think we got some SunChips.

CAROLINE: Oh those low-fat?

JOSH: I don't know, man, I'm not a label reader. Read the thing.

> *She gives him an ornery look and sees the book. She charges at him – he tries to hide it but drops it at her feet. She quickly grabs it.*

CAROLINE: Oh my God. What are you reading? Oh my God! YOU'RE READING THIS? NO OH MY GOD! *THIS IS A SIGN! THIS IS A SIGN!* WHERE'D YOU GET THIS? WHY ARE YOU READING THIS?

JOSH: We just sell it man, I just grabbed it off the thing –

CAROLINE: This is the most remarkable coincidence I've ever heard of in my life!

JOSH: Really?

CAROLINE: I'm on my way to New Orleans, *right now,* to compete in an international pageant to become Miss Scarlett O'Hara!

JOSH: *(Looking at the parking lot on the CCTV monitors.)* Where's your car?

CAROLINE: Crashed it. But I figure that's gonna make a great Scarlett O'Hara story. How many of them other girls are going to come out of flaming wreckage on their way there?

> *Beat.*

What does Scarlett O'Hara mean to you?

JOSH: What, you recording this or something –

CAROLINE: No, it's just a question that they ask, this'll, like research –

JOSH: Sexy. Strong... *(CAROLINE "mms" in agreement.)* Uh, Red?

CAROLINE: Red and sexy... Ask me!

JOSH: What does Scarlett–

CAROLINE: Scarlett-O'Hara-is-a-self-made-woman-and-a-true-female-American-role-model-thank-you!
I have this whole... I have this one dress – that I wanna wear during the –

JOSH: So them dresses were like...
They were big, right?

CAROLINE: Oh. THEY WERE HUGE!
Like the size of two of your desk!

JOSH: Why were they so big?

CAROLINE: I think it was for protection. Like, oh, try to get close to me.

JOSH comes towards her a step.

K, you'd be all over my dress right there! So, I'd be, I just come walking down here like this – oh, and them other girls will be lined up back there, listenin' to me–

JOSH: So them other girls just lined up over there?

CAROLINE: Yeah, right over–

JOSH: I'll just, I'll be one of them.

CAROLINE: You wanna be one of the girls?

JOSH shrugs and nods his head slightly.

CAROLINE: *(Tickled.)* Okay, HERE! You be one of them girls.

She puts a flower from her suitcase behind his ear.

Okay, so I come down, I come down like this and I say,
Ladies and Gentlemen.
I know what it is to be Miss Scarlett O'Hara because I have seen my entire life go down in flames around me. I know what it is to watch and plant and persevere in the face of struggle and strife – I know what it is to genuinely work at something for your entire life–

JOSH: Hey man, it's hitting me kinda harsh, you know…

CAROLINE: Harsh?

JOSH: Yeah, I mean that's how it's hitting me, you know? I think you maybe wanna soften your edges a little bit.

CAROLINE: Soften my edges.

JOSH: Yeah–

CAROLINE: How far are you in that book?

JOSH: I'm at the barbeque.

CAROLINE: Okay, you want barbeque Scarlett?

JOSH: Yeah.

CAROLINE: *(Seducing JOSH, total transformation.)* I would make the best Scarlett O'Hara, because I know what it is to walk into a room, and have everybody fall at my feet.

I know how to give one little smile, and to have everybody nearby feel their little heart going something like this...

> *She does a fluttering gesture. A long lingering moment. Then she drops it suddenly.*

Barbecue Scarlett O'Hara.

> *JOSH is nodding, wide eyed.*

> *A moment.*

> *JOSH hands her back the flower from his hair, and she takes it, almost catching his hand in desperation.*

You wanna dance with me?

> *Music from somewhere.*

> *She and JOSH make a tiny move towards each other, but are still far apart. They begin to sway. Each of them just rotating their imagined hoop skirt. Watching each other. Beautiful and quiet.*

CAROLINE: How old are you?

JOSH: Guess.

CAROLINE: 27. *(He motions up.)* 32. *(He motions down.)* 30. *(Down.)* 29. 29. Can I tell you something?

JOSH: Alright.

CAROLINE: My daddy died two weeks ago.
And I have never been... by myself.
You alone a lot?

JOSH: Yeah.

CAROLINE: You got a car?

JOSH: Yeah.

CAROLINE: You wanna come with me?

JOSH: *(Immediately.)* Yeah.

CAROLINE: Really?

JOSH: Yeah. *(Points to a CCTV security monitor.)* You see that monitor right there, just tell me when it cuts off.

Now? *(CAROLINE: No.)*

Now?! *(CAROLINE: No!)*

CAROLINE: It's OFF! It's OFF!

JOSH: Hey! Get some snacks!

CAROLINE: Ok!

> *JOSH and CAROLINE grab some snacks and run off laughing.*

JOSH: Let's go!

> *The Sunoco sits empty for a moment.*

> *FRANKLIN DELMORE MCKINLEY enters the empty Sunoco station and rings the service bell. He is puzzled by no one being there. Rings bell again.*

FRANKLIN: Hello? Hello?

> *During the following VIDEO scene Franklin goes behind the counter, looks at CCTV's and begins to read the copy of Gone With the Wind. At the sound of someone entering the gas station he hides. Blackout on the gas station.*

> *On VIDEO: CAROLINE and JOSH driving at night.*

> *NOTE: VIDEO serves primarily as a time passage device throughout this section.*

CAROLINE: *(In the middle of laughing at something previous.)* My daddy said I was...

JOSH: That so?

CAROLINE: This is an ode to Margaret Mitchell. For Margaret Mitchell:

> *CAROLINE sings "Georgia On My Mind."*

> *JOSH and CAROLINE enter onstage and drive. Song continues live with CAROLINE singing as the VIDEO fades out.*

JOSH: Pretty good.

CAROLINE: Do you sing?

JOSH: To myself.

CAROLINE: Sing somethin'!

JOSH: No.

CAROLINE: C'mon, sing something.

JOSH: No.

CAROLINE: Josh! Pretend I am yourself.
Hey! You should come to LA with me after this.

JOSH: Nah.

CAROLINE: Why not?! We'll be drinkin' margaritas by the sea, papacita.

JOSH: I gotta work on Friday, so.

CAROLINE: At the Sunoco?

JOSH: Yup.

CAROLINE: Josh, I do not think you should count on that job being there
for you on Friday.

JOSH: It will be. My grandpa owns the place.

CAROLINE: Your grandpa owns Sunoco??!! Oh my God–

JOSH: No, no, no, not the whole thing. Just that station, man. It's a
franchise, you know. Like McDonald's.

CAROLINE: I love McDonald's.

JOSH: I hate McDonald's. *(Long beat.)*
But I love it.

CAROLINE: This is really it for me. This pageant. I'm 24, so… You can't
compete in any of the big pageants once you're 25, so. I don't know
what I'll do if… well, I know what I'll do if I win! I'll go to LA, I'll get
representation. I'll make a couple of movies, and I'll probably record
something later this year. If I don't I'll… I'm turning a corner! … I feel
hopeful. I feel really… hopeful!

> *Lights fade on stage.*

> *On VIDEO: JOSH and CAROLINE driving, singing along with Elvis'
> "Heartbreak Hotel" on the radio.*

CAROLINE: *(On video.)* I love Elvis. My daddy, loved Elvis.

JOSH: *(On video.)* My daddy hated Elvis.

BACK TO STAGE: JOSH plays guitar, even though he is technically still in the driver's seat.

CAROLINE: *(Singing.)*
  Blowin' Away
  Blowin' Away
  Sometimes a burnin' makes everything grow
  Up even healthier than it was before that day
  Blowin' Away
  Blowin' Away
  If my heart is heavy I'm gonna keep it inside
  Hop in your car and we'll head on down the highway

> *Slowly she moves over to the microphone. Out of the darkness rises huge applause that won't die. We are transforming from a quiet car sing-a-long to a dream of CAROLINE performing at the pageant.*

  Blowin' Away
  Blowin' Away
  Everything I touch is gonna turn into gold
  I am not average and I am not old, no way!
  Blowin' Away...

> *The applause continues to build. CAROLINE is overwhelmed.*

Thank you! Thank you!
I want to thank you all so much! Thank you for letting me represent Scarlett O'Hara for you today. Scarlett said, "As God is my witness, I will never be hungry again!" And, ladies and gentlemen of the jury, tonight I am so full!

MARGARET: Will you make it?

> *The dream begins to turn.*

CAROLINE: Who are you?

MARGARET: Never mind that. Let's play scenario. Everything you love is gone. Caroline Dixon, you believe you have what it takes?

JOSH: You dreaming?

> *Suddenly back in the car.*

CAROLINE: No.

JOSH: You woke up real quick...

CAROLINE: I know.

JOSH: You alright?

CAROLINE: Yeah.

JOSH: Man you was long gone. You was snoring and twitchin' and shit.

CAROLINE: Shut up.
    You wanna switch turns?

JOSH: No.

CAROLINE: That was a crazy dream... I dreamed that I was in front of the
    pageant panel – but it was like I was auditioning for the movie. And
    I was doing the "As God is my witness I will never go hungry again"
    scene. And I was crying my eyes out... And I just kept hearing this
    voice behind me saying, "Caroline, honey? You do not have what it
    takes. You just are not the genuine article..."

JOSH: That's awful.

CAROLINE: And then I turned around and I think it was my dad...

    She begins crying. JOSH quietly observes.

JOSH: That's grief. That'll pass.

CAROLINE: What does your dad do?

JOSH: He has emphysema.

CAROLINE: Oh. How long?

JOSH: Twelve years.

CAROLINE: Twelve years! God. Does he even have any lungs left?

JOSH: He's got one. *(CAROLINE: Jeez!)* It's why I quit smokin'.

CAROLINE: Yeah. You get along with him?

JOSH: Yea. Pretty good.

CAROLINE: You have a good relationship.

JOSH: Yeah. He was the general manager of the Sunoco. So now I'm the
    GM.

CAROLINE: Does it feel different being the GM instead of an M?

JOSH: Nope.

CAROLINE: It's like I just turned 24 and it doesn't feel any different than 23. Though I guess if you compare the beginning of 23 to the end of 24, then you'd have something.

> *Silence.*

He live near you?

JOSH: Yup.

CAROLINE: He in a home, or... ?

JOSH: Yeah, he lives in a house...
That I live in too.

CAROLINE: So you take care of him? Or does he have a nurse?

JOSH: Nah. My aunt's there, we take care of him.

CAROLINE: What does your mom do?

JOSH: You wanna talk about somethin' else?

> *On VIDEO: CAROLINE at a gas station requesting a large beverage from the driver's seat.*

> *Back to stage, CAROLINE sings along with a fully produced recorded track.*

CAROLINE:
>*It's a special time*
>*When you find*
>*Someone who's*
>*Gonna share your life*

>*And I found mine*
>*By the side of the road*
>*Shinin' like*
>*A new dime*

>*And I apologize*
>*For the stupid grin*
>*That crosses my face*
>*When I look at him*

>*And I know you*

Are shy
But I'm not gonna
Pass you by

So we'll just drive
Until it grows
Into something
You're ready to show

We'll just drive...

> *JOSH gets guitar. He begins playing and CAROLINE falls asleep,*
> *contented, on his shoulder. The track slowly fades away.*

> *MALE SCARLETT enters quietly from the darkness.*

JOSH: *(Singing.)*
Highway drive
Late at night
And you pretend
To fall asleep

And all the while
I can feel you
Listening
To me breathe

And I apologize
For lookin at you
Right in the eyes
So many times

And I know I
I love you
But not the way
That you love me...

MARGARET: Is that your song?

> *JOSH is profoundly startled and quickly tries to hide the guitar.*
> *MARGARET is quietly watching him from behind.*

> *MALE SCARLETT pulls back, but is still visible, turning in the darkness.*

I like it. You remind me of someone...

JOSH: I do?

MARGARET: Whoa! Don't look at me, look at the road.

JOSH: Yes Ma'am.

MARGARET: Ma'am. *(Laughing at this.)* Good boy. You always been a good boy?

JOSH: Ma'am?

MARGARET: Done what your parents taught you? Worked?

JOSH: I guess.

MARGARET: You ever been in love?

JOSH: ...yes Ma'am.

MARGARET: ...Interesting. You are not a man of many words.

JOSH: Guess not.

MARGARET: That's alright. I am a woman of many words.

JOSH: *(A bit of a dare.)* I'm reading your book. Margaret.

MARGARET: Yes... You can call me Peggy.

JOSH: Peggy Mitchell.

MARGARET: *(To herself.)* Gumption.

JOSH: What?

MARGARET: *(Ever so kind. So gentle.)* Nothing, Joshua. You gonna lead my people out of the desert into the promised land?

JOSH: I'm sorry, Ma'am?

MARGARET: Never mind. *(Pause.)* So, you are reading my book. I sure hope you like it?

JOSH: Yeah. I'm only at the barbeque, but—

MARGARET: Well that's okay, it's good to read it slow. Take your time.

JOSH: Yeah, yeah. It's real good.

MARGARET: Can you elaborate?

JOSH: Yeah. I like the way the world feels just, real alive you know, and passionate.

I like the way that them people speak, you know, all elegant and stuff. I like them big dresses.

MARGARET: You know when I was a child I used to wear pants. So I called myself Jimmy.

JOSH: You wanted to be a man?

MARGARET: No. No – Well, sometimes. Yes.

JOSH: Like Scarlett.

MARGARET: I suppose.

JOSH: You ever been in love?

MARGARET: What do you think?

JOSH: Well, I think you probably have. Probably had it like a motherfucker too.

MARGARET: Oh!

JOSH: *(Embarrassed.)* Sorry. Is that your house there?

MARGARET: Yes it is.

JOSH: Don't look too good.

MARGARET: Yes, well… People keep burning it down.

JOSH: How come?

MARGARET: Well I suppose I don't exactly know.

JOSH: I'm a little worried about you.

MARGARET: I'm worried about you.

JOSH: I'm fine.

MARGARET: Will you dance for me?

JOSH: Hey, you going to be at that pageant too, Peggy?

MARGARET: Pageant?

> *Sudden jump back into reality.*
>
> *Harsh light of day. JOSH and CAROLINE in New Orleans.*

JOSH: I think we're here. Man, you ever been to New Orleans before?

CAROLINE: When I was a kid. Didn't look anything like this. Look at all these new houses: they're so shiny.

JOSH: So, where's this pageant at?

CAROLINE: I don't know. I think we took a wrong turn on Annunciation.

JOSH: I'm starving man.

CAROLINE: Me too.

> *CARRIE enters wearing work clothes.*

CAROLINE: Oh there's someone – ask them where the pageant is. I'm gonna get us something at McDonald's.

JOSH: Hey excuse me sir –

CAROLINE: Josh, it's a girl.

JOSH: Sorry. Excuse me –

> *MARGARET enters, following CARRIE.*

CARRIE: *(To JOSH.)* Look, this is a restricted area.

JOSH: You alright? *(Seeing MARGARET.)* Peggy?

> *MARGARET stares at JOSH, not speaking.*
>
> *CARRIE exits.*

CAROLINE: *(Shouting from offstage.)* Josh? You want supersize?

> *JOSH exits in the direction CAROLINE has gone.*
>
> *MARGARET is alone onstage. A transition in time/place/vibe.*
>
> *On VIDEO: MARGARET is being interviewed by SCOTT (off camera) for the DVD extra features for the movie. On stage MARGARET watches herself on VIDEO.*

MARGARET: *(On VIDEO, extremely hesitant and uncomfortable.)* Well, a uh, novelist must be many things at once. Like a child she must believe contradictory facts to be true.

SCOTT: *(Off, whispering.)* Little louder –

MARGARET: Who?

SCOTT: *(Off, whispering.)* Little louder –

MARGARET: *(A little louder.)* A… An Historian need not sympathize with anyone, least of all her characters. Therefore the writing of a novel is an entirely different BEAST than the writing of a history –

SCOTT: Yeah. Let's – let's move forward if we could –

The sound of rustling papers.

A jump cut. CAROL is leaning partially into the shot, showing MARGARET the last question that she is to answer. She steps away. MARGARET focuses on the camera.

MARGARET: *(On VIDEO.)* Who should see this movie? I don't know. I don't know. It was a huge seller in Germany.

Anyone who knows about war…

MARGARET: *(On stage and on VIDEO.)* I know a lot about loss. So I –

MARGARET: *(On stage finishing the sentence that on video she was interrupted during.)* – wrote about that.

MARGARET: *(On VIDEO.)* – Excuse me? What was that question again? Something ludicrous about my feelings on race?

I dare you to ask me it again young man.

I dare you to insult my intelligence again.

VIDEO cuts abruptly out.

On stage.

MARGARET: I have something to add. I am not quite finished. I have an announcement.

I have a written a sequel.

This is the Ballad of Franklin Delmore McKinley. *(Music.)*

A sequel. People have been begging me for the sequel for years. This is it.

To start: A preface. A sequel does not require the revisiting of a former story. It does not necessitate you pick up where a deliberately severed narrative left off. I cannot say whether Scarlett gets Rhett in the end, and will not answer that question here. I only know that we must all answer for our actions sometime or other. And this sequel, this sequel is my answer.

This country is changing and Franklin's father has gone missing.

FRANKLIN enters and enacts the narration.

FRANKLIN DELMORE MCKINLEY! If I had a neon sign with his name on it I would light it now, has left New Orleans. His entire family left after Katrina to St. Louis where the old people have started dying and the young people have taken permanent jobs and will never again return to Louisiana. Franklin's house was marked for destruction, but he fought for it to stay. Then after nobody returned to his neighborhood, his was now the only old house standing in his Ward. So Franklin decided to pick up and take off with no other real plans than to somehow single-handedly remind his nation that an entire city had been left to rot.

FRANKLIN quietly sings the spiritual, "Were You There When They Crucified My Lord?" MARGARET observes him for a few beats.

MARGARET: With no money he starts hitchhiking across a country that he sees as scarred at every turn by injustices to black people.

This is a landscape that could be mapped topographically by travesties to humanity small and large. And on a lonely stretch of highway in Arkansas, Franklin couldn't get another ride. Nobody would pick him up.

He waits for a ride at the gas station that Josh works at, and no ride comes for days. Eventually Josh tells Franklin that twenty years ago a white man picked up a black hitcher in that area and was then found hanging dead in a tree. That hitcher was never caught, and since then it has been common understanding that nobody picks up a black hitcher. In that area.

Then Caroline shows up. She wants Josh to come with her to New Orleans and Josh decides mmmmmmmm fuck it, I'm goin' to New Orleans with Caroline. Franklin remains behind.

And thus begins Franklin Delmore McKinley's life at the Sunoco station. If I had another neon sign with his name on it, I would light it now. The constant fluorescent lights. The muzak. The slow and steady stream of customers. The girl who works the night shift at Texaco across the highway. The ghosts of his city rising in the Arkansas mists. The ghosts of his ancestry sitting in the thick trees surrounding the station.

Franklin begins capturing clips and images of the customers who pass through on the CCTV monitors, and he plays them to ward off the loneliness.

VIDEO begins to play images of characters from throughout the play on CCTV. Ghostly.

He finds a closet full of old CCTV monitors in the back, all kinda busted, but workable. They just distort the color and image a bit. Eventually Franklin has a wall of CCTV monitors inhabited by fabricated friends and disciples.

Franklin hasn't slept.

The customers stop coming in. Shipments stop coming in. No cars on the highway. The sun does not rise. Crickets come. And someone is whistling Dixie in the woods.

Music with a heavy beat begins.

We see Franklin returning from various excursions outside of that station.

MARGARET and FRANKLIN begin to move slowly to the music, at first just walking.

He is unaware of her presence.

He has met the people who live in the night woods. He has learned the old Negro spirituals. He has learned the old names of places. He has learned the Voodoo magics. Franklin returns to the station. He gathers up his many CCTV friends, tinted varying degrees of dark, into an army, and he leads a forced march back to New Orleans.

The music begins blaring.

FRANKLIN breaks into a savage, full solo dance of the march.

The entire cast emerges to watch him. Then they begin to join him in waves.

He the Major General, and is leading a forced march back to New Orleans. A march that gets confused about what year it is. It is at times a Civil War march, burning everything in its wake; at times a Mardi Gras march, sweeping everything it passes into its bellowing furnaces; at times a Civil Rights march, arm-in-arm, impervious to the world.

The march dance cycles, disintegrates. MARGARET loops the above text like a cassette being eaten by a player.

It all devolves eventually into stillness and panting.

The sound of rain. Slow at first.

FRANKLIN sings quietly, and begins walking as if through rising water. He is hopping from solid surface to solid surface. The cast begins to sing quietly underneath him.

FRANKLIN and ALL: *(Singing.)*
Build your house on a rock, boy!
Build your house on a stone!

These lines repeat and grow in power, until they break into the full song, all sung a capella.

Well they built my house on the sand brother,
Built by the mouth of the mad mother river.
They built my house on the sand brother,
Built my house on the sand!

This song begins to bleed with "Admirable Things." Metabolism begins to accelerate.

The slow gathering of so much lost.

MARGARET: *(Singing.)*
Admirable things.
Admirable things.
Yeah I am interested in
Some honest enterprises

ALL: *(Singing.)*
No, I've been to the devil

MARGARET: *(Singing.)*
And he is very dull.
I am interested in
Something that sounds foreign
Something like surrender
Foreign like surrender
Foreign like surrender
Foreign like surrender

ALL of this is building to a massive movement/montage sequence that fuses images from Hurricane Katrina and its aftermath, to images from Gone With the Wind, *and moments throughout the play.*

ALL: *(Waving to helicopters overhead.)* Help! Hey! Over here!

ALL: *(Singing.)*
Foreign like surrender!

> *NOTE: Each line in the following chaotic sequence corresponded to a whole nonverbal moment/tableau that gathered around it. For the most part, only the spoken dialogue is included below.*

FRANKLIN: Hello, my name is Franklin Delmore McKinley.

MELANIE: *(Singing.)* **One more victory and the war is over!**

MARGARET: Tomorrow is another day.

MELANIE: *(To MARGARET.)* You have got to be kidding me.

SCARLETT: *(To MELLY.)* You never were a sister to me.

> *A melodramatic scene in which JOSH plays RHETT and MALE SCARLETT plays SCARLETT.*

RHETT: How old are you my dear?

MALE SCARLETT: Twenty-eight.

RHETT: That's not a vast age to have gained the whole world and lost your soul.

MALE SCARLETT: All I know is that you do not love me anymore.

MARGARET and CARRIE: *(Together, on their knees.)* "Pray for us sinners now and in the hour of our death. Amen."

> *FEMALE SCARLETT and MELANIE do the rebel yell as they run at each other.*

MARGARET: *(To CARRIE.)* They asked me, "Tell us your feelings on race?"

CARRIE: Knock knock.

MARGARET: They said, "We have 30 seconds left. Can you tell us your feelings on RACE." You can't hear *them* on the camera!

CARRIE: Sounds a little leading, misleading. I fucking hate the press.

MARGARET: I love the South.

> *JOHN is dragging a drunken SCOTT following the Academy Awards.*

JOHN: The thing is, Scott, I just don't like you very much.

SCOTT: I don't like you either, but we're winners. We won!

JOHN: Sorry I didn't thank you in my speech.

SCOTT: What a night.

JOHN: I forgot.

SCOTT: Where's my headset?

> *FEMALE SCARLETT drags MELANIE across the stage.*

MELANIE: You'll look after him, won't you?

SCARLETT: I will.

MELANIE: Oh Scarlett, you're so smart. So brave.

ALL BUT SCARLETT: *(At SCARLETT.)* You've always been so good to me, Scarlett!

SCARLETT: *(To the audience.)* Money is the most important thing in this world and, as God is my witness, I don't ever intend to be without it again.

MELLY: *(Singing.)*
  Yes I'm here, every single night.
  Doesn't mean I'm just passing my time.
  Just because I always say I'm fine!
  Doesn't mean I've got nothing on my –
  (Spoken, in total dismay.) **My bar!**

CARRIE: Put on your masks… Put on your masks!

> *The demolition of the set/the Oasis Bar/a TND home/FRANKLIN's home begins.*

SCARLETT: Look for it in books, celluloid, VHS and DVD, collector's editions, autographed copies. Purchase a doll and a set of plates. Buy the trading cards and give them to your babies. They come with a chocolate, a little chocolate baby you can suck on.

MARGARET: Please, oxygen! Please! My mom can't swim!

MALE SCARLETT: *(Suddenly in JOSH's arms.)* All I know is you don't love me anymore. So what am I supposed do? Where am I supposed to go?

JOSH/RHETT: My dear, I don't give a damn.

> *JOSH and MALE SCARLETT kiss passionately.*

Then MALE SCARLETT throws his hoop skirt onto Josh.

SCARLETT: *(To AUDIENCE.)* For it is more than a dream remembered. "Come, Come With the Wind!"

> *SCARLETT charges over to CARRIE, wearing a blazer and looking absolutely fierce. She hands her a business card.*

My name is Katie Scarlett O'Hara. I hear there's so much money in real estate.

MARGARET: In a moment of weakness I have written a...

> *The blaring dance music dies down. Quiet music plays in the background as the sun rises.*

> *ALL but FRANKLIN and MARGARET exit as MARGARET returns to narrating her sequel, exhausted.*

MARGARET: Franklin Delmore McKinley arrives in New Orleans as the sun rises for the first time in months only to find that it has been turned into a walled suburban community. Artificially raised above the flood lines.

(Singing.) **Little boxes on the hillside...**

The pattern of the streets is overlaid with a sprawling maze of cul-de-sacs. Well, Franklin's house is still standing!!
As a cultural curio.
There is a spiffily dressed band that plays New Orleans Jazz in his living room, and a wet bar serving Hurricanes on weekends.
Franklin walks in. And addresses the tourists.

FRANKLIN: Thank you all for coming. My father would have been so proud.

> *Flames begin. Quietly.*

MARGARET: Franklin Delmore McKinley burns his house to the ground.
Franklin Delmore McKinley burns his house to the ground.
And walks West.
Heading to Mexico.

> *The fire burns.*

> *It grows unbelievably big, engulfing the stage.*

> *The centerpiece of Phoenix Meadows is burning to the ground.*

CARRIE enters and sees what is happening.

CARRIE: Oh. My god. The house. Ohmygod. Call the police. NOOOOO!

MARGARET grabs her, followed quickly by HENRY. The two hold her back as she thrashes, preventing her from running straight into the flames to try to save something.

MARGARET: *(Holding CARRIE back.)* They've all moved to Houston.

CARRIE: No no no no no no—

HENRY: This is magnificent! Well done, Carrie!

CARRIE: Are you crazy? This isn't – I didn't do this. This was supposed to be—

MARGARET: It's okay. People keep burning my house down too. It's therapeutic.

CARRIE: This house was supposed to be – it was supposed to be the memorial. It was supposed to be – I was going to –

HENRY: This *is* the memorial, Carrie. It's okay. This *is* a memorial.

CARRIE: No no no no no no no…

They watch it burn, and slowly sink to the ground.

In the glow of the flames, CAROLINE walks slowly to the mic, speaking something impossible to hear over the roar.

Suddenly the sound cuts out. We are at the "Miss Scarlett O'Hara" pageant, where CAROLINE is dressed beautifully, and just wrapping up an answer.

CAROLINE: I believe Scarlett O'Hara is a self-made woman and a true female American role model. Thank you.

MARGARET: *(Slowly, stoically.)* Thank you Caroline.

CAROLINE: *(Completely crushed, but still smiling.)* Oh… is that all?

MARGARET: Yes.
Who is next?

JOSH: *(Enters in hoop skirt and corset.)* I think I'm next.

CAROLINE: Josh?

JOSH: Hi.

CAROLINE: You're in a dress.

JOSH: Yeah.

CAROLINE: But I thought we... Oh my God! Why did you do this? Where am I gonna go?

JOSH: I can't go back, man...

MARGARET: Are we okay to move on?

CAROLINE: No.

JOSH: Yes.

CAROLINE: No.

JOSH: Yes.

> *They stare at each other. Then JOSH slowly crosses to the mic.*

I'm taking the necessary steps to make sure I can't ever go back to being the way I was. Thank you.

MARGARET: Okay...
Historical novel.
You are standing in the middle of a field of red earth.

JOSH: Blood red after the rain?

MARGARET: *(Quiet.)* That's right.
And, let's say, you look behind you. And back there, in the distance, by the forest, you look...
Look Joshua.
And you see your home, Tara...
You see your home is burning down. And the flames are making your face hot, as everything you ever loved, everything you ever held in your heart, is gone.
Now. Look the other way.

JOSH: *(In tears.)* What is it?

MARGARET: What do you see?

HENRY: *(To CARRIE, who is still by the burned out home.)* What do you see?

> *The worlds are all beginning to blend.*

CARRIE: I see open space.

JOSH: I see open space.

CAROLINE: *(Quietly, backstage at the pageant.)* What am I gonna do…

JOSH: There's nothing but open…

CARRIE: *(To audience.)* Ladies and Gentlemen, I am truly thrilled to welcome you all here tonight.

MARGARET: You ready to take us out of here Joshua?

HENRY: *(To the audience.)* This – This is a Dynamic Theory of History.

> *The image of the Dynamo spins.*

JOSH: I'm hot.

MARGARET: Yeah. It's hot down here.

CAROLINE: Where will I go? I won't think of it now.

CARRIE: Phoenix Meadows is unlike any neighborhood seen before, and an opportunity unlike anything that will come again. It is a memorial. It is a recovery. It is a new American city.

MELLY: *(Standing outside the burned out shell of the Oasis.)* My bar.

JOSH: And I see all of God's materials.

CARRIE: Let me take you through what you are looking at.

HENRY: Like most theories it begins by begging the question: WHAT IS PROGRESS?

MARGARET: *(To JOSH and CARRIE.)* I think I'm ready.

JOSH: I see sand and bricks and shovels and mortars.

CARRIE: What may not look quite finished is in fact a completely new vision of the American dream.

CAROLINE and MELLY: I won't think of it now.

CAROLINE: I'll go home and think of it tomorrow.

HENRY: The world is demanding a new man!

CARRIE and JOSH: I'm dizzy.

MARGARET: Motion sickness.

MARGARET and HENRY: It's alright.

MARGARET: Burdens are made for shoulders strong enough to carry them.

CARRIE: This is architecture that responds to zones of crisis.

JOSH: And I see fresh water.

HENRY: And all of the new forces are demanding a new type of man.

MARGARET: I'm dizzy.

HENRY: For the old man has plainly reached the end of his strength, and his failures have become… catastrophic.

CAROLINE and MELLY: I'll think of it all tomorrow. I can stand it then.

CARRIE: The supreme aim of any creative activity is architecture – to build is to create events.

JOSH: And I see
Vegetation.
Of all kinds.

> *JOSH begins to change out of his corset and back into his work clothes.*

CARRIE: Ladies and gentlemen, I believe that our future cities must be constructed out of the precise conditions that exist in the present. You are looking <u>right now</u> at the past, at the present and future all at once.

> *MAMMY enters, walking slowly and inevitably towards MARGARET.*

MARGARET: Mammy? Can I ask you a question? Did you mean it when you said you don't like me very much?

MAMMY: Yas'm Miss Mitchell. Yas… and no.

> *MAMMY picks MARGARET up like a baby and carries her offstage.*

JOSH: And I see people.

CARRIE: As you can see all day long the sun will flood the workspace.

JOSH: I see people sitting.
And waiting…
They're waiting for a plan.

> *A sail ascends into the sky – lifted by CARRIE and JOSH. A massive scenic gesture (that should fit the destruction/construction aesthetic of the design). It should feel a bit like the spire of a cathedral.*
>
> *CAROLINE begins to exit. JOSH runs up to her, post pageant.*

JOSH: Where you going?

CAROLINE: I don't know.

JOSH: I don't know.

> *CAROLINE exits. HENRY re-enters.*

HENRY: Carrie?

CARRIE: Yes?

HENRY: What did one architect say to the other architect?

CARRIE: I don't know.

HENRY: …Welcome home.

CARRIE: There is something about entrances.

> *LUCY enters, dropping her keys on the way in.*
>
> *Sudden silence.*

LUCY: Shit.

CARRIE/HENRY/JOSH: Shit.

> *CARRIE, HENRY and JOSH exit. LUCY finally finds her key, and enters the burned out shell of the McKinley home.*

LUCY: Hello! Anybody, anybody.

So…

> *LUCY takes out her notes and begins practicing her speech. She uses the audience directly. Should have the awkward feel of standup comedy.*

Welcome… WHAT a NIGHT, huh? An INNOVATIVE new neighborhood is almost completed in New Orleans.
N'orleans.
New Orleans.
N'orleans, USA.
New Orleans.

> *She makes a note about the most successful pronunciation.*

As homes are completed later this year, it may look like a trip back in time. That's the idea. Phoenix Meadows – (I should have slides.)

> *She begins to click and gesture as if she had slides.*

Phoenix Meadows! Emerging on a 220-acre parcel of land on the southeast corner of Elysian Fields and Burgundy St. is a TRADITIONAL NEIGHBORHOOD DEVELOPMENT. A TND, a style of new urbanism rapidly gaining in popularity. Nearly 400 TND's – whoops – over 400 TND's are under construction across the country today. Phoenix Meadows features many recognizable characteristics of TND's, including innovation mansion-plexes (I need to google that), well landscaped common areas, wetlands, a variety of home styles, often with porches, five-foot wide sidewalks will border every street, and you will never lose yourself in this traditional neighborhood structure with a discernable center.

She is standing center stage.

It's a little bit of overkill if I'm right in the middle when I say that. *(She adjusts.)*
There are no limits. Only edges in this closed community with an open heart.

Lots will be sold expressly through the builder. A place where you can bicycle and leave your doors unlocked at night. A place like this is capable of producing thought in a way that no contemporary community is capable of fostering. We can raise a whole generation of Norman Rockwells and Jackson Pollocks here. This is a place of openness and a place of sheer perfection, to counteract the normal imperfections of daily human life.

(Leaning in.) How many unthinking people did you have to pass by in the street on your way here tonight?
And how much harder did you have to think to make up the gap?
My associate and friend, Carrie Campbell…

Gesturing to "CARRIE" who is not present.

And this is where Carrie will enter, if she ever calls me back. She will say "Hello! My name is Carrie Campbell, you may recognize my name, I was a child genius! My father is Steve – whoops… *(Making note, sadly.)* My father was Steve Campbell." Blah blah blah.

CARRIE: *(Emerging from the darkness.)* Blah. Blah. Blah.

LUCY: *(Stunned.)* Hello.

CARRIE: Hi Lucy.

LUCY: There you are. You're here.

CARRIE: I'm here.

LUCY: They told me you weren't here.
Nobody has seen you since the fire.

CARRIE: It was a shock.

LUCY: *(After a beat.)* I think the historic center is a great idea.

CARRIE: Thank you.

LUCY: Probably better anyway. This place probably wasn't going to last the year anyway, it looked like.

CARRIE: It would have stood up.

LUCY: *(Uncomfortable silence.)* So… you got my emails?

CARRIE: Yeah. Rec Center.

LUCY: And you'll be there at… *(Gestures "6:00.")*

CARRIE and LUCY: Six.

LUCY: Right.

CARRIE: Right.

LUCY: We'll send you the script.

CARRIE: I actually have a few things I wanted to say.

LUCY: Of course you do. Of course. You can improvise. A little. Just keep it to the point Carrie. These people aren't builders. They're buyers.

> LUCY *exits.*
>
> CARRIE *slowly surveys the damage. There's a lot of damage.*
>
> HENRY *slowly enters.*

HENRY: Cleaning up?

CARRIE: We have people that will do that. I'm just looking. Looking.

HENRY: Will the fire have set you back?

CARRIE: Just a bit. The clean up will be done in a couple days. The building will take another few months to be fully complete, but new families will already be in here by then. There will be cars, and then there will be bikes.

And rollerskates…

I don't know if you read in the paper, but we're going to build a historic center in place of the old house so that people will know what was once here.

And hopefully in ten years the toxicity level will be down in the soil, and people might be able to plant things in the ground again. And we made space for a community garden so that eventually people can eat community grown food.

I like the landscapers, you know, cuz they don't even know what it's going to look like…their part of the architecture isn't actually complete for fifty or one hundred years. It has to grow in. To grow up.

She looks at the space. Overwhelmed.

HENRY: What are you seeing?

CARRIE: Space. I see open space.

HENRY: That's poisoned ground.

CARRIE: *(Shaking her head.)* Open space.

HENRY: What is it?

CARRIE: It's a memorial. Something – a… it's a vast building.

She suddenly recognizes it. Finally. Quietly.

It's a cathedral. It's a cathedral. In the building of which everybody will help who has lost his identity.

HENRY: Religious?

CARRIE: No. Yes. There will be a mass. There will be masses for the dead. Here. This will all happen here. And there will be rose windows and gargoyles and there will be prayers. And hymns. And more and more and more people will come and it will grow into a kind of moaning and a chattering – with a sort of murderous in…in…

HENRY: Insouciance?

CARRIE: Insouciance. Everyone saying over and over again, "I'm sorry," and "I forgive you." I'm sorry. I'm sorry. I'm sorry and I forgive you. There will be confessions. People will leap out of their seats – people will run up and down the aisles CONFESSING. Horses will gallop up and down the aisles. People will scream and weep, you can scream and you can weep, and you can butt your head against the walls, they won't give. And you can pray in any language that you choose. Or you can just curl up outside and go to sleep.

It will be enormous. ENORMOUS.

This cathedral.

This memorial.

This place.

Huge.

And it will last a thousand years at least. And there will never be another like it. There will be no replica. For the builders will all be dead, and the formula too.

But we will have postcards made. And organize tours. Towns will grow up around it, outside it. For miles and miles and miles.

We have no need for genius. The genius is dead. Here… here on this ground, in this place we need strong hands. We need spirits who are willing to give up the ghost, and put on flesh.

> *On VIDEO and around the ruined space, as CARRIE looks, shards of the cathedral become visible.*
>
> *BLACKOUT.*

MISSION DRIFT

WRITTEN BY
JESSICA ALMASY, FRANK BOYD, RACHEL CHAVKIN, HEATHER
CHRISTIAN, JILL FRUTKIN, SARAH GANCHER, AMBER GRAY,
BRIAN HASTERT, MATT HUBBS, LIBBY KING, IAN LASSITER, JAKE
MARGOLIN, DAVE POLATO, AND KRISTEN SIEH

WITH
JAKE HEINRICHS and NICK VAUGHAN

MUSIC BY
HEATHER CHRISTIAN

LYRICS BY
HEATHER CHRISTIAN and THE TEAM

Mission Drift was co-produced by the Almeida Theatre, Performance Space 122, and Culturgest.

It was made possible with support from the Greenwall Foundation, the Panta Rhea Foundation, the JMJ Family Fund, the Jerome Foundation, A.R.T./NY and subsidized studio space provided by the A.R.T./New York Creative Space Grant, supported by the Andrew W. Mellon Foundation, and the Mid Atlantic Arts Foundation (through USArtists International in partnership with the National Endowment for the Arts and the Andrew W. Mellon Foundation). It was supported, in part, by public funds from the New York City Department of Cultural Affairs in Partnership with the City Council, the National Endowment for the Arts, and the New York State Council on the Arts.

It was developed at the Almeida Theatre, BRIClab, the University of Nevada Las Vegas, LMCC's Swing Space Grant at Building 110 on Governors Island, the Orchard Project, Soho Think Tank's Ice Factory Festival, and ArtsEmerson.

Mission Drift was first presented at Culturgest in Lisbon, Portugal on July 14, 2011.

The World Premiere took place at the Traverse Theatre, in Edinburgh, Scotland on August 7, 2011 with the following cast:

CATALINA RAPALJE	Libby King
JORIS RAPALJE	Brian Hastert
MISS ATOMIC	Heather Christian
JOAN	Amber Gray
CHRIS /ATIATONHARÓNKWEN	Mikaal Sulaiman

And with musicians:

Piano	Heather Christian
Drums	Matthew Bogdanow
Guitar, Bass	Gabriel Gordon

The U.S. Premiere of *Mission Drift* took place in New York City on January 8, 2012 at the Connelly Theatre, as part of Performance Space 122's COIL Festival. The cast was as follows:

CATALINA RAPALJE	Libby King
JORIS RAPALJE	Brian Hastert
MISS ATOMIC	Heather Christian
JOAN	Amber Gray
CHRIS /ATIATONHARÓNKWEN	Ian Lassiter

And with musicians:

Piano	Heather Christian
Drums	Matthew Bogdanow
Guitar, Bass	Gabriel Gordon

Rachel Chavkin	*Director*
Heather Christian	*Composer/Co-Lyricist*
Nick Vaughan	*Set Design*
Brenda Abbandandolo	*Costume Design*
Matt Hubbs	*Sound Design*
Jake Heinrichs	*Lighting Design*
Séan Linehan	*Associate Lighting Design*
Jake Margolin	*Additional Choreography*
Dave Polato	*Production Stage Manager*
Paz Pardo, Jenny Worton	*Dramaturgs*
Ben Gullard	*Assistant Director*
Nate Koch	*Producing Director*
Michael Mushalla, Double M Arts & Events	*Tour Producer*

Mission Drift **was awarded** a 2011 *Scotsman* Fringe First Award, the Edinburgh International Festival Fringe Prize, and a *Herald* Angel Award.

CAST OF CHARACTERS

CATALINA RAPALJE, an immortal Dutch teenager, wife of Joris

JORIS RAPALJE, an immortal Dutch teenager, husband of Catalina

MISS ATOMIC, a 1950s beauty-queen,
Las Vegas lounge performer, and goddess of some kind

JOAN, a cocktail waitress in Las Vegas

CHRIS, a cowboy who lives in the desert outside of Las Vegas

ATIATONHARÓNKWEN, a Mohawk Indian trader

Names in the text not appearing in the character breakdown are the names of the performers assigned to those pieces of text in the production.

In the production "The LIZARD" was played by Stage Manager Dave Polato.

"VICKI" is the name of a computer-generated voice from a speech-to-text program included in most Macintosh computers.

Lines left blank such as

JOAN:

indicate a nonverbal reaction that takes up the rhythmic space of a line of dialogue.

The phonetic pronunciation of the name Atiatonharónkwen is

Akya·doo(n)·ha·ROO(n)·gwuh.

The (n) is a swallowed "n" sound.

We also recommend for further guidance on pronunciation that artists contact the Saint Regis Mohawk Tribe. Up-to-date contact information can be found through the tribal directory on the National Congress of American Indians' website www.NCAI.org.

A studio recording of the original music may be purchased online through the TEAM's website or through the iTunes store.

The creation of *Mission Drift* began unofficially in May 2008 with the question "What defines American capitalism specifically, versus capitalism as it took shape anywhere else in the world?" The question was actually inspired by *Architecting*, and our work on the fiercely capitalist Scarlett O'Hara. And then the stock market crashed in September.

Jake Margolin directed our focus towards Las Vegas, which had been the fastest growing city in America at the turn of the millennium, and was suddenly the epicenter of the housing crisis. This provided our first stake in the ground, and in June 2010 we traveled there for a month-long residency at the University of Nevada.

Our residence was a foreclosed home – marked by a piece of paper taped to the door. Nearly every third house in our neighborhood had one. We took daily field trips, and generated material each afternoon. We spoke with members of the Culinary Workers Union (Local 226) about the past and present casino and hospitality economy. We learned about the Nevada Proving Grounds, just 60 miles north, where atomic bombs were tested into the 90s. We visited a 60-year-old pig farm that was being fined because homeowners in the new, gated communities surrounding it were complaining about the stench. At the Springs Preserve, we learned that Las Vegas was once a lush and fertile valley, and was now on track to run out of water by mid-century.

The second foundation for the play came from *The Island at the Center of the World: The Epic Story of Dutch Manhattan and the Forgotten Colony that Shaped America*, by Russell Shorto. This introduced us to Catalina and Joris Rapalje, teenage Dutch settlers who spawned over a million descendants, including allegedly the man who fired the first shot in the American Revolution. Richard Slotkin's monumental trilogy about westerns and western mythology also were invaluable. Frederick Jackson Turner in *The Significance of the Frontier in American History* wrote that the story of America is the story of people moving further and further west, becoming less European and more American with every mile. For hundreds of years there was a pervasive belief that America was limitless; that resources were so plentiful that one could pursue profit endlessly, and without consequence. This is, of course, a myth belied by both slavery and the near annihilation of the American Indian population.

Mission Drift is not a straight analysis of the financial collapse. It instead occupies this space – between the myth of the frontier and the reality of its costs – which is the undercurrent of so much American identity.

– Rachel Chavkin, Summer 2013

Heather Christian in *Mission Drift*, Culturgest, 2011
Photo: Rachel Chavkin

ACT ONE

MISS ATOMIC in her lair over the stage. Nighttime in Vegas. She is looking out over the valley.

MISS ATOMIC: *(On mic.)* Good evening, pagans, Vegans, insomniacs, gorgeous lizards, hospitality peddlers, sweethearts, assassins.

Grab your drink baby, we're gonna be here for a while.

No seriously, grab your drink, it's dry out here.

We are desert people. We make our homes in impossibility. We hallucinate regularly. We might have magic lamps, or we may be the type, myself included, to play the genies. Let me illustrate. If you will, a little snap-er-oo.

She snaps.

VICKI: WELCOME TO LAS VEGAS.

MISS ATOMIC: Welcome to fabulous Las Vegas! Las Meadows. A resting stop for Mexican traders, for Mormon missionaries, for folks looking to start over get a leg up, find a way out. Our oasis in the desert.

There's a story round these parts. I know it from the inside. Before time there were two twin brothers. Mythic, beast brothers. Big scale. They slept between mountains with their legs in separate valleys. Their names were Love and Wrestling. I'm not being poetic. Those were their names.

Wrestling liked heavy things. He set records and broke them. Lifting hurling pushing pulling dragging pieces of world across the continent as dead weights. What use is a god, after all, unless he's strong.

Love had the soul of an artist, and kept mostly to himself. The Mojave was his secret sandbox. And he was wild with his work.

Now Wrestling, as the firstborn, had inherited the land from their giant beast father. And over time Love grew angry. What good is force without talent? "Fuck sand," he said. He turned to limestone. Sandstone. Shale. Granite. Erecting elaborate countries that baked under the sun. Big as a continent. Sharp and bright and complicated.

So late one night while hurling boulders Wrestling discovered his brother's work. A *secret country* carved in his brother's hand. And it pushed him into the red.

"Fuck you Love," he thinks.

And he hurls a rock, blasts the tops of Love's castles. He bowls. Makes gullies and forks. Sits on pyramids. Splits and tears and shakes the earth with belly flops.

Love awoke the next morning.

And saw what his brother had done.

Family is funny.

Sometimes it's just not possible to work shit out.

So the two brothers call it Splitsville. Separate ways. Rivals.

Love did everything he could to build up the fucking land: dams, canals, hotels, high rises, casinos. And Wrestling did everything he could to raze the fuckers down. Tornados, earthquakes, explosions, whatever. And on they went, until ONE day, Love realized, "What the hell? Why don't I get these fucking humans to do my work?" So Love put the lust for improvement and development and expansion...and expansion into the hearts of humans, and claimed his Lazy-boy throne in the sky.

And then he changed his name.

To Steve Wynn.

Smiles.

Fucking bastard...

Everybody's heart has two houses. Two brothers living inside...

A snap-er-oo.

She snaps.

LIBBY: The outskirts of the city of Las Vegas. Metropolitan population –

LIBBY and VICKY: 1,951,269.

LIBBY: This is Joan, a cocktail waitress with a mortgage and a car loan. She just got laid off.

She's in the darkness now off North Las Vegas Boulevard, in a place called the Neon Boneyard, alone with only the lizards for company. Before her are the signs of long gone casinos: the Desert Inn, the Stardust. The fragile bones of electric dinosaurs.

She looks at the new skyline, at the bronzed Wynn casino, at the golden Mandalay Bay, at the 40 billion-candle-power beam of light streaming upwards from a black glass pyramid.

JOAN looks out, a quiet desert moment.

She looks at the frozen construction sites... The cranes look like animals in the dark.

MISS ATOMIC (and JOAN): *(Singing quietly, almost like a voice on the wind in JOAN's mind. JOAN joins her for the second line.)*
I think somebody is Burning Down this Place I built
But if you believe in Vegas...

JOAN: Fuck.

LIBBY: Two days ago at a casino, south on the Strip.

A flashback. A casino, glowing, humming, buzzing. JOAN is working as a waitress, which she is very good at. CHRIS, a modern cowboy, walks in, dumping sand out of his boot.

JOAN: Hey. *Hey.* YOU NEED TO WEAR SHOES IN HERE.

CHRIS: *(His voice raspy and dry from dust.)* In here?

JOAN: Yeah, "in here." We don't have a lot of rules, go crazy, you know, but you do have to wear shoes.

CHRIS: *(Unable to speak through dryness.)* I'm sorry – I – *(Coughing fit.)*

JOAN: Are you okay?

CHRIS: I just came in to – *(Coughing.)*

JOAN: Do you need a drink?

CHRIS: *(Through dust in throat.)* I didn't bring my wallet.

JOAN: If you've got a dollar for the slots all drinks are on the house. *(He gulps water.)* It's your first time in a casino.

CHRIS: Yeah.

JOAN: Yeah. *(She looks at him a moment, slightly too long. Shaking herself, walking away.)* You're covered in dust.

CHRIS: You smell like horses.

Western theme begins.

JOAN: Where are you in from?

CHRIS: Born. Here.

JOAN: You don't look like you're from Las Vegas.

CHRIS: Desert. Outside of.

BRIAN: She wants to ask why, if he's from Las Vegas, he's never been inside a casino. Why he's got desert in his shoes. But then she thinks, it's been a long time since she saw a real cowboy…

CHRIS: What are you *doing* here?

JOAN: I've been here a long time. Third-generation HouWoo.

CHRIS: HouWoo?

JOAN: House Through The Woods Incorporated? They own this place. My mom used to –

CHRIS: But what are *you* doing here?

JOAN: I'm – working.

CHRIS: So how much is your life worth?

JOAN: *(Beat.)* That's private.

CHRIS: *(Quiet, anger underneath.)* No.

JOAN: *(Beat. A shifting.)* With or without my house?

CHRIS: Just you.

Western theme fades. Casino sounds rush back.

JOAN: *(A beat.)* Four sixty-five ($4.65) an hour, plus tips and benefits. And I'm gonna be made a manager when they finish the Ark –

CHRIS: The Ark?

JOAN: There is no way you're from Vegas.

CHRIS:

JOAN: *(She points.)* The Ark! You can't miss the construction site. They imploded 3 old places to make the space.

The sounds of a crowd.

BRIAN: New Year's Eve, 2007.

Flashback. JORIS stands at a microphone, basking in a bright light. CATALINA looks on.

CATALINA: I want to now introduce my husband! My partner, the CEO to my CFO, my own house through the woods, Chick Darling.

JORIS: *(Speaking to the crowd.)* The frontier is the birthright of every American, and it's at the heart of this project. This year we imploded the Shining City – HouWoo's first baby. We imploded the magnificent Stardust. And tonight we implode the New Frontier casino, and launch a new era in this valley. From the ashes of these casinos will rise a vessel unlike anything you've seen before. A primeval ship composed of light, and glass. And she will be blinding. Ladies and Gentlemen, it is time to make way for The Ark. Cat?

CATALINA: Raise your glasses everyone! To the New Year – and to the Ark. *(Signaling ALL to count.)* 10 9 8 7 6 5 4 3 2 1!!

An implosion rockets through – see the actual implosion of the New Frontier in Las Vegas for a sense of the show. It is thrilling.

The flashback dissolves. The sounds of the casino come rushing back.

JOAN: It's gonna be big.

CHRIS: Big.

JOAN: *(Looking at him.)* Unbelievable. It's gonna have the biggest forest in the state of Nevada inside.
Underground.
And it'll have condos, and schools.
And it's gonna look like a boat. Like…

CHRIS: Like an Ark. Like Noah.

JOAN: Like it just ran aground in the middle of the desert.

Like it was always there, just waiting to be discovered.

CHRIS: It sounds awful.

JOAN: *(Starting to exit.)* Kay, well I work for tips and not talk so –

CHRIS: Wait!

JOAN: *(Exiting.)* Enjoy your stay.

CHRIS: I do like your way. Of talking about it.

JOAN:

CHRIS: I'm staying down off 15 on Sunset, at the La Quinta.

JOAN: Okay.

CHRIS: Room 206.

BRIAN: The next day the stock market collapsed in New York. And the day after that out west Joan got laid off, along with several thousand HouWoo employees. And construction on the Ark froze. And Vegas froze. And now –

Flashing forward again to the present.

The outskirts of the city of Las Vegas.
This is Joan in the Neon Boneyard.

JOAN: Fuck. You.

BRIAN: And she is looking at her city.

JOAN: Fuck this place.

BRIAN: It's the first time she's ever said those words.

MISS ATOMIC: I know you're hurting out there tonight in the valley my Vegans.

BRIAN: Joan imagines a light brighter than a thousand suns exploding over the skyline. She imagines Vegas burning.

MISS ATOMIC: But you know what? I like it when I'm down. I like it when I'm down cause that's when I get creative. The cranes may have stopped, but remember: The one thing you can't outsource –

LIBBY, BRIAN and IAN: Is hospitality!

MISS ATOMIC: This is Miss Atomic coming at you live, reminding you to just keep on rolling, like a good shooter. Yeah shooter! Good girl!

MISS ATOMIC: *(Singing.)*
   I think somebody is burnin' down Las Vegas
   I think somebody is tryin' to snatch my house

I think somebody is burnin' down this place I built

MISS ATOMIC and JOAN:
But if you believe in Vegas, then you believe in God

MISS ATOMIC and ALL:
I think somebody is burning down my country
I think somebody is burning out my heart
I think somebody has smoked me out and gassed my mouth
But if you believe in money, then you believe in God
I think somebody is burning down this place I built
But if you believe in Vegas, then you believe in God
Said if you believe in Vegas, then you believe in –

Last note sustains and becomes something else, a hymn.

MISS ATOMIC:
Woh Sinner
Brethren Kin
Walk in the way of the well spring
Yay Amen

Tonight we are dried up. Washed out. But this place used to be wet. Las Meadows. Whole rivers used to run underground here with spring mounds on top to mark the path. Oh God. We gotta go some place different. Follow the water back… A girl.

CATALINA enters to the sound of water.

IAN: A girl is standing on a dock beside a big wooden ship.
She is 14. But she's big sized for 14 because that is the way Dutch people are.
THIS… Is Amsterdam.
The year is 1624.
Catalina prefers sunsets to sunrises. She just quit her job doing the books for a brothel in the Red Light District. (She always got numbers.) She's got good teeth. And she's an eligible bachelorette.

Shouting down to her.

CATALINA!!

CATALINA shouts back at her in Dutch the way you would if you got catcalled by someone on the street. Gives her the finger.

CATALINA: Krijg kanker en ga dood, hoer! (Get cancer and die, asshole!)

She is approached by JORIS.

He watches her.

AMBER: A serious young man stands apart from the crowd and looks at her.

CATALINA: What?

JORIS: Hey.
I'm Joris Rapalje.

IAN: "Rapalje" roughly translates to white trash. I'm not being poetic. That's just what it means.

JORIS: If I received a nickel for every time I saw someone as beautiful as you, I'd have five cents.

CATALINA: Gross.

JORIS: I'm gonna be on your boat –

CATALINA: I don't care.

JORIS: Who are you?

CATALINA: What? No! I won't marry you.

JORIS: How did you know I was gonna ask –

CATALINA: You're the eighth person to ask me that today.

JORIS: Who are you going to pick?

CATALINA: I'll marry an Indian when I get there.

JORIS: Is that a joke?

CATALINA: Serious.

JORIS: I have a cousin who works for the company. We will have first pick of the land when we arrive and access to the first livestock shipments. I will work as a trader, and you will tend the farm. I believe a strong wife is vital to a strong household.

CATALINA: Uh-huh.

JORIS: In six years, when the contract finishes we will return home and I will be offered an in-house position at the company. I expect a starting salary of –

CATALINA: Show me your _____.

JORIS: What?

CATALINA: *(Gesturing to his crotch.)*
Show me your _____.

JORIS: What are you –

CATALINA: Fine, thanks, bye.

JORIS: Okay! Okay, yes!

> *JORIS begins to walk offstage to a hidden spot. Realizes CATALINA is not following. Beat.*

JORIS: In front of all these people?

> *He relents. Unbuttons.*

CATALINA: *(To the audience.)* I was told. I was told you can see a lot by the size of a man's...and the width. My boss at the brothel told me exactly what to look for. But... Uh-huh...

> *(Looking closer.)* It's not like what she described...

JORIS: It looks different –

CATALINA: I see –

JORIS: At different times.

CATALINA: *(Quickly.)* Yes – It looks fine –

JORIS: *(Quickly, pissed. Buttoning up.)* Like right now it's very cold by the water –

CATALINA: It was very nice –

JORIS: Your mother told you this?!

CATALINA: What? No! God no! She was, uh...like an aunt.

JORIS: *(Charging forward.)* How old are you?

CATALINA: F-fourteen.

JORIS: I am as well. What's in your bag?

CATALINA: Back off.

JORIS: I want to know what you chose to bring.

CATALINA: Seeds. A couple coins...
(A secret.) Tulip bulbs.

JORIS: For trade.

CATALINA: YES. I purchased 5 right before the boom –

JORIS: That's very practical.

CATALINA: Well I'm very practical. Now would you please –

JORIS: You have nice teeth.

She is shy about this for a moment. Covers her mouth.

CATALINA: Thanks...
Can I –

Before she finishes JORIS drops to one knee and allows her to look inside his mouth.

The gesture is grand but he performs it simply.

Easy generosity.

A quiet moment.

You have nice teeth too.

JORIS: Thank you. This one's silver.

CATALINA: Oh. *(JORIS stands.)*
You're tall.

JORIS: Five foot eleven and three-quarters.

CATALINA: Is your family sickly?

JORIS: All my grandparents lived past seventy.

CATALINA: *(Really impressed. Trying to be cool.)*
Cool...
What did you bring?

JORIS: *(Beat.)* Honestly not a lot.

CATALINA: Oh.

JORIS: And I've not yet met my cousin –
But I am a man of faith.

CATALINA: Yes.

JORIS: I take this step with tremendous faith in the life to come. I will honor you as my wife, and respect you as my partner, in this –

CATALINA: Leap?

JORIS: This venture.

CATALINA: Adventure.

THEME SONG tonal strains begin low and slow under this. MISS ATOMIC "Oohs."

JORIS: My name is Joris Rapalje.

CATALINA: Joris Rapalje...
Yes.

JORIS: Will you...

CATALINA: Uh, Catalina.

JORIS: Catalina. Will you marry me?

MISS ATOMIC:
Take me to the rock

CATALINA: Yes.

MISS ATOMIC:
And if there's any luck I want it all my own
Brick, brick brick build your box
Cause I've worked hard to build it to make it all my own

MISS ATOMIC: Catalina and Joris did it right there, got married right there on the dock. They took one step onto that leaky boat and they looked west. Now! This is back when even the East was the West, and we couldn't wait to put our footprints all over it.

MISS ATOMIC and ALL:
Take me to the start
The boat, the leagues, the starboard will point me close to home
Brick brick brick in the heart
Yes yes, it will progress till the getting's done.

MISS ATOMIC: The trip took 4 months! They drank beer, ate biscuits, played cards, told dirty jokes. 12 people died, 1 baby was born, joy and fear and sweat and tears all in anticipation of that great green unknown. The dead rolled over and got lost in the wake, and Catalina…

CATALINA: I'm pregnant!

DUTCH MAN:

THE ONLY WAY TO AVOID THIS SHIPWRECK –

Loud crash of waves.

WE MUST BE CLOSE-KNIT TOGETHER –

Another loud crash of waves.

IN THIS WORK –

Another loud crash of waves.

AS ONE MAN!!!!!

MISS ATOMIC and ALL:
Land you hard, hey
Walk you west, ho
Look you up, higher
Look you loooooooonger
Jump the shark, hey
Jump the frontier
Back to land, ho
We'll make millions here

OOOOhhhhh/AAAAhhhhh

CATALINA looks at the new land.

CATALINA: JORIS!!!

CATALINA begins to panic.

AMBER: And there it was…

CATALINA: JORIS!!!

AMBER and IAN: Kaaahhhh-Powwwwwwww!

JORIS: Catalina??! *(Finding her. Then seeing the land.)* Oh my –

CATALINA: *(Terrified.)* It's huge.

JORIS: *(Thrilled.)* It's massive!

CATALINA: I pictured more people.

JORIS: There are plenty of people out there.

CATALINA: No, I meant Dutch people. I think I'm going to be sick.

JORIS: Catalina. Look at me. LOOK AT ME. This is happening.

CATALINA: It is.

JORIS: You are here.

Beat as CATALINA looks slowly up at the shore again.

CATALINA: I'm here.

(Looking.) It's beautiful.

JORIS: It's unbelievable. Catalina this is unbelievable.

The music swells.

CATALINA: I love you.

JORIS: I love you.

Song finishes with Oooohhh/Aaaahhh swell.

An American Indian chant begins to play.

ATIATONHARÓNKWEN: *(A nightmarish standup routine.)* So! A white man and a medicine man meet at a line in the forest. And the white man says to the medicine man, "Give me all your glass beads. And your secrets." And the medicine man says, "Hey man, I can't do that man." And so the white man says "Hey. I'm new here. I'm a pi-o-neer, give me all your glass beads and your secrets." And the medicine man says "Hey man, I can't do that man." And so the white man says –

ATIATONHARÓNKWEN & CATALINA & JORIS: EVERYBODY PUT YOUR HANDS ON THE GROUND AND GIVE ME EVERYTHING YOU FUCKING HAVE!!!

CATALINA and JOAN: AAAHHHHHHHHHHH!!!!

The scene drops out. We are in modern Las Vegas.

BRIAN:

Joan.

Wakes up in her half-empty gated community in a haze of cocktails and
unemployment and so much debt
She gets out of bed.
She looks in the mirror.
Her head hurts.
She goes downstairs to the fridge.
She opens it.
She closes it.
She opens it.
She takes out a beer.
She downs it.
She wishes she still smoked.
She turns on her radio.
She stares at the door.
She picks up the phone.
She calls information.
She asks the time.

JOAN quietly speaks these questions into the phone as BRIAN narrates.

They tell it to her.
She hangs up.
She calls again and asks about classes at the local community college.
She calls again and asks about work programs.
She just wants to talk.
She calls again asks for the number to the La Quinta Inn down on 15.
She asks to please be connected to room 206.
She looks across the highway at a cheap motel called the North Star
with a neon sign flashing backwards in the window Vacancy No
Vacancy Vacancy No Vacancy –

CHRIS: *(Answering the phone.)* Hello?

JOAN: *(Still a bit slurry.)* Hi…uh, Hi.
This is the waitress who told you to put your shoes on?
(Silence.)
Hello?

CHRIS: Hello.

JOAN: You told me your room number. *(Silence.)*
I got laid off.

CHRIS:

JOAN: You're supposed to say you're sorry. Hello?

CHRIS: You okay?

JOAN: No.

CHRIS: Yeah. What's your name?

JOAN: I go by Joan.

CHRIS: Go by?

JOAN: My given name is Onidah.

CHRIS: What sort of name is that?

JOAN: It's an American name?

CHRIS: Like Indian?

JOAN: Like Mormon? *(Beat.)* It means people of stone.

CHRIS: I go by Chris.

JOAN: "Go by?"

CHRIS: My given name is Cier. From my grandfather.
It's a bird that used to live in these mountains.
So...Mormon.

JOAN: Well. I'm sort of –

CHRIS: Fallen?

JOAN: Falling. Like freefall. Like splat.
I've been thinking...*bad* things. About Vegas.

CHRIS: That sounds okay.

JOAN: But this is my home.

CHRIS: Third-generation.

JOAN: Yes! (Good memory, by the way.) My grandparents worked at the Shining City. My grandpa was a dealer, which meant something back then. And my grandma once got Elvis a peanut-butter banana bacon sandwich.
So what are you doing at a motel? If you're from here and all.

CHRIS: Lost my house.

JOAN: That's terrible. You're like the 3rd person I know –

CHRIS: Can I come over?

Light fades on CHRIS.

Light on MISS ATOMIC, on the radio.

MISS ATOMIC: Well it's another clear sky under another hot moon babies, and we are celebrating! Tonight is the fiftieth anniversary of the Luna nuclear test! Do mamma a favor – imagine it is 1958 and you are wearing sunglasses in the dark. You've been *DANCING* and I've been *SINGING*, and now WE are outside in the cool desert night. We got our atomic cocktails, and we are looking north. And here comes the countdown…

(Whispering.) 10…

LIBBY: The sound of sand under tires.
The sound of sand under boots.

CHRIS knocks.

LIBBY: Joan goes to the door.
She opens it.
She smiles at Chris.

JOAN: I'm sorry about your house.

A beat. CHRIS begins to walk towards JOAN.

Now you say I'm sorry about your job.
This place feels really fucked up right now.
I feel really –

CHRIS kisses JOAN.

LIBBY: Joan makes love for the first time in a long time.

MISS ATOMIC: There's a flash of light. And then it's like…dawn come early. All because two little protons came together to try something new. Two by two, as on the Ark…

LIBBY: They share a beer. Chris leaves.

CHRIS leaves.

MISS ATOMIC: *(Directly to AMBER.)* Was that nice?

AMBER looks at MISS ATOMIC.

Whoo! All this romance is getting to me! Even my fingertips feel good. New Amsterdam.

AMBER: Catalina and Joris are assigned land across the river.
Catalina is pregnant.

JAMES JOHN begins.

During and in time with the song CATALINA sets up the house, while JORIS chops wood.

MISS ATOMIC: *(Singing.)*
Half circle on a straight line
Tight lasso on a new time

CATALINA: Hey, babe. Moving day.

MISS ATOMIC:
Dough, lily-white and clean knees
Forever see what he sees

CATALINA: We're home.

MISS ATOMIC and JOAN:
Fat ankles on my own land
Red sod between his toes, my little man
My story light in his face
Alight even when I'm gone, immortal grace

CATALINA: How you doin babe? Can I get you a beer?

JORIS: I would kill for a beer.

CATALINA: *(To LIZARD.)* Can I get a beer?

Drinks, spit-take.

I'm not supposed to be drinking. I'm pregnant. Shhh.
Here ya go babe?

JORIS: Thank you.

CATALINA: I've been working on baby names.

JORIS: What have you got so far?

MISS ATOMIC and JOAN:
Franklin Fredrick Jacob Joshua Jermaine George Tom

Searching for names, CATALINA calls out to the audience.

CATALINA: Help me! *(She calls out to a male audience member.)* What's your name? What's your name?

The audience member gives his name. CATALINA repeats it back to him.

[Name]? *(She tries out the name, the feel of it in her mouth.)* [Name.] *(Calling as if to a child.)* [Name] get in here and help your mom set up this furniture! Help your mother [Name]. Help!

CATALINA beckons to the audience member, gets him to join her onstage.
One day when these flat-land valleys fill with light
No receding tides or predator in sight
Only starling brand-new things forever in this home
on the porch and in the kitchen
and the portraits of his mother
like an eagle or the north—star.

Onstage, the audience member helps CATALINA set up her new house. When they are finished, CATALINA beams.

CATALINA: Look [Name], we invented the couch!

CATALINA digs into her purse, pulls out something concealed in her hand.

This is a tulip bulb. It is worth so much money. It's called a perennial. It's very special because it comes back year after year.

CATALINA gently teaches the audience member how to plant the tulip bulb and water it.

Grown upwards at a fierce pace
No resemblance to his dad– just my face
Ten brothers and a fair fawn
Black arrow pointing straight on and on and on

CATALINA kisses the audience member on the cheek and returns him to the audience. As the song ends, she sits, struck by a sudden thought.

CATALINA: What if it's a girl?

Daniel Benjamin Tim Christopher Bernard James John

In CATALINA and JORIS' home. ATIATONHARÓNKWEN, a Mohawk Indian, negotiates with JORIS.

ATIATONHARÓNKWEN: And that's non-negotiable, you understand. You will be our full allies in wars and skirmishes with any of the Algonquin people –

JORIS: For defensive purposes –

ATIATONHARÓNKWEN: All purposes.

JORIS: The company said defensive only.

CATALINA: Would you like a beer? We have Heineken and Amstel Light – old family recipes.

ATIATONHARÓNKWEN: No. But thank you, Catalina? Is that right? Catalina?

CATALINA: Yes. Akwee…?

ATIATONHARÓNKWEN: Atiatonharónkwen. You will supply us with weapons and ammunition, as well as regular instruction and maintenance. In return we will supply 750 pelts monthly, mainly beaver –

JORIS: You said, now wait a minute, we agreed on 1000 pelts a month –

CATALINA: With at least a 2% annual increase –

ATIATONHARÓNKWEN: I don't think we could go any higher than…800.

JORIS: *(Beat.)* But we agree this is an exclusive relationship. We are to be the sole –

ATIATONHARÓNKWEN: You want us to stop trading with the British.

JORIS: The British are fanatics. They don't know how to do business. They make it emotional – this is not emotional.

ATIATONHARÓNKWEN: You seem emotional.

JORIS: No.

ATIATONHARÓNKWEN: As for your living arrangements, we will allow you to stay here –

JORIS: We will purchase –

ATIATONHARÓNKWEN: At the very southern tip of the Island, and here on the southwestern corner of Marechkawick.

JORIS: Breukelen.

ATIATONHARÓNKWEN: *(Beat.)* Any additional pelts we may bring or land you may wish to use will require separate and further settlements of wampum. Do we have a deal?

JORIS: I can get my boss to sign off on this. Even at the lower rate –

ATIATONHARÓNKWEN: Good.

JORIS: *If.* Your people can agree that the land we purchase is *ours*. You are not to loiter –

ATIATONHARÓNKWEN: Loiter.

JORIS: We have heard about what's been happening upriver. Fifty of your people showing up at a farm, staying for days, demanding tribute –

ATIATONHARÓNKWEN: You people don't understand how real estate works. The land is shared. This is a partnership.

JORIS: We will not have that here. But we will be your exclusive partners in war and trade.

ATIATONHARÓNKWEN: *(After a beat.)* I will discuss it with my people.

They stand and shake hands.

JORIS: We'll meet again in ten days at the fort.

CATALINA: You're leaving? You may stay if you wish.

JORIS: Catalina.

CATALINA: He is a business associate Joris. It's nearly dark.

JORIS: He needs to bring word back to his aqua-

ATIATONHARÓNKWEN: Aquayanderen.

JORIS: Aquayanderen.

ATIATONHARÓNKWEN: Good.

JORIS: *(Aside to CATALINA.)* This is a very big deal. *(To ATIATONHARÓNKWEN.)* Discuss it with your people, and we will celebrate at the fort. *(Shaking ATIATONHARÓNKWEN's hand.)*

CATALINA: *(Aside.)* You're glowing.

JORIS: I'm so happy. We should celebrate.

CATALINA: Will you get some more wood? *(At JORIS' look.)* I will see him out.

JORIS: Travel safe.

He leaves. As ATIATONHARÓNKWEN prepares to go:

CATALINA: Do you have everything you need?

ATIATONHARÓNKWEN: I do, yes –

CATALINA: I've never seen an Indian up close before.

ATIATONHARÓNKWEN: Do I look how you thought I would?

CATALINA: No. Much stronger looking.

ATIATONHARÓNKWEN: You look very young.

CATALINA: I'm fourteen.

ATIATONHARÓNKWEN: I'm nineteen.

CATALINA: I'm pregnant.

ATIATONHARÓNKWEN: Congratulations. You're stronger looking than I expected as well.

CATALINA: You've only seen British women.

ATIATONHARÓNKWEN: *(Laughing.)* Maybe. What are you doing here?

CATALINA: What?

ATIATONHARÓNKWEN: It isn't very safe. There have been –

ATIATONHARÓNKWEN and CATALINA: Kidnappings.

CATALINA: I know. I heard. Up north.

ATIATONHARÓNKWEN: And there've been wars. I know your husband is here for pelts.

CATALINA: Yes. We are employees.

ATIATONHARÓNKWEN: But I don't understand why a woman would come. The traders are filthy –

CATALINA: I thought it would be exciting.

ATIATONHARÓNKWEN: How have you found it?

CATALINA: *(Beat.)* I haven't really…I haven't left our farm yet. Do you travel much?

ATIATONHARÓNKWEN: For trade, yes.

CATALINA: I would be terrified. *(Beat.)* I get terrified sometimes. It's so empty –

MISS ATOMIC begins gentle underscoring.

ATIATONHARÓNKWEN: It isn't empty.

CATALINA: Compared to Amsterdam it is. I would be worried about getting lost. *(ATIATONHARÓNKWEN laughs.)* What?

ATIATONHARÓNKWEN: It's just a funny thought. You would get to know it. The land becomes familiar. You'd learn the waters. The rivers are like veins. Where I live, four days travel from here –

CATALINA: Which way? *(He points.)* West?

ATIATONHARÓNKWEN: And north. Where I live we have the most beautiful waterfalls you've ever seen.

CATALINA: How far west do you think it goes?

ATIATONHARÓNKWEN: Very far.
Good evening.

CATALINA: Good evening.

ATIATONHARÓNKWEN leaves. A moment.

Very far…
Very far…

A cross-fading.

BRIAN: Joan looks out at the darkness.

CHRIS: You're up.

JOAN: *(Startled.)* What?

CHRIS: Can't sleep?

JOAN: No. Uh, no.
What time is it?

CHRIS: Three-fifteen.

BRIAN: She sits on her small green lawn that borders the desert.
It's hot.

CHRIS gets a beer.

CHRIS: Thanks again. For letting me, you know.

JOAN: You were here most nights anyway. Motel was a waste of money.

CHRIS: That's very practical.

JOAN: Well I'm very practical.

BRIAN: She looks at the moon over Red Rock. She wonders whether, if
she'd gone to college, she would feel this old at 32.

JOAN: What are you thinking about?

CHRIS: I wish it was darker out here.

JOAN: What do you mean?

BRIAN: Chris sits silent. Joan tries to be cool with that. Joan tries to slow
down, to breathe…

CHRIS: Our land used to be so dark.
Desert sounds.
Static on the radio.

You open the screen door.
You walk to the lawn chair.
You sit down.
You watch the dark.
You run the sand between your toes.
You think about lizards.
You think about them out there in the dark.

JOAN: Yeah.
I kinda got a thing about lizards. My grandma used to tell stories about
sitting on her roof the nights they tested the bomb. The whole sky
would just, *light up* with this flash.

CHRIS: The human body can't function without total darkness. We've got
these rhythms.

JOAN: They're gonna have sensory deprivation chambers inside the Ark.

A quiet moment.

JOAN: You ever been married?

CHRIS: Yeah.

JOAN: She wasn't the right one.

CHRIS: No. She was. But maybe you are also the right one.
Do you want to go with me to Montana?

JOAN: What?

CHRIS: Move with me to Montana.

Beat. Perhaps laughter.

I got a cousin there. Got a bunch of land. Far from everything. Off the grid.

JOAN: *(Playful.)* I like the grid.

CHRIS: I gotta get out of here.

Dropping in.

JOAN: You're serious. Woh – Wait, when are you going?

CHRIS: End of the week?

JOAN: When were you going to tell me?

CHRIS: I'm telling you.

JOAN: Chris, I can't just pick up and move like that.

CHRIS: You're out of work.

JOAN: I'll find another job.

CHRIS: Where?

JOAN: When the Ark opens –

CHRIS: Construction's frozen.

JOAN: Not forever. And my family is here.

CHRIS: You haven't seen them in months.

JOAN: My house is here. My life is here. You can't just walk away from your entire life!

CHRIS: You *can.* Just walk away. Half the houses here are empty anyway. And this place is a piece of shit.

JOAN: Hey –

CHRIS: You owe more than it's ever gonna be worth –

JOAN: Chris, I *just* met you.

CHRIS: And I've said more to you in two weeks than I have to anyone in five years.
You like the dark.
Montana is dark.

JOAN: It's just not that easy. I have my volunteering! My shifts at the Neon Boneyard.

CHRIS: You're gonna stay here for a volunteer job guarding some useless old junk?

JOAN:

CHRIS: Sorry. I shouldn't have –

JOAN: No. You shouldn't have.

CHRIS: Look, the city gave me $160,000 for my grandfather's house. I have $160,000.

JOAN: I – I can't go with you because you have money.

CHRIS: Why not? It's as good a reason as any.

Beat. She is seriously considering "Why not?"

JOAN: I have to think about it. You should probably not stay here tonight.

CHRIS: Joan –

JOAN: I need some space.

CHRIS: Now just hear me out –

JOAN: I think you should leave now.

CHRIS: It's three-fifteen in the –

JOAN: I think you should leave.

LIBBY: Chris leaves.

CHRIS places his hat on JOAN's head and leaves. Her head is spinning, trying to figure out what just happened.

JOAN: Fuck.

CATALINA: "Thank you for your kind words regarding my promotion. I look forward to representing the company over the next 5 years before returning to the home offices in the Hague."

JORIS: "In the Hague?" Scratch that. They know they're in the Hague.

CATALINA: "I have begun compiling a manual about what I've learned here concerning the negotiating of treaties with the Mohawk, the Mahican, the Mannahattas, and the Lenni-Lenape – "

JORIS: *(JORIS corrects her on her pronunciation).* Lenni-Lenape.

CATALINA: *(Correctly.)* Lenni-Lenape. "The politics between the tribes are as delicate as the politics between us and they require…" *(Looking at JORIS.)* "Nerves of steel?"

JORIS: "Fortitude and care to exploit… To effectively exploit the divisions between them."
I should say something about the new slave trade –

CATALINA: "I am extremely eager to– "

JORIS: "Ecstatic". I look forward. Greatly. To returning at the end of this contract to the land of my birth. My home. My homeland. *(CATALINA has stopped writing.)* To the Dutch Republic. I look forward to taking your jobs. How would you like to see me someday in a fine white wig. *(She throws down her pen and paper.)* What's wrong?

CATALINA: I'm going to miss it.

JORIS: Playing house in the woods?

CATALINA: Pardon me but I can't get excited about you becoming a glorified clerk.

JORIS: This promotion comes with money Catalina, like you've only heard of.

CATALINA: You look old when you say that.

JORIS: Well you look very young.

CATALINA: I'm fourteen.

JORIS: So am I.

CATALINA: And you're boring me.

JORIS: You are being ridiculous. The loneliness hasn't been good for you. When we get back to Amsterdam –

CATALINA: *(Sudden.)* I'm not going back.

JORIS:

CATALINA: I'm not. *(Realizing.)* I don't want to move to the fort. I don't even want to work for the company any more. I don't ever want to go back to Amsterdam.

JORIS: You want to die here, thousands of miles from home? Catalina I've just gotten a promotion not even a year into starting with the company, and when we return –

CATALINA: You won't be happy in an office.

JORIS: This is what I've always wanted.

CATALINA: Well, I didn't know that.

JORIS: I told you that when we first met.

CATALINA: Well I didn't *know* that!
You should…
You should have that then, Joris – you should do that. This. I won't –

Pained.

I mean, this is a contract right? So…so you can go – I release you – you can go and I can stay and we can break this contract.

JORIS: But I don't want to do that. I want to grow old with you.

CATALINA: Well I don't want to grow old Joris.

MISS ATOMIC begins beat.

I never intended to go back there and just die. And if I had any intention of dying I don't need to cross an ocean to do it either. There are people going further – in the other direction. There's good land, there's good soil, and plenty of space.

JORIS: You're pregnant!

CATALINA: Who cares?!

JORIS: We can't take a baby into the wilderness.

CATALINA: This baby won't be Dutch Joris. We won't be Dutch. Forget the boat. Forget the canals. Look out there. Look at the forest. What do you want? Imagine you're HERE. What do you want.

ALL begin feeding into beat.

JORIS: I don't know.

CATALINA: You do. You know.

JORIS: Catalina please –

CATALINA: You just need to say it. I want. Say it – "I want…"

JORIS: I want…I want. My own land.

CATALINA: Good. Good. What else? Come on Joris!

JORIS: And I want to kill a buffalo.

CATALINA: YES! I want to see you kill a buffalo baby. What else?

JORIS: I want, I want to…

CATALINA: I want to have a thousand babies!! And I want to give them each a piece of this land. And I wanna do you on every acre of this continent.

JORIS: I want that! And I want to found something. I want to have something named after me. A, uh…a street.

CATALINA: A town.

JORIS: A river!

CATALINA: The river Joris!!

JORIS: You're so beautiful here.

CATALINA: I am.

JORIS: You're strong. Stronger than me.

CATALINA: No. I'm not.

JORIS: I would like to kiss you now.

They kiss.

JORIS: Your mouth is wet.

CATALINA: Like a wildfire.

JORIS: What?

CATALINA: You catch through me. Like a wildfire.

MISS ATOMIC: Okay, I'm takin' over for a bit babies! It's time to get moving.
And so it was!!

MUSIC to FIGHT IT FOOT FORWARD begins.

On that day, Joris and Catalina were again married and originated.

CATALINA: I name you Husband.

JORIS: I name you Wife.

MISS ATOMIC: They peel off each other's skins.

JORIS: I name you the Eternal Frontier.

CATALINA: I name you the Wealth of Nations.

MISS ATOMIC: And give birth to one another again.

JORIS: I name you Catherine.

CATALINA: I name you Jonathan.

MISS ATOMIC: Fuck the pilgrims. The pilgrims were witch burning prudes in itchy pantaloons trying to build white bread fucking Jerusalem. Joris and Catalina are EMPLOYEES of the FIRST multinational corporation. And THEY are changing.

JOAN: *(On the phone, plugging ears as if in a noisy place.)* I'm not blaming the union, I'm just asking, are you negotiating with HouWoo? Will there be any new hires?

MISS ATOMIC: Ahem.

JOAN: What about the Ark? Don't laugh!

MISS ATOMIC: Excuse me! *(Quickly summarizing for audience.)* Chris moves back to the motel, Joan keeps looking for work, time passes. Time moves different in the present tense. We're gonna focus over here for a while! On the day before her 15th birthday Catalina ripped her tulip bulbs out of the earth.

JORIS: Two for the horses.

CATALINA: I wanna ride bareback.

JORIS: Two for the wagon and one for the grain.

MISS ATOMIC: They go to market, try to make a trade, only to discover that the bulbs are now worthless –

JORIS: What the fuck.

MISS ATOMIC: They proceed to steal what they need. Now Catalina should have died at 84 in Long Island surrounded by her family. Joris should have died at 59, a magistrate! But as they ride like Hell out of New Amsterdam –

CATALINA: I love you baby.

JORIS: I love you.

MISS ATOMIC: Time stops. Just two little atoms…
There is something nuclear about their adolescence!
And it shines in the dark.

ALL: *(Singing.)*
Stagger
Sunken
Soldier
Blow your
Trumpet
Low

fight it foot forward foot forward
foot feet feet it
fight it foot forward foot forward foot forward
foot feet feet it
fight it foot forward foot forward
foot feet feet it
fight it foot forward foot forward foot forward
foot feet feet it

JOAN: I'm actually calling on the off chance you're hiring? I don't know my typing speed…

MISS ATOMIC: Catalina and Joris dive into the wilderness. We're in Pennsylvania, shooter.

JORIS: Look at those woods. Virgin woods.

CATALINA: Virgin. *(CATALINA howls.)*

MISS ATOMIC: And something unlocks.

JORIS: I'm going to need a bigger axe.

MISS ATOMIC: Clicks.

JORIS: We have so much work to do. It's beautiful

CATALINA: You're beautiful. You're lovely here Joris. You make a fine Indian.

JORIS: I'll never be an Indian.

CATALINA: I shall be the Indian then. I shall have a line running through my body. On that side – civilization! Wave goodbye to civilization Joris!

JORIS: Jonathan.

CATALINA: I mean, Jonathan.

MISS ATOMIC: Aren't they brilliant? They will never grow old, fourteen forever.

JOAN: I need an extension on my payment? Yeah, I know it's overdue.

MISS ATOMIC: Who is to tell them they cannot have what they want?

JORIS: You have to think about a continuous need. So, not something like a table and chairs. Because once you have that, you have that.

CATALINA: The men at the sawmill stink.

JORIS: You know what they need here?

CATALINA: Yeah, wives?

JORIS: Beer.

CATALINA: Whores.

JORIS: A bar!

CATALINA: We could call it House Through the Woods.

JORIS: House Through the Woods…

CATALINA: *(Announcing.)* Tonight! At the House Through the Woods –

MISS ATOMIC: Hou-Woo!

CATALINA: Half off a whiskey and an octoroon!

MISS ATOMIC: Catalina and Joris pour pints as miners strip the forests. Bye bye trees.

ATIATONHARÓNKWEN: A US senator and a medicine man meet at a line where the forest used to be.

CATALINA: Oh my God. The woods. Look at them.

MISS ATOMIC: Bye bye logging industry.

JORIS: Our customers. We're fucked.

CATALINA: We've gotta move faster.

JORIS: What?

CATALINA: It's time to go.

JORIS: But the bar.

CATALINA: We'll sell it.

JORIS: To who?

CATALINA: We'll burn it!

JORIS: The insurance –

CATALINA: We'll take the money. We'll change our names.

MISS ATOMIC: *(Calling to them, like subliminal messaging.)* This is the Sound of the Bang, and I am Miss Atomic coming at you live! Coal is booming.

JORIS: Coal is booming.

CATALINA: West Virginia?

JORIS: I name you Caite.

CATALINA: I name you Jordan.

MISS ATOMIC: They shed their skins again and now the dice are really starting to roll. Before their eyes the continent begins to vomit coal. Cotton. Cattle. Steel. Oil. Gold.

It becomes a dry heave.

JOAN: I'm calling about retraining? Refinancing? Credit counseling? Well is there a waiting list? Is there anything I can do?

MISS ATOMIC: It becomes a dry heave.

JOAN: No, I understand. Thanks anyway.

MISS ATOMIC: And Joris and Catalina move on.

ALL: *(Singing.)*
 Ramble
 Black Beaked
 Starling
 Rapture
 Ready
 Go (Hey Now)

 fight it foot forward foot forward
 foot feet feet it
 fight it foot forward foot forward foot forward
 foot feet feet it
 fight it foot forward foot forward
 foot feet feet it
 fight it foot forward foot forward foot forward
 foot feet feet it

 BIG STOMPING SECTION.

 fight it foot forward foot forward
 foot feet feet it
 fight it foot forward foot forward foot forward
 foot feet feet it
 fight it foot forward foot forward
 foot feet feet it
 fight it foot forward foot forward foot forward
 foot feet feet it

MISS ATOMIC: Hearts race here! When you wake up you take one blink
 at the sun, and then the next time you blink you see the roulette wheel
 spinning and you see...
 Dollar signs.

 A ticking begins.
 Stock market dance.

MISS ATOMIC: Before time and Las Vegas there were two brothers fighting.
 This continent was their arena. One was a creator, and one was a

destroyer. But as they raced from east to west, it got hard to tell which was which. Love bolts down railroad tracks like stitches. Wrestling pops them like rotten teeth. Love blasts holes in mountain sides. Wrestling crushes them and the miners inside like tin cans. Love bends a river to feed a city. Wrestling makes the waters overflow.

ATIATONHARÓNKWEN: A homesteader and a Choctaw Chief meet at a line in the territory. And the white man says HEY MAN! LOOK AT MY FLAG!

MISS ATOMIC: Caite and Jordan hit sunny California!

JOAN: *(Singing.)*
Millions...

JORIS: Welcome to the Golden Bar, No Credit, We are Armed! I got into a fistfight with a guy last night. Won a rock of gold from him the size of one of your tulip bulbs. I think we should use it to build a hotel above the bar. Charge $60 a night and add a craps table. I got into fights back in Amsterdam but here the winner gets to make a building!

CATALINA: I think it's time to get going.

JORIS: We just got here.

CATALINA: Along with half of China and the forty-niners. The easy gold's gone. And everyone is on top of each other.

JORIS: You're pregnant.

CATALINA: I'm always pregnant! I want west.

JORIS: We're in California, Caite.

CATALINA: And I'm ready for a new name.

JORIS: Okay. Cate.

CATALINA: Please try harder.

JORIS: Lina.

CATALINA: Better.

JORIS: Lina Lina Catalina.

MISS ATOMIC: We expand. Mushroom. Grow.

JOAN: I just need things to slow down for a second.

CATALINA: The middle is empty.

JORIS: The Great American Desert.

CATALINA: The Great Plains!

JOAN: Everything's hitting at once.

MISS ATOMIC: How do you stop a chain reaction?

CATALINA: I wanna ride bareback!

JORIS: I wanna ride a railroad.

CATALINA: I wanna to buy some longhorns!

JORIS: I want to buy a river!

ALL: *(Singing.)*
LAND YOU HARD HEY

JORIS: The River Joris.

Silence.

CATALINA: The River Jordan. You make a fine cowboy Joris.

JORIS: I shall always be a cowboy.

CATALINA: Chase me!!

*Band does dizzying progression in quick five during as CATALINA and JORIS and
ALL run across the stage. Spraying sand, exuberant dancing.*

ALL: *(Singing.)*
WALK YOU WEST HO

JORIS: I saw the most beautiful thing just now! A river! A river of cattle.
Thousands of 'em.

CATALINA: Welcome to sunny Montana. Home of a million future farms.
Look at this place!
Cowboys!
Ranchers!
Indians!

*A massive quartet/couple oriented dance section that combines JORIS' dance with
the stock market dance.*

JOAN: Can I please be connected to room 206?

ATIATONHARÓNKWEN: *(Overlapping.)* A civil war veteran and an Indian prophet meet at a line on the prairie. And the veteran says to the prophet –

JORIS and CATALINA: You're really spooking us with your dancing.

JOAN: Can I leave a message for him?

ATIATONHARÓNKWEN: And the prophet says, "But we dance to raise the dead." And so the veteran says –

JORIS and CATALINA: Sure man, we know man, but you're really spooking us with your dancing.

JOAN: What do you mean you don't know if he's checked out?!

ATIATONHARÓNKWEN: And so the prophet says, "But I have had a vision of the future. And so we dance to raise the dead!" And so the veteran says –

MISS ATOMIC: Ready boys. Five, four, three, two, one.

A bugle. The deafening sound of a stampede. Movement with increasingly savage energy. They all struggle to keep up.

The movement dies down in a fit of cramps and panting.

MISS ATOMIC: 1890. Crazed from war and exhaustion, from counting money not yet made, a little bruised, a little battered, a little tired, covered in coal dust, in cow shit, in gold flecks, in Indians' blood, Joris and Catalina come to a stop. In the desert. Jack picks up a newspaper. Cat is pregnant.

JORIS: The frontier's closed.

CATALINA: *(Reading.)* "Up to and including 1880 the country had a frontier of settlement that divided savagery from civilization. But at present, the unsettled area has been so broken into by settlers that there can hardly be said to be a frontier…"

Long Beat.

Where do we go now?

CATALINA can't continue. She doubles over.

CATALINA: *(Rising panic.)* Ow – ow –

JORIS: Cat…Lina…Catalina…

MISS ATOMIC: And Catalina loses a baby for the first time.

JORIS picks her up and holds her in his arms.

CANNONBALL *music begins.*

MISS ATOMIC/ALL:
> **Cannonball**
> **My testament and guide**
> **Aim and fall and crevices divide**

JOAN sees CHRIS.

CHRIS: Hey.

JOAN: Hey.

CHRIS: I just came by to grab my stuff.

JOAN: Okay. There's a lot – it's not so easy for me to just give up and leave.

CHRIS: *(CHRIS nods.)* Here. *(Hands JOAN the letter.)*

JOAN: What is this?

CHRIS: It's a letter, Joan. I'll be quick.

MISS ATOMIC:
> **Waterfall, the beacon lights the grain**
> **Cut your loss and grant me what remains**
> **Screaming here for always Eternity I see**
> **And God my God, in rivers wide with me**

MISS ATOMIC and ALL:
> **We walk we tire**
> **We walk we tire**
> **We walk we tire**
> **We walk we tire**
>
> **Release me**
> **Release me**
> **Release me**
> **Release me**

IAN: Joan sets the letter down. She picks up a handle of cheap gin.

MISS ATOMIC: Catalina and Joris wandered west and east, and tried and lost…they just kept trying –
Until.

IAN: 1905. The railroad was sponsoring a land auction to set up a new *city* somewhere between Salt Lake and California. On a *green* patch in the middle of the Mojave.

JORIS: It's a hundred and ten degrees.

MISS ATOMIC: Las Meadows…

JORIS: *(He notices CATALINA staring hard at something out in the distance.)* What are you looking at? Cat?

CATALINA: *(Seeing something.)* There's something…

IAN: She said it as the sun was setting and it was breathtaking. This orange blue hazy kinda sky, and the distance…

CATALINA: *(Staring into the desert.)* I can see myself walking…just taking off my shoes and walking off into that…

MISS ATOMIC: We spread into the soil.

JORIS: Let's stay.

CATALINA: What? No.

MISS ATOMIC: We branched into the sky.

JORIS: Let's stay here for a while. I'm tired Cat. And you're exhausted. That's why you / lost –

CATALINA: Don't.

MISS ATOMIC: *(Singing.)*
Talk to me…

JORIS: I know that's why. We just need some time. No one's gonna care what we do here. It's a desert! There's no taxes. No one watching…

CATALINA: Please let's keep moving. I have a bad feeling –

JORIS: Baby, you know what they need here? Beer. Ice cold beer.

MISS ATOMIC: *(Singing.)*
Talk to me…

JORIS: *(Sharply.)* Look at me Catalina.

CATALINA: *(Suddenly, focusing.)* Yes Joris. Jordan. Jonathan. Jack.

JORIS: Chick.

CATALINA: Chick.

JORIS: Yeah, Chick Darling.

CATALINA:

JORIS: I'm staying. I think it can all happen here. I don't need to move anymore.
So will you – uh, Mrs. Darling?

CATALINA: Cat. I think I'll just stick with Cat.

JORIS: Okay, Cat. Will you please stay with me?

MISS ATOMIC breaking back into Act opening energy. Maybe even slamming the piano in excitement. Playful.

MISS ATOMIC: So they stay babies! Dig their toes into that Las Meadows dirt, and Groooowwww...
Up.

Build up. And double down.

That's intermission babies. We're gonna take 15. Grab a cocktail.

– INTERMISSION –

ACT TWO

MISS ATOMIC enters, with cast following behind.

MISS ATOMIC: Hi! Did you miss me? You all look better than you did
 when I left! That's some Kriss Angel shit!
 Alright. You ready?

She rekindles the spell that ended Act One.

MISS ATOMIC: *(Singing.)*
 Talk to Me…

IAN: *(Under last chorus.)* Night. Joan is in Red Rock Canyon, looking at her
 city through a haze of gin and tonics.

JOAN breathes.

MISS ATOMIC: *(Singing.)*
 Talk to Me…

IAN: She looks at her unfinished housing development in Summerlin.
 Towards her folks' house on the north end of town.
 She looks at the golf courses. All that open space where Brad Pitt will
 never build a casino, and where the M will likely stay a small family
 place.

JORIS: All that open space…

IAN: She pictures the valley before all this.

JORIS: Unbelievable.

IAN: She thinks about lizards. She thinks about them, out there, in the dark.

JOAN closes her eyes.

MISS ATOMIC: *(Singing.)*
 Talk to Me
 Vegas

JORIS: Moving day…
 Sing me your strange song
 Bring me your tired your poor
 I am home to the weary and the wrong
 Do you feel lucky?

I can be your oasis in the heat
And I'm not your mama
But I can be your sweet release

Talk to me you tigers, you midnight angels and you lambs
I will be your conduit
I can shape you from a minion to a man
Cause once you get lucky
You will never be the same
And if you're down,
I can comfort you and remind you how far you came.

JORIS also witnesses this song. It is a siren call to both. He will build his casino during this, as CATALINA earlier built her home during JAMES JOHN.

The following dialogue overlaps quietly with the second verse.

JORIS: How's it going?

CATALINA: I'm hot.

JORIS: You want a pop?

CATALINA: I'd kill for a pop.

JORIS: What'd the doctor say?

CATALINA: He said there's nothing *medically* wrong with me.

JORIS: I've been thinking about names.

CATALINA: Joris, I'm not, I can't –

JORIS: For the casino. For the casino.

Just before the big choral breaks, they walk out, transformed.

You ready?

CATALINA: Let's go.

They enter the casino lobby. A massive light cue. The place looks like millions…

MISS ATOMIC:
Well! One shining morning a fierce and brilliant light
Will come and wake you from your troubled sleep
And all your future roads are paved with dreams and dice
And all it takes is courage and one – one blessed faithful leap

And Oh! I'll be waiting at the canyon for you
With open arms and hold and rock you in your trembling grace

And here I stand, here I stand screaming out to you
Oh
In my high heels
and my sweet smile and my crown — oooooh tell me what you want of
me poppa!

Oh tell me what you want of me.
I am the surest sign of life for a thousand miles
I am the ocean that you think of in reverie
Far as you fathom
And wider than you dream

Deep as a canyon
Deep as a canyon
Deep as a canyon

I am your –

JOAN: This is the –

MISS ATOMIC: *(MISS ATOMIC holds a finger up to JOAN for a moment.)*
key

JORIS: *(He names it.)* The Shining City.

MISS ATOMIC: The Shining City. 1952.

Sound of shmoozey band finale. Canned applause. MISS ATOMIC begins quick costume change to showgirl.

JORIS: Thank you Miss Atomic! Let's give her a hand!

Real moment for audience to applaud MISS ATOMIC.

She is the winner of last night's beauty pageant, and the symbol of this valley's new atomic age. She'll be appearing every weekend here at the Shining City. I am your host Chick Darling, and this is my beautiful wife Cat.

CATALINA: Hi everybody! I hope you are enjoying the food! We want to just say a quick thank you to Don and Dolores and Betty and Francis and everybody else at the Golden Cup bakery for the beautiful cakes, and to Lloyd over at Sparkling Hills for the wine and champagne. Drink up everyone.

She leads an applause. ALL participate politely.

JORIS: C'mon down here Miss Atomic.

MISS ATOMIC has come down to the deck, perhaps for the first time. In full regalia. She is so bouncy, sparkly, like a perfect 1950s showgirl should be.

JORIS: Tell the folks out there your real name.

MISS ATOMIC: Leigh.

JORIS: Leigh that was just beautiful. Tell me Leigh, are you from Las Vegas?

MISS ATOMIC: My daddy worked here on the Hoover Dam but I grew up in northern California.

JORIS: Grew up? How old are you Leigh?

MISS ATOMIC: Well, a lady never discusses that, right Cat?

A strange moment passes between CATALINA and MISS ATOMIC.

JORIS: Are you excited for this morning's test?

MISS ATOMIC: I sure am Mr. Darling.

JORIS: What do you think it's gonna look like?

MISS ATOMIC: Well, I saw the pictures from Nagasaki and Hiroshima, and I've heard they just keep making these things bigger! So I think it's gonna be big.

JORIS: Big?

MISS ATOMIC: Huge. I think we're gonna feel it from here. And I think it's gonna hit us all right in the face.

JORIS: Well, we just got word from the Proving Grounds that it is time! Miss Atomic? I believe the honor is yours.

He passes her the mic.

MISS ATOMIC: Grab your glasses Joan.

JOAN: What?

MISS ATOMIC: You heard me.

JOAN: How do you know my –

MISS ATOMIC: GLASSES! *(With a big grin.)* 10! 9! 8! 7! 6! 5! 4! 3! 2! 1!

JOAN has followed JORIS to grab her glasses. She runs into CHRIS, who hands her glasses and spins her around to watch the blast.

JOAN: *(Shouting over countdown, as if over helicopter.)* Chris?! WHAT ARE YOU DOING HERE??

A bomb ricochets through the landscape. It takes a very long time.

JOAN: Unbelievable…

The shockwave arrives, blasting sand in everyone's face.

MISS ATOMIC: *(To the band.)* A five, six!!

A reprise of 'Talk to Me Vegas' is launched. Pink snow falls from the ceiling. Like a New Year's party. CATALINA and JORIS dance.

CHRIS kisses JOAN and they dance.

MISS ATOMIC: Bonanza…

JORIS: There's so much we're gonna do here Cat. I saw it all this morning, when that bomb just kept exploding and exploding.

CATALINA: You really are glowing.

JORIS: I'm so fucking happy. They're gonna be testing these things almost every month, and I think we should celebrate each one here.

CATALINA: *(Beat.)* You make a fine businessman Joris.

JORIS: Chick.

CATALINA: Chick.

JORIS: You're happy we stayed right?

CATALINA: *(Dodging with a smile, an invitation to dance.)* Chase me.

JORIS accepts. They dance.

CHRIS: You're glowing.

JOAN: I'm so fucking happy! This is what it looks like –

MISS ATOMIC: Looked like. Your grandmother is over there holding a tray of appetizers.

JOAN: My grandma…

MISS ATOMIC: She's pregnant with your momma, and do you know what *she's* dreaming about?

JOAN: What?

MISS ATOMIC: A *bigger* house. It's gonna be big. Filling up all that open space...

JORIS: You look beautiful tonight.

CATALINA: *(Unhappy.)* I feel like a wife.

JORIS: You are a wife.

CATALINA: I feel *only* like a wife...

Tell me your idea for the new sign.

JORIS: It's gonna be big.

CATALINA: How big?

JORIS: A neon sculpture as big as the building. It'll be a beacon in the desert. And people will follow it –

CATALINA: Like a mirage.

MISS ATOMIC: It's beautiful here, isn't it Joan?

JOAN: This is where I belong.

MISS ATOMIC: Too bad we can't stay.

JOAN: Why?

MISS ATOMIC: You stay in one place for too long you start to slide backwards.

CATALINA: I want to take over financial operations.

MISS ATOMIC: HELLO!

JORIS: What?

MISS ATOMIC: Here we go.

JOAN: I'm not ready to go yet.

CATALINA: I think I've been bored.

JORIS: You need your rest Cat. The doctors said if we want another –

CATALINA: I'm fine.

JORIS: We can keep trying –

CATALINA: *(Firmly.)* I want <u>this</u>.

  I'm fine, baby.

  Besides I miss numbers. *(Flirting, trying to make JORIS smile.)* I'll make them grow big and strong, bigger and bigger…

JOAN: Can't it just stay like this?

MISS ATOMIC: Oh, but we are JUST GETTING STARTED.

JORIS and CATALINA: *(Sloppily running on together.)*

  And bigger and bigger and bigger…

  CATALINA and JORIS grab each other.

CATALINA and JORIS: We are gonna make so much MONEY!

MISS ATOMIC: Are you radioactive now daddy? Are you radioactive now?

  (To her band.) Shut up.

  Let's take it up a few notches.

  VEGAS MEDLEY begins. This is a massive extended freeform musical section. CATALINA and JORIS transform into show-people tiger trainers. It is bizarre, glorious and scary.

  MISS ATOMIC begins singing the opening verse of Elvis' "Viva Las Vegas" under the following text.

MISS ATOMIC:

  Bright light city gonna set my soul, gonna set my soul on fire…

JORIS: Tonight, at House Through the Woods!

CATALINA: New Year's!

JORIS: Tonight, at House Through the Woods!

CATALINA: Boxing!

JORIS: Tonight, at House Through the Woods!

CATALINA: Topless Showgirls!

JORIS: Tonight, at House Through the Woods!

CATALINA: IPO!

  Mic chord/tiger training whiplash.

JORIS: Tonight, from House Through the Woods Incorporated!

CATALINA: 6,000 new rooms!

JORIS: Tonight, from HouWoo International!

CATALINA: Luxury suites! Marble Floors! Private concierge!

JORIS: Tonight, from HouWoo Homes!

CATALINA: Time Share! Condo! Single Family Subdivision!

JORIS: Tonight, from HouWoo Financial!

CATALINA: A-R-M! M-B-S! C-D-O! S-I-V!

MISS ATOMIC: Yeah, Shooter! We got that tiger by the tail, and we are
  burning bright! BUILD ME! *(Applause.)*
  Boys, make some room!

Implosion sound effect. MISS ATOMIC squeals with delight.

MISS ATOMIC: I love a good implosion. Don't you?
  1993! Bye bye Dunes Hotel! Hello Bellagio!
  Hit it boys!

Implosion. Music changes to "Fly Me to the Moon."

MISS ATOMIC:
  Fly me to the moon and let me sail among the stars...

JOAN: *(Beginning to see what's lost.)* The Landmark...

MISS ATOMIC: The Landmark Hotel in 1995. The Landmark a Landmark
  no more. Now a parking lot for our glorious new convention center.
  The Sands in '96 – Take your last curtain call, Sammy, Dean, Frank!

Implosion.

MISS ATOMIC:
  In other words...

JOAN: Unbelievable...

MISS ATOMIC: You know Joan, very, very few people ever have the
  opportunity to be a part of something that grows so fast that you can
  see it, and feel it, and be afraid of it.

Music changes to "Vehicle."

MISS ATOMIC drives JOAN offstage.

The Aladdin. In 1998. Imploded.

The El Rancho in 2000.

The Desert Inn in 2001.

The Boardwalk in '06.

The Bourbon Street in '06.

Castaways in '06.

And in 2007 we made way for House Through the Woods' greatest triumph…

Music changes to Celine Dion's "My Heart Will Go On". MISS ATOMIC does an exaggerated impression of Celine Dion.

MISS ATOMIC:

I am here in your heart and my heart will go on and on…

Music changes to Elvis' "Suspicious Minds". MISS ATOMIC sings underneath the following dialogue.

MISS ATOMIC:

We're caught in a trap…

JOAN re-enters.

She is transformed into a tiger: sexy and disturbing in a short print dress. CATALINA and JORIS lead her like tiger trainers. A nightmarish act.

ATIATONHARÓNKWEN: So! A half-black Mormon waitress and an immortal Dutch teenager meet at a line in the desert. And the teenager says –

During the course of the act, it becomes harder and harder for CATALINA and JORIS to control JOAN.

JORIS: We're here today to implode HouWoo's first baby the Shining City and start clearing the path for a revolution in this town. Cat?

CATALINA makes a grand gesture, signaling "Hit it." SOUND of an IMPLOSION ROCKETS THROUGH THE THEATRE.

JORIS: We're here today to implode the magnificent Stardust –

JOAN, shocked by the violence, attempts to run away. CATALINA catches her quickly and JORIS whips his microphone. Recovering:

The magnificent STARDUST! Cat and I want to take you on this leap – this venture – this adventure! Come with us! Cat?

CATALINA makes a grand gesture, signaling "Hit it." SOUND of an IMPLOSION ROCKETS THROUGH THE THEATRE. JOAN is more disturbed. She bolts for the door and CATALINA tackles her and wrestles her to the chair.

JORIS: We're here to implode the New Frontier casino. Ladies and gentlemen, it's time to make way for the Ark!

A grand gesture: "Hit it." SOUND of an IMPLOSION ROCKETS THROUGH THE THEATRE. The MEDLEY is ratcheting to its insane conclusion.

JOAN, disturbed as the tiger and herself by the lights and the implosions and CATALINA and JORIS' thoughtless joy attacks. She mauls JORIS and CATALINA, leaves them trembling on the floor.

VICKI: 10 9 8 7 6 5 4 3 2 1. You are getting your face ripped off.

The MEDLEY comes down to a quiet hovering point as JOAN comes to — trembling — and realizes what she has done.

JOAN: This is a nightmare.
I want to kill these people! Kill them in the FACE!

MISS ATOMIC: *(Panting.)* They cannot be killed Joan. They are the light pulsing in every bulb in this town. They are the self-sustaining chain reaction. They're immortal, as long as they want to be. Even if you rip their faces off. ONE, TWO, come on babies.

The band resumes the chorus of "Suspicious Minds" at an aggressive pace. On the lyric "because I love you too much," MISS ATOMIC raises CATALINA and JORIS from the dead, and the MEDLEY reaches an insane apex.

JORIS rises.

CATALINA struggles, staggers.

JORIS and CATALINA: Tonight, at The Ark Arena!

MISS ATOMIC: They just keep going.

JORIS and CATALINA: Tonight, at the Ark Speedway!

MISS ATOMIC: And going.

JORIS and CATALINA: Tonight, at the Ark Ski Slopes!

MISS ATOMIC: And going.

JORIS and CATALINA: Tonight, at the Ark!

MISS ATOMIC cuts off the music. A low hum or low feedback.

She doubles over.

MISS ATOMIC: *(Through terrible cramps.)* Ow. *(Stretches.)* 2008.

Silence. The following takes place in a terrible silence; rushed words, the sense of listening in on a whispered conversation.

CATALINA: Dubai is out.

JORIS: What?

IAN: *(Low.)* Joan wakes up in a haze of Singapore Slings.

CATALINA: It's official. They're pulling the plug on the Ark.

IAN: Joan wakes up in a haze of Gin and Tonics.

JORIS: Who did you speak to? I was just at the Ark site. They can't –

CATALINA: They can.

JORIS: This is a joint venture!

CATALINA: BABY! They want a billion back.

Cell phone ring.

JORIS: We don't have it.

CATALINA: I said.

JORIS: And?

CATALINA: They're suing.

Cell phone ring.

CHRIS: JOAN!

A sudden silence.

JOAN: What the –

JOAN is awake. She coughs. Looks around.

IAN: Joan.

LIBBY: Joan.

BRIAN: Joan. Wakes up on the ground off a dusty highway shoulder in Red Rock Canyon.
It is dark.

She is thirsty.

She sits up.

She lays back down.

She sits up again more slowly.

She wonders how she got here.

She makes a phone call and asks to please be connected to –

JOAN: He checked out? Already?

BRIAN: She notices she has a message.

CHRIS: *(A voicemail.)* Joan. It's my last night in town. I went by your house. I...

I'm at the Stateside now. Over by the Boneyard.

I – I don't want to bother you. I won't call again.

BRIAN: Joan looks at the city's glow.

She walks to the car.

She puts the keys in the ignition.

She doesn't want to go to her house.

She wants to go to the place that feels like home.

She turns on the radio.

On the radio:

IAN: Can you confirm rumors that all construction at the Ark site has frozen?

JORIS: Uh, I was just there this morning, and everything is on track. Obviously we're taking stock of recent market/ events –

IAN: Meltdown.

JORIS: Events. That's – there's no reason to say "meltdown," let's not / you know

IAN: Where's your wife?

JORIS: *(Caught off guard.)* Uh... Cat's not feeling well –

IAN: You're here today to quell investor fears that the Ark is facing bankruptcy.

JORIS: We're here to present the plans –

IAN: And your CFO is missing. Has she quit?

JORIS: She's just sick today – everyone's under a lot of pressure – But let's back up for a minute. We're here today to unveil –

IAN: Is HouWoo International prepared to acknowledge rumors that Dubai World has just pulled out from the most expensive private project ever undertaken in the Western hemisphere / leaving the project potentially –

In another world, JORIS is in a bar, listening to himself on the radio.

JORIS: Hey! HEY! Can we turn this shit off?

It cuts out.

JORIS: Thank you. The lady is playing!

MISS ATOMIC piano flourish.

Besides, they've already played that clip twenty times tonight. Humiliating.

AMBER: Nighttime. A piano bar off Silverado.

MISS ATOMIC: *(To the audience.)* Yes, baby, we still exist.

MISS ATOMIC plays the piano, a lounge act, an old woman, a used-up ashtray. She finishes. JORIS applauds loudly.

MISS ATOMIC: Thank y'all. Thank you. I would like to say a quick thank you to CTIA Wireless and AARP and the American Frozen Food Institute and Monsanto for flying in to be with us this weekend. I do hope y'all got window seats. If anyone's a local, I'll be appearing every weekend here at the Rock Bottom. We're gonna take a breather. Don't go far.
(To JORIS as she leaves the stage.) You didn't look so good up there.

JORIS: How am I supposed to do a press conference like that without her? I don't know how to answer all those questions, the financial stuff. That's her area. She always got numbers.

AMBER: Joris nurses a Heineken.
He is alone.
For the first time in a long time.

JORIS: She just…walked out. Said she needed space.

MISS ATOMIC: I had a husband once. Big real estate tycoon. Fucking bastard, pardon my Mandarin. I followed him like a Pekingese.

JORIS: She told me it would look bad if she came to work as drunk as she was about to get. You know when we got here there was no one but Mormons and Okies building the Hoover Dam. We grew a shack into a string of resorts you can see from space. *That's* what I should have said up there! Goddammit. I feel like shit.

MISS ATOMIC: Yeah, well take a number. We all feel like shit tonight.

JORIS: I fucked up. I don't – I don't even know how...

MISS ATOMIC: Stop. Makes you sick thinking of it.

JORIS: She said we can't finish it. That we won't be able. We've never *not...* *(Beat.)* I was going to name it the Catalina? Boats are always named after women you know.

MISS ATOMIC: I thought you were building it for me.

A magnetic moment between the two of them.

JORIS: Do I know you?

MISS ATOMIC: If you don't, baby, nobody does.

JORIS: I should go.

MISS ATOMIC: Take the money, change your name.

JORIS: I have to go find my wife.

MISS ATOMIC: Goodbye, Joris Rapalje.

JORIS: You. I know you.

MISS ATOMIC: Not like me. I am an anchor in the desert. I am chained to this place. In 50 years this city will dry up, you will leave and everyone else will move to PHOENIX and I will be stuck here, singing to the lizards, an ancient city baking in the sun. Praying for the floods to come and wash us all away –

JORIS: Hey.

MISS ATOMIC: What.

JORIS: Nobody is walking away.

MISS ATOMIC: You are. You and Cat. Isn't that what you just said?

JORIS: We have to figure something / out.

MISS ATOMIC: Sure –

JORIS: *(A decision.)* But nobody's going anywhere. Don't you know what we are – ?

We are building an Ark in the desert.

At its heart is a place called the New Amsterdam

Experience. You reach it through a steel elevator that descends deep into the desert rock because the park doubles as a bomb shelter. Then the doors open and you emerge into an ocean of tulips. A Dutch girl in a dirndl approaches you and offers you a credit card that comes with a single golden ticket.

You board a full-size ocean vessel that sails through a great, simulated storm, until you arrive on land and are taught to creep silently through thick synthetic woods, and to trade pelts with a robotic Indian.

You board a rollercoaster that takes you in a covered wagon towards impassible mountains so fast you think you'll crash, until, at the very last minute the mountain blasts a hole in itself to let you through.

You ride over forests, over deserts that explode into wheat fields, and across plains covered as far as the eye can see with rivers of life-size, animatronic buffalo until finally you arrive in sunny California where you can drift up a lazy river lined with underwater slot machines filled with water piped straight from the Pacific Ocean.

On a tiny island a beautiful Indian girl sings in her lost language a sad song, made more heartbreaking by the fact that you cannot, can never understand the words. And this girl notices you weeping like a child, and your complete understanding of her pain so moves her that she cries. And just at the moment that you lock eyes, and you feel that you finally understand America…a recorded voice informs you that a picture has been taken, capturing this sacred moment of communion. And in 25 minutes, that photo can be purchased in the gift shop.

That is what we are building. And no one is walking away.

MISS ATOMIC: Thank you Joris.

She begins to play WATERFALL, underscoring this last bit of dialogue. Over the top of this:

JORIS: Hey Leigh?

MISS ATOMIC: Hey Chick?

JORIS: We have been doing this for 400 years. We just need to be patient.

JORIS exits. CATALINA is in a bar talking to the LIZARD bartender.

CATALINA: Hey Lizard face. Hit me.

He pours her another drink.

I hit a guy in the face with a calculator today. I was in my office and everyone was talking around the desk. We've got every armchair quarterback in the country short-selling us, fucking us, and Joris just keeps saying WE'RE UP THREE POINTS YESTERDAY, and I'm like DEAD CAT BOUNCE, and this GUY! This *guy* keeps leaning over me, like over the desk, to point out the numbers, and they're not adding up, and he's IN MY SPACE so I –

MISS ATOMIC: *(Singing.)*
Waterfall
One way down
Electric your seed in the weed of now all that's done
And pop pop and fizzle and making its wet way –

CATALINA: WOULD YOU TURN THAT SHIT OFF!

MISS ATOMIC abruptly stops playing.

MISS ATOMIC: Gladly.

CATALINA: BARTENDER! DON'T YOU HAVE ANY RAP MUSIC? Play something about MONEY!

Rap music. To whoever changed the music:

I love you!

AMBER: Cat at a bar called the Stateside, north end of town.

CATALINA: I used to ride horses! *Coyote Ugly* – you ever seen it?? The 1600s – you ever heard of it?

Putting in a quarter into a mechanical bull.

Git along Bessie. I came over on the TIGER in 1624. Not the Nina the Pinta the La Quinta – the TIGER!! I could have died on that boat. You can't *fathom* my boat. I brought my starter dough, my work dresses, my Sunday dress, two pair of thick-soled shoes, a hatchet, a chamber pot, what else, cheese cultures – WHAT ELSE? Oh, goods for trading with the Native People! I was told my tulip bulbs would be good for this.

She spies CHRIS across the bar.

Akwee?! Akwee!!! I am so fucking happy to see you!!

She rushes over to embrace him. He stops her.

CHRIS: Woh, woh kid – you don't know me –

CATALINA: *(Playing along.)* Okay, sure, what's your name?

CHRIS: Chris. What's yours?

CATALINA: *(Giggling.)* Good question.

She slams a drink.

CHRIS: How many is that?

CATALINA: Yahtzee.

CHRIS: Maybe you should slow down.

CATALINA: It's called a binge, not a slow.

CHRIS: You don't look old enough to be in here.

CATALINA: 14. But who's counting?

CHRIS: You shouldn't be here.

CATALINA: I know. I should be working. We need 200 to get the contractors off our nuts. *(Giggling.)* 200 MEEEL-LIONS. *(Tries to burp.)*

CATALINA jumps on the mechanical bull.

CHRIS: You don't seem 14. Who are you?

CATALINA: I'm the House! As in the House Through the Woods? As in the House Always Wins.

Her bull stops.

Can I have a quarter?

CHRIS produces a quarter. CATALINA eagerly runs to the machine.

EAT MY QUARTER YOU FUCKING COW. EAT MY STUPID FUCKING QUARTER YOU PIECE OF SHIT METAL. Ow. I think I'm bleeding.

Jumping on the now moving bull.

It may not look like it, but I own all this. THIS IS mine. This glass – the ice in this glass – the bartender who pours it, the bottle, the bar, who carved it, who painted it – I own you, these people, the money in their pockets their clothes their shoes how much they're all worth – I decide…

CHRIS: So how much am I worth?

CATALINA: Seventeen dollars and eighty-five cents.

CHRIS: Nope.

CATALINA: *(Beat.)* What are you doing here?

CHRIS: I was waiting for someone.

CHRIS starts to leave.

CATALINA: Hey. HEY! Where are you going? We were just getting started.

CHRIS: *(Putting on his coat.)* Very far.

CATALINA: Can I come?
(Cracking.) Can I come?

CHRIS: *(Beat.)* No.

Beat. She turns into a lost little girl.

CATALINA: Heads or tails?

CHRIS: What's riding on this?

CATALINA: Heads you die. *(She flips the coin.)*
Tails. Piece of shit.

She kisses him hard. He pulls her off.

CHRIS: You need to sleep this off.

She steps back, furious.

CATALINA: Please don't TALK to me like I'm a GROWNUP! *(She hisses at him like a rattlesnake.)*

CHRIS: That's it – I'm fucking out of here.

CHRIS storms out.

CATALINA: Let's all get out shall we???

MISS ATOMIC stands.

Time to hit the road Jack I mean Jonathan I mean Jordan I mean Chick! Stay in one place for too long and you will start to slide backwards.

MISS ATOMIC: Catalina stumbles out of the Stateside onto North Las Vegas Boulevard.

Beat. A lighting shift.

Chris is gone. It's getting light. She looks across the street –

CATALINA: Hey.

MISS ATOMIC: *(Continuing.)* And sees a parking lot filled with dusty neon sculptures. Big as buildings. A woman stands behind the gate.

CATALINA: HEY! HEY YOU!

MISS ATOMIC: A cocktail waitress with a mortgage and a car loan.

JOAN: Can I help you?

CATALINA: Is this place open?

MISS ATOMIC: It's late.

JOAN: It's 6am.

CATALINA: I'll pay. I'll pay. You work here?

JOAN: Sort of – But we're not open yet.

CATALINA: Well you're here aren't you.

JOAN: I'm just – I just felt like being here.

CATALINA: Well I want to see the signs.

JOAN: Come back at 10am.

CATALINA: I want to see the signs.

JOAN: We're closed.

CATALINA: I made them. They're mine. I wanna see them.

JOAN: Holy shit.

CATALINA: *(Little girl.)* PLEEEEEEEEAAAAASSEEEE!!! Please please please –

JOAN: You're Cat Darling.

CATALINA: What's it to you?

JOAN: I work for you. Worked for you. You laid me off.

CATALINA: Look, I'll pay you for a tour. Let me hire you. You have a special skill right? You work here right so you have special skills? Let me pay you for your special skills.

JOAN: Fuck you.

CATALINA: Hey I've got two thousand bucks! I won two thousand bucks at roulette tonight. I'm very good at roulette.

JOAN: Nobody's good at roulette.

CATALINA: I am. To an embarrassing degree. Here.

JOAN: I don't need –

CATALINA: It's 6am and you're in a parking lot with a buncha JUNK IN IT! You must need something right?

JOAN: It's a museum.

CATALINA: So give me a tour. I'll – I can pay. I just want to see them before I go.

JOAN: You're going?

CATALINA: Yeah.

JOAN: Where? Dubai?

CATALINA: Sure.

JOAN: Macau?

CATALINA: All of the above.

JOAN: And then?

CATALINA: *(Repeating the gesture, delusional.)* Very far…

JOAN: *(Beat.)* Unbelievable.

CATALINA: Look, are you gonna let me in or not?

MISS ATOMIC: Joan opens the gate.

JOAN: *(After a moment.)* Give me the money. *(She does.)* Let's go. *(Heart not really in it.)* Welcome to the Neon Boneyard.

This is the museum.

CATALINA: The Desert Inn. The Stardust. These places are dead.

JOAN: Imploded. And this is what's left. The fragile bones of electric dinosaurs.

CATALINA: S'poetic.

JOAN: *(Grim.)* Yeah. C'mere. You'll recognize this one. We found out from Holly Madison's TWEET that you were imploding –

CATALINA: The Shining City. *(Beat. Seeing JOAN, who has a strange look in her eyes.)* What?

JOAN: Nothing. My grandmother…nothing.

MISS ATOMIC: *(Singing.)*
Waterfall
One way down
Electric your seed in the weed of now all that's done
And pop pop and fizzle and making its wet way on

JOAN: Royal Nevada casino! Home of –

JOAN and CATALINA: The dancing water.

JOAN: When I can't sleep I think about how you made water dance in the '60s.

All the signs are she's, except for the King of the coin palace, the logger, and the Ugly Duckling.

This is the unfortunate. People think this font is Helvetica but it's actually Futura bold. And this is the original atomic font over here – the Russians launched Sputnik the year before the Stardust opened…

There's a family living there.

CATALINA: What?

MISS ATOMIC: *(Singing.)*
Use my skin
Take my hide
I am a creature marooned in your silent spill
And centuries catapult aimed at your great divide

Fall fall fall fall fall...

JOAN: In the "S" from the Stardust. We get a lot of homeless here. Lost a sign last year when a guy built a fire one night to keep warm. They're very flammable.

CATALINA: Was he –

JOAN: He was okay. Just lost the sign.

This news lands on CATALINA as JOAN continues.

A sign doesn't have to have words. It can also be an idea of space.

The Moulin Rouge. First integrated casino. The designer was the only female in a pack of men. And she said she wanted it to be the most beautiful sign she ever designed because she knew what purpose it would serve. So she goes to the library to research illuminated manuscripts.

I love this metal genie teapot because it makes me think of Texas instruments. Make a wish.

JOAN closes and then covers her eyes, overwhelmed.

ALL: *(Chorus of song starts to creep in on "illuminated manuscripts" of JOAN's line above, whispered under the company's breath.)*

Treat me now with kindness
Though the odds be staggering
I will keep its memory
Here beside through anything
Intersected roads and rainy rocks and muttering
Kicking up the dirt where
I'll be left remembering
Scratching on the vine and
Jumping on a trampoline
Getting old and dying
Getting old despite all we
Dropped when we were faster
Lost when we were foraging
Left when we got taller
Sold when we were pillaging
Needed in the flood
Hungered for in tourmaline

Needed for trip we
Drifted from when we were king

ALL:

Fall fall fall fall fall fall
Fall fall fall fall
Fall fall fall fall fall fall
Fall fall fall fall
Fall fall
Fall
Fall
Fall

Underscore trails...

CATALINA: *(Seeing JOAN upset. Defensive, unsure how to feel about all this.)*
What?

JOAN: *(Worked up.)* This was a tiny western desert town where my mom
grew up riding horses. And the types of designs that came out of this
place governed and shaped an entire image of America. When we get
neon benders in here they fall to their knees.

CATALINA: You know this isn't going to go back to being a small town.

JOAN: I know that.

CATALINA: It grew. It's a big city now. Like any other big city.

JOAN: And so what, you're just gonna pick another one? Look at what you
made! Look at the history of this city.

CATALINA: Look, I have to go find my husband.

JOAN: You have a responsibility. There are people living in tent farms up
by Red Rock. It's like the *Grapes of Wrath* some mornings.

CATALINA: We'll do better next time.

JOAN: No you won't.

CATALINA: You'll see. Chick and I, we're just gonna pack up and go
somewhere else –

JOAN: You don't get to just make a WRECK AND GO SOMEWHERE
ELSE ANYMORE!

CATALINA: WHY NOT I'VE BEEN DOING IT FOR THE LAST 400
YEARS??!!! I'm gonna be sick –
Can I have some water?

JOAN: GET UP.

CATALINA: We'll do better next time.

JOAN: GET UP. GO.

CATALINA: Please –

JOAN: You can't be here anymore.

CATALINA: I know.

JOAN: GO! GET OUT – I can't even look at you. GO TAKE A
FUCKING WALK. *LOOK* AT THIS CITY. IF YOU'RE LUCKY
IT'LL MAKE YOU THROW UP.

*JOAN nearly or actually shoves CATALINA. CATALINA stumbles out. Both women
are heaving.*

The march begins. They walk tensely. THIS HOUSE IS EMPTY.

MISS ATOMIC: Catalina leaves the Neon Boneyard and starts walking.
Her tongue is swollen with the wreck of last night's G & Ts.
She's thirsty.

JOAN: *(Singing quietly.)*
This House is Empty
This House is

MISS ATOMIC: She gets lost in a sea of cul de sacs and identical
communities. Foreclosure notices hang from blue tape. Half-finished
model homes stand beside skeletons. Paved driveways with no houses.
Street signs with no names. It's like the film set for a western ghost
town.

JOAN: *(Singing.)*
This House is Foreclosed
This House

MISS ATOMIC: She wanders into a tent city.
She is lost now, somewhere between resurrection and the land of the
dead.

JOAN: *(Singing.)*

That whole neighborhood
Areas never finished
Areas where there once was none
Beautiful homes over there

JOAN: Joan reaches out, touches the glass, the channel that guides the internal incandescent light. She stops. Pulls out Chris' letter.

MISS ATOMIC is changing the march.

MISS ATOMIC: Catalina begins to climb. Walking up the hills of the valley, looking back on her city below. All that open space.

CHRIS: Dear Joan,

I am sorry I did not explain myself better. I'm sorry that you cannot go. I wondered this morning while packing, what my life would be like if I'd grown up in the cold. Would I, for instance, play competitive sports? Would I have gone to college? Would I remember people's birthdays and write thank you notes? Would I be able to explain myself better?

There is a man who wears a suit and no tie and sunglasses that aren't very dark. He comes by one day at sunset. He had papers that had my name and address and his name and his signature and the signature of the Commissioner of the Las Vegas Water Authority. I told him that I don't live in Las Vegas. And he said that I do. A tricky thing.

He insisted that Las Vegas had grown out and that my land is now encompassed by the city of Las Vegas. I told him that maybe I was surrounded by Las Vegas, that I can't control where people build. But that my house is not in Las Vegas. My grandfather's house is in the desert outside of Las Vegas. He talked about Las Vegas like it was a person. A person with the right to grow.

I have an uneasy relationship with the concept of "rights." It strikes me that the basic ones make sense: A right to life. A right to own things. But why a right to boundless growth?

Joan, I am leaving now. But I am writing so that you know that a man who lived in the desert, outside of Las Vegas, hopes that you live where you want to live and that you are happy.

Sincerely and with best regards.

JOAN: Chris.

MISS ATOMIC stops THIS HOUSE IS EMPTY entirely. Silence.

She looks at CATALINA, who gasps.

MISS ATOMIC: Catalina stands on the ridge of Red Rock Canyon by an old house in the desert outside of.

AMBER: Catalina looks at her skin. She sees it is peeling back, like a lizard's. She sees that underneath is dust. She sees that her canvas is tearing off her frame.

CATALINA peels back her wig to reveal pure white hair.

JORIS: Catalina?

CATALINA: Hey handsome.

JORIS: Oh my G-d.

AMBER: In the half-built forest at the center of the New Amsterdam experience.

CATALINA: Is it that bad?

JORIS: What happened to you?

CATALINA: I think I got tired.

JORIS: Where were you?

CATALINA: I was just walking –

JORIS: You didn't come to work. You didn't come home.

CATALINA: I went out Joris. That's all. I got trashed –

JORIS: *(Tight, trembling with anger and upset.)* You look terrible.

CATALINA: My skin feels odd – like lace –
(She goes to touch her face.)

JORIS: Don't.

CATALINA: *(Terrified and stunned.)* You look like you're seeing a ghost.

JORIS: Am I – *(Going up to touch his own face.)*

CATALINA: *(Quickly.)* You look like the day we met.

JORIS: I'm sure we can find you a doctor.

CATALINA: I don't need a doctor

JORIS: I've seen people, who work hard day after day, and when they stop they just, they lose their momentum, and they come down with a a a cold, the flu –

CATALINA: I – I don't think I have the flu, Joris.

JORIS: *(Quickly.)* I spoke to the lawyers. They think we can get a consortium together to guarantee a loan.

CATALINA: Do you think it's worth it?

JORIS: What?

CATALINA: I –

AMBER: Catalina takes a drink of water. And for the first time in 400 years she thinks about never seeing Joris again, and is hit with a pang of so much missing him.

CATALINA: *(Urgently.)* I think it's time for us to go.

JORIS: You want us to just leave the half-finished hull sitting in the middle of Las Vegas Boulevard?

CATALINA: Yeah – let someone else finish it.

JORIS: Stop it. We'll – you're dehydrated – we'll take you to a doctor –

CATALINA: I don't need a doctor Joris –

JORIS: You do – you don't know what you're saying and you probably are just tired –

CATALINA: Joris we have to get out of here –

JORIS: You probably are just tired –

CATALINA: Joris look at me. LOOK AT ME.

JORIS:

CATALINA: I'm…I'm old.

JORIS: You're not.

CATALINA: I am baby.

JORIS: You're hallucinating –

CATALINA: No. No. No. No. No I'm not. This is happening.

AMBER: Like a flood Joris remembers the first day they came to the valley when such a small town lay inside…

JORIS: You said you could see yourself walking –

CATALINA: *(Overlapping.)* Just walking off into the desert. You should have believed me.

JORIS: You're leaving me.

CATALINA: Come with me.

JORIS: Where?

CATALINA: We'll take off our shoes and we'll just walk.

JORIS: We're so close Cat. Let's just finish this, please.

CATALINA: You're building a boat in a desert.

JORIS: That's how much I love you.

CATALINA: And I love you.

Realizing the implications.

And so…so I think I will go now.

Because I think that if I come to work tomorrow I will shoot you.

JORIS: I am OK with that, as long as you come to work.

AMBER: Joris thinks of Catalina's skin becoming hard and lizard-like under the sun.

JORIS: You can't leave.

CATALINA: I have to. I think there is something wrong about the two of us. Together. Here, anyway. I think, if we left, if we went off –

JORIS: Who are you?

CATALINA: What?

JORIS: Who are you? My wife wouldn't do this to me.

CATALINA: Joris please.

JORIS: My name is Chick. And I have a contract with my wife. She is my partner. She looks outward and I look up, and I am careful and she is free, and I am building this Ark for her. So I'll know. If you walk out of here, if you walk out on this. I'll know you're not her.

CATALINA: Here are my shoes.

She begins to remove her shoes, as he goes to get his axe.

JORIS: I'm going back to work. I'll –

He halts, seeing her arms outstretched, offering her shoes.

I'll see you there?

He begins chopping wood, which will continue for the rest of the show. Music for REBIRTH begins.

CATALINA nearly collapses, the weight of goodbye sinks in.

CATALINA: Goodbye Joris.

MISS ATOMIC: Catalina put one foot in front of the other and started walking. She walked so long her feet bled.
You hear about it, but it actually happens.
She lost her name around mile 3 and her fingernails at mile 5. She stopped sweating.
She thought about the way things worked. She took apart a cactus. She killed a lizard, ripped it apart to see where the bones connected to the tissues.

ALL:
Hands, skin to the nail to the skeleton
Blood highway buh-byway buh-bone
Old butterfly song of destruction
Ca-carry ca-carry me home

(Aaaaah)
(Aaaaah)
Miiiileeeeeeons.

MISS ATOMIC: She stopped.

CATALINA: *(She laughs.)* "I stand tonight facing west." Which way's west?

Everyone points.

"I – I stand tonight! Facing west! On what was once the last frontier!"

Laughing. Jumping. Something physical. She screams.

AAAAhhhhhhhhhh!

It vanishes into the distance. She watches.

Okay. Now which way's east?

Everyone onstage, including the band, points.

MISS ATOMIC: Catalina starts to run.

JOAN: Joan walks out of the Boneyard, gets in her car, and starts to drive towards Montana.

ALL:
I am traveling traveling traveling
No one here remembers my song (Millions)
My ghost is forgotten and so it be
Come swiftly
Come high
Come bury me
Throw desert over me
World turning over me
World turning over me
World turn

JOAN: The sun sets in her rearview mirror as the Las Vegas skyline disappears from view.

CATALINA: Hello?

MISS ATOMIC: And in the distance, Catalina sees something –

CATALINA: Hello?

MISS ATOMIC: Like it was always there, just waiting for her to come home.

CATALINA: Is someone –

A DUTCH PIONEER WOMAN in impeccable period garb enters the space. She is dumbstruck by the sight of CATALINA.

DUTCH PIONEER WOMAN: *(All in Dutch.)* HALLO?! (Hello?!) *(Horrified.)* Oh! (Oh my) – Waar kom jij vandaan? (Where did you come from?)

CATALINA: What?

DUTCH PIONEER WOMAN: Ben je gevangen genomen? (Were you captured?)

CATALINA: I don't –

DUTCH PIONEER WOMAN: Hebben de Indianen – (Did the Indians)

CATALINA: The Indians?

DUTCH PIONEER WOMAN: Shhhh. Je bent in alle staten. (You're in a state.)

CATALINA: Where am I?

DUTCH PIONEER WOMAN: Dit is Niew Amsterdam. (This is New Amsterdam.)

CATALINA: Oh. But I've already done this before – *(CATALINA begins coughing, totally dry.)*

DUTCH PIONEER WOMAN: Wacht even. (Hold on.)

The PIONEER goes to get water. Hands it to CATALINA.

Hier. (Here.)
Waar kom je vandaan? (Where are you from?)

CATALINA points.

Uit het westen? (You're from the West?)

CATALINA: Yeah.

DUTCH PIONEER WOMAN: Laat me eens naar je voeten kijken. (Let me see your feet.)

CATALINA tentatively extends her bare feet. PIONEER grimaces at how terrible they look.

Heb je veel gelopen? (You've been walking?)

CATALINA: I don't remember.

MISS ATOMIC: I do.

CATALINA: *(Having heard MISS ATOMIC, as if a ghost.)* Hello!?

DUTCH PIONEER WOMAN: Shhh. Vertel me erover? (Will you tell me about it?)

CATALINA: Tell you about what?

DUTCH PIONEER WOMAN: Het Westen. Mijn man en ik gaan er heen. (The west. My – my husband and I are going there.)

CATALINA: Oh…that's good. *(Laughing.)* You should go there. Everyone should…

DUTCH PIONEER WOMAN: Hoe is het daar? (What is it like?)

CATALINA: There will be less trees.

DUTCH PIONEER WOMAN: Minder? (Less?)

CATALINA: No trees. There won't be any trees. And the water –

DUTCH PIONEER WOMAN: We blijven het water volgen. (We're going to stay along the water.)

CATALINA: The water goes away at some point. But it comes back, pops up in places. Look for the mounds.

DUTCH PIONEER WOMAN: Bergen? (Mounds?)

CATALINA: Where there's water there will be a mound. Cause the wind blows the dust. And the dust sticks where it's wet – where the ground is wet. And it forms a mound.

DUTCH PIONEER WOMAN: Wat nog meer? (What else?)

CATALINA: It's hot!

DUTCH PIONEER WOMAN: Is dat zo? (It is?)

CATALINA: Yes.

DUTCH PIONEER WOMAN: Ga dor. (Keep going.)

CATALINA: The sky, it's big… It's huge actually. And time feels different there. And it sort of feels – like there's every possibility…

Lights fade, the chopping of wood continues.

BLACKOUT.

ACKNOWLEDGMENTS

We would not have made it without the support and encouragement of our friends and family and colleagues.

Thank you to the current and past members of the TEAM's board of directors for their guidance and support:
Danielle Amedeo, Jeremy Blocker, Carly Hoogendyk, Will Hunter, Jaime King, Nathan V. Koch, Karina Mangu-Ward, Nicole Simoneaux, Ryan West

Thank you to the individuals and theaters that have helped us to create and produce our work (in a quasi timeline):
Chashama; Shelley Hastings and our Battersea Arts Centre family; Jackie Wylie and the whole staff of the Arches; Lorne Campbell and Laura Collier, and past and present Traverse Theatre staff; Robert Lyons, Erich Jungwirth, Vanessa Sparling, Aaron Lemon-Strauss and folks at the Old and New Ohio Theatres; Ric Watts; Tommy Kriegsmann; Caroline Newall, John Tiffany, Vicky Featherstone, Neil Murray, and everyone past and present at the National Theatre of Scotland; Michael Mushalla and Double M Arts & Events; Vallejo Gantner, Derek Lloyd, Andy Horowitz, and everyone at PS122, past and present; Helen Cook, Jean Andzulis, and Playwrights Horizons Theater School; Jack Walsh, Stephanie Pacheco and the staff at BRIC; Jenny Worton and the Almeida Theatre; Frank Hentschker and the Martin E. Segal Theatre Center/ Prelude Festival; Ari Edelson, Dean Strober, and everyone at The Orchard Project; 3LD; Oskar Eustis, Mark Russell, Liz Frankel, and everyone at Under the Radar and the Public Theater; Francisco Frazão and Culturgest; Philip Arnoult; LMCC; Rob Orchard and ArtsEmerson; Ben Power, Sarah Murray, and everyone at the National Theatre and National Theatre Studio; Chris Haydon, Clare Slater, and the Gate Theatre; Kansas City Repertory Theatre; Joseph Haj, Jeff Meanza, and PlayMakers Repertory Company; Noel Allain, Sue Kessler, and the staff of The Bushwick Starr; Sarah Stern and the Vineyard Theatre.

Thank you to the funders that have made our work possible:
Ginny Louloudes and the incredible staff of The Alliance of Resident Theatres/New York, The American Theatre Wing, Creative Capital, The Drama League, Edinburgh International Festival, The Greenwall Foundation, The Jerome Foundation, The JMJ Family Fund, The Lower Manhattan Cultural Council, The Panta Rhea Foundation, The Puffin Foundation, The Mid Atlantic

Arts Foundation through USArtists International in partnership with the National Endowment for the Arts and the Andrew W. Mellon Foundation, and the Global Connections – In The Lab program, funded by The Andrew W. Mellon Foundation and administered by Theatre Communications Group. The TEAM has also been supported with public funds from the National Endowment for the Arts, the New York State Council on the Arts with the support of Governor Andrew Cuomo and the New York State Legislature and from the New York City Department of Cultural Affairs in partnership with the City Council.

Thank you to the individuals who have contributed their time, talent, feedback, and/or manpower to the making and staging of these plays (in no particular order):
Heather Christian, Amber Gray, Ian Lassiter, Sarah Gancher, Mikaal Sulaiman; Jacqui Kaiser; Renee Blinkwolt; and Taylor Mac; Davey Anderson; Lucy Kendrick Smith; Lana Lesley, Kirk Lynn, Shawn Sides, Thomas Graves and the Rude Mechs; Nathan Wright; Brian Scott; Chantal Pavageaux; Michael Rohd, Rebecca Martinez, Bobby Bermea, Sonya Nankani, Alisha Tonsic, Heather Schmucker and Sojourn Theatre; Paz Pardo; Ben Gullard; Annie Tippe; Kevin Hourigan; Will Detlefsen; Dan Rothenberg, Dito Van Reigersberg, and Pig Iron; Jen McGrath; Anna Hodgart, Meg Kelly, Genevieve Taricco, Liz Rogers, and Kailee Ayyar; Jay Sterkel, Joe Cantalupo, Seán Linehan, Doug Filomena and the entire Lighting Syndicate; T. Stowe Nelson; Brian Bender, Sasha Brown, Matt Bogdanow, Josh Myers, Jonathan Anderson, and Spencer Cohen; Brenda Abbandandolo; Stephanie Wright Thompson; Bryce Gill; Brian Ferguson; Sandy Grierson; Jason Kaiser; Rachel Karpf, Billy Hart, and Natalya Krimgold; Richard Slotkin; Max Rubin; Boo Froebel; Jimmy Bendernagel; Jeremy Reff; Jessica Jelliffe and Jason Craig; Brandon Powers; Alex Kveton; Stacy Levine; Bradley King; Asa Wember; Colbert Davis IV; Danielle Monica Long King; Danielle Kelly, Erin Stellmon and the Neon Museum; Samuel Savalli, Mukul Kumar, Jacob Goldberg, and Culinary Workers Union Local 226; Nancy Deaner, Valerie Davis, and the Office of Cultural Affairs City of Las Vegas; Karen Green and the Atomic Testing Museum; R.C. Farms in North Las Vegas; Brackley Frayer, Kenn McLeod & the University of Nevada Las Vegas; Josh Heine, Nate Schenkkan, Nick Cisik, Tim Peper, and Heather Girardi; Rebecca Spinac; Miki McCoy; Rachel Shukert; Ben Morris; Tom Attenborough; Kate Rusek; Jim Schmiedel; Peiyi Wong; Mark Russo; Paul Ford; Emily Eagen; Adam Rapp; Louis Scheeder; Michael Krass; Patrick Daly; Ashima Jain; Anne Bogart; Brian Kulick; Jay Indik; Leighton

Mitchell; Anik Meijer-Werner; John Clancy; Nikkole Salter; Kate Rusek; Emily Davis; Jennie Liu; Bev Mitchell; Eamonn Farrell and the community at Montgomery Gardens. And a special thanks to Paulette Douglas for documenting our process so beautifully in *The TEAM Makes a Play*.

Thank you to our families, who have hosted us, fed us, and nurtured us in so many ways.

And thank you to everyone who has helped support the TEAM in so many ways over the past 10 years:
Brenda Abbandandolo, Lauren Adleman, Akiko Aizawa, Carlo Alban, William Allis, Donald & Christine Almasy, Emily Alpren, Ryan Amador, Jerome & Carol Amedeo, Danielle Amedeo & Jason Adler, Victoria Andujar, Jean Andzulis, Joe Angio, Sarah Anton, Arnold Aronson, Peter Aspden, Richard & Joanna Atkinson, Mathew August, Sandra & Joseph Augustine, Sanda Balaban, Natalie   Baribeault, Blake Barrett, Douglas Beck, Ellen Beckerman, Paul Bedard, Nick Benacerraf, James & Alicia Bendernagel, Karen Benelli, Eliza Bent, Lawrence Berger, Susan Bernfield, Shakti Bhagchandani, Anna Bierbrauer, David Binder, Paula Marie Black, Renee Blinkwolt, Jeremy & Miriam Blocker, Holly Blomquist, Frank Boudreaux & Megan Gaffney, Marc Bovino, Chris Bowser, Kerry Boyd, Margaret Boyd, Stephen Boyd, Stephen Brackett, Andrew Bragen & Crystal Finn, Alison Burpee, David Call, Shannon Cameron, Lorne Campbell, David Cannon, Chris Cariker, Salvatore Caristo & Robin Geller, Polly Carl, Melissa & William Carter, Terry & Patsy Carter, Vinny Catalano, Christine Causey, Steven Chaikelson, David Chapman, David Chavkin, Peter & Nancy Chavkin, Shirley & Herbert Chavkin, Jess Chayes & Ben Beckley, James Chen, Cosmin Chivu, Laurie Chock & Lawrence Goldman, Paul Choi, Heather Christian, Matthew Citron, James Clark, Katie Clark, Libby Clearfield, Alexis Clements, Tamara Cohen, Emily Coit, Gwendolyn Coleman, John Collins, Hannah Cook, Helen Cook, Jack Coplen, Catherine Coray, Acacia Cormier, Anna Corrigan, Lorenz & Jane Costello, Amelia Cox, Steve Cramer, Maria Crocker, Julie Crosby, Anna Crouch, Michael Crowley, David Cugell, Patrick Daly, Summer Damon, Jennifer Conley Darling, Emma De Crespigny, Lear deBessonet, Patricia Decker, James DeJesus & Iva Locorriere, Will Detlefsen, Henry & Lisa Devlin, Curzon Dobell, Maureen Donohue, Paulette Douglas and Woody Freiman, Jill Du Boff, Alec Duffy, Patrick Dugan, Bridgette Dunlap, Christian James Durso, Jason Eagan, Rebecca Easton, Sarah Ehlinger, David Elbaum, Maria Elena & Michael Hardma, Anna Elliott, Elizabeth T. Elliott, Jerome Ellis, Dina

Emerson, Anne Erwin, Oskar Eustis, Eleanore Everdell & Jason
Friedman, Jeremy Falk, Katherine Falzon, Ben Famiglietti, Andrew
Farmer, J.S. Fauquet & Joseph Papa, Amanda Feldman, Brian
Ferguson, Douglas Filomena, Aubrie Fine, Desiree Fischer, William
Fisher, Peter Flynn, Alona Fogel, Dustin Fontaine, Ann Marie Foss,
Jeffrey Frace, David Frank, Andrea Frankle, Gibson Frazier,
Francisco Frazão, Anna Frenkel, Renata Friedman, Hannah
Friedstein, Scott Friedstein, Kyle Frisina, James Frutkin, William
Fugman, Maya Galbis, Sarah Gancher, Vallejo Gantner, Philip M.
Gardiner, Joshua Gelb, Robin H. Geller-Caristo, Barbara A. Genco,
Sanaz Ghajarrahimi, Megan Ghiroli, Gian-Murray Gianino, Eileen
Giardina, Nicola Giardina, Karen Gibson, Nancy Gibson, Robert
Gillespie, Molly Gillis, Michael Gionfriddo, Di Glazer & Risa
Shoup, Katie Jo Glover, Montego Glover, Anna Godbersen, Barry
Goldstein & Sue Stubbs, Maria Goyanes, Matthew Gray, Kathryn
Grody & Mandy Patinkin, Rinne Groff & David Becker, Denise
Guerra, Ben Gullard, Anne Hamburger, Seth Hamlin, Alicia
Hancock, Rob Handel, Luke Harlan, Jackie Harris, Victoria Hart,
Charlie Hastert, David Haupert, Dan Hawkins Sr., Danny Hawkins
Jr., Leslye Headland, Denise Heinrichs, Elizabeth Heinrichs, Joseph
Heinrichs, Hannah Heller, Rebecca Henderson, Chris Henry, Leah
Herman, Jeremy Hersh, Josh Higgason, William Hill, Douglas
Hitchner, Anna Hodgart, Al Hoffman, Mike Holmes, Carly
Hoogendyk, Jill Hoogendyk, Zac Hoogendyk, Anna Hopkins,
Andrew Horwitz, Kevin Hourigan, Sharon Hourigan, Doria Howe,
Wilfred & Jessie Hoyt, Stephen A. Hubbs, Matthew Humphreys,
Merlyn Hurd, Chisa Hutchinson, Jay Indik, Michael Iveson, Lucy
Jackson, Feygele Jacobs, Shashi & Prithvi Jain, G.T. Janssen,
Stephanie Janssen & Wally Krantz, Jake Jeppson, Isaiah Johnson,
Kay Johnson, Stephanie Johnstone, Tonya Jones, Kathleen Jones &
Tait Miller, Marla Joy, Lisa Joyce, Erich Jungwirth, Liam Kaas-
Lentz, Howard & Janet Kagan, Greg & Danielle Kaiser, Jacqui
Kaiser, Christopher Kaminstein, Alison Jill Kaplow, Kelsey
Kapolnek, Kendall Karg, Susan & John Karlin, Bob Kelly, Meg
Kelly, Alexander Kelly, Richard Kingdom, Fran Kirmser, Jaci &
Jason Klein, T.R. Knight & Patrick Leahy, Todd Knudson, Amanda
Koch, Nancy Koch, Nate Koch, Jenny Koons, Michael Krass,
Tommy Kriegsmann & Shanta Thake, Daniel Joshua Kriess,
Kimberley & Robert Lamountain, Barbara Lanciers, Robert
Landau, Aaron Landsman, Susan Lang, John Lavelle & Chloe
Whiteford, Georgette & Jimmy Lawlor, Nila K. Leigh, Joseph
Leonard, Sarah Leonard, Kristina Leonetti, Ruby Lerner, Lauren
Letman, Staci Levine, Heather Lind, Seán Linehan, Rebecca
Lingafelter, Alicia Looney, Ruth Lopert, Kaite Lowes, Patricia

Mactaggart, Jason Mahler, Nigel J. Maister, Jimmy Maize, Melissa Malde, Dave Malloy, Randy Malloy, Karina Mangu-Ward, Mike & Susan Manternach, Anthony Marble, Malcolm & Rina Margolin, Reuben H. Margolin, William Margolin, David Margulies & Lois Smith, Lauren Marks, Carol Martin, Jerry & Linda Martin, Rebecca Martinez, Kristin Marting, Donnie Mather, Henry & Barbara Matusik, Johannah Maynard, Matthew Mazur, Barbara McAdams, David McGee, Kate McGinnis, Jackie McGlone, Jennifer McGrath, Nancy McKim, Annie McVey, Tyler Mercer, Thya Merz, Suzy Meyers, Stacy Mikell & Drew Tinnin, Alexandra Milak, Katie Miles, Steve Miller, Sharon Miller & Gary Roebart, Meg Miroshnik, Belina Mizrahi, Thomas Stephen Molloy, Chris Morgan, Caitlin Morris, Harry Moses, Betty Lynn Moulton, Colin Murphy, Michael J. Murphy & Brigid K. Glackin, Michael Mushalla, Mary Myers, Frederick Nagel, Soneela Nankani, Stowe Nelson, Lila Neugebauer, Robert J. Neumann, Laura Newman, Jeffery Norman, Julie Oh, Alex Orbovich, Stephanie Pacheco, Natalie Palamides, Dave Palmer, Paz Pardo, Louis Trabb Pardo & Sharmon Hilfinger, Chris Passasvia, Chantal Pavageux, Celeste Pechous, Jennifer Pehr & Jonathan Adam Ross, Emily Perkins, Sam Pinkleton, Nick Polato, Robert & Jennifer Portman, Brianna Privett, Sara Quin, Bobbin Ramsey, Karla Ramsey, Alice Reagan, Jeremy Reff, Sarah Richardson, Megan Riordan, Rebecca Robinson, Heather Rogers, Jackie Rogers, Amy Rogoway, Michael Rohd, Edith Rosenbaum, Ellen Rosenbaum, Sara Rosenbaum, Selma Rosenbaum, Andrew Rosenthal, Matt & Alyssa Ross, Alice Rost, Alexandra Kissel Roth, Gabriel Roth, Dan Rothenberg, Janet T. Roy, Rosemary Roy, Nina Rubin, Janice Rubin & Charles Wiese, Kathy Rucker, Pesha Rudnick, Winthrop Jordan Ruml, Kate Rusek, Rowena Russell, Leanne Russo, William Russo, Raphael Sacks, Rafael Salas, Julian Sands, Gregory Sargent, E. Patterson Scarlett, Kate Scelsa, Kaneza Schaal, Magin Schantz, Richard Schechner, Noah Schechter, Lucia Scheckner & Robert Lovering, Louis Scheeder, Alan Schimpff, Jenny Schwartz, Shawn Shafner, Katya Shapiro, Kara Sheffel, Chris Shelley, Betina Shepard, Scott Shepherd, Rachel Shukert, Caitlin Sieh, Michael Silverstone & Abby Browde, Sara Simmonds, Sarah Simmons, David & Judy E. Sisk, Crystal Skillman, Kristin Slaysman, Erin Smith Dennis, Sonya Sobieski & Robert Davenport, Colleen Sonosky, Phillipa Soo, James Sparber, Paul Sparks, Tony Speciale, Karen Spector, Jenny Spencer, Ash & Emily Sroka-Groves, Deborah Stein, Bruce Steinberg, Bonnie Stephens, Richard Stinson, Joe Stipek, Caitlin Sullivan, Carol Tambor, JD Taylor, Rusty Thelin, Jake Thomas, Natalie Thomas, Nick Thomas, Joseph & Mary Ann Thompson, Stephanie Wright Thompson, Paul Thureen, Alex

Timbers, Traci Timmons, Eric Ting, Annie Tippe, Claire Titelman,
Colleen Toole, Maureen Towey, Ricardo Trindade, Rosemarie
Troche, Lindsey Trout, Lindsey Turteltaub, Kurosh Valanejad,
Kathryn Valk, Dito van Reigersberg, David & Tiffany Vander Ploeg,
Mitch Vanneman, Victoria Vazquez, Angelina Velasquez, Patricia
Voight, Sandra Ward, Charles Wardell, James Watkins, Emily
Watson, Ric Watts, Dorothy Weber, Kim Weild, Ryan West, Darron
West, Alyssa White, Stuart White, Margi Whitmore, Lily Whitsitt,
Peter Wiese, Ben Williams, Naomi Williamson, Verna Willis, Nathan
Wright, Jackie Wylie, Ben Yalom, Julian Yap, Christine & Hanson
Yates, Guy Yedwab, Peter Yeung, Madani Younis, Pirronne
Yousefzadeh, Mohammad Yousuf, Anatol Yusef, Chad Zimmerman,
Harmon Zuckerman, Pavel Zustiak.